Bullies in the Workplace

Bullies in the Workplace

Seeing and Stopping Adults
Who Abuse Their Co-Workers
and Employees

Michele A. Paludi, Editor

Foreword by Philip E. Poitier

Women's Psychology
Michele A. Paludi, Series Editor

PRAEGER™

An Imprint of ABC-CLIO, LLC
Santa Barbara, California • Denver, Colorado

Library of Congress Cataloging-in-Publication Data

Bullies in the workplace : seeing and stopping adults who abuse their co-workers and employees / Michele A. Paludi, editor ; foreword by Philip E. Poitier.

    pages cm.—(Women's psychology)

    Includes index.

    ISBN 978-1-4408-3253-6 (alk. paper) – ISBN 978-1-4408-3254-3 (ebook)

1. Bullying in the workplace.   I. Paludi, Michele Antoinette.

   HF5549.5.E43B835   2015

    658.3′82–dc23   2015008678

ISBN: 978-1-4408-3253-6

EISBN: 978-1-4408-3254-3

19 18 17 16 15   1 2 3 4 5

This book is also available on the World Wide Web as an eBook.
Visit www.abc-clio.com for details.

Praeger
An Imprint of ABC-CLIO, LLC

ABC-CLIO, LLC
130 Cremona Drive, P.O. Box 1911
Santa Barbara, California 93116-1911

This book is printed on acid-free paper ∞
Manufactured in the United States of America

For Benjamin Brown, Ella Mastriano, Gina Seggos, Lily Seggos, and Paige Seggos. You teach me about what I have left to do to eliminate bullying in the schools and in the workplace.

Contents

PART IV: BULLYING ACROSS THE LIFE CYCLE: SCHOOLYARD BULLIES BECOME WORKPLACE BULLIES

Series Foreword

Michele A. Paludi

Because women's work is never done and is underpaid or unpaid or boring or repetitious and we're the first to get fired and what we look like is more important than what we do and if we get raped it's our fault and if we get beaten we must have provoked it and if we raise our voices we're nagging bitches and if we enjoy sex we're nymphos and if we don't we're frigid and if we love women it's because we can't get a "real" man and if we ask our doctor too many questions we're neurotic and/or pushy and if we expect childcare we're selfish and if we stand up for our rights we're aggressive and "unfeminine" and if we don't we're typical weak females and if we want to get married we're out to trap a man and if we don't we're unnatural and because we still can't get an adequate safe contraceptive but men can walk on the moon and if we can't cope or don't want a pregnancy we're made to feel guilty about abortion and . . . for lots of other reasons we are part of the women's liberation movement.

(Author unknown, quoted in *The Torch*, September 14, 1987)

This sentiment underlies the major goals of Praeger's book series "Women's Psychology":

1. Valuing women. The books in this series value women by valuing children and working for affordable child care; valuing women by respecting all physiques, not just placing value on slender women;

valuing women by acknowledging older women's wisdom, beauty, aging; valuing women who have been sexually victimized and viewing them as survivors; valuing women who work inside and outside of the home; and valuing women by respecting their choices of careers, of whom they mentor, of their reproductive rights, their spirituality and their sexuality.

2. Treating women as the norm. Thus the books in this series make up for women's issues typically being omitted, trivialized, or dismissed from other books on psychology.

3. Taking a non-Eurocentric view of women's experiences. The books in this series integrate the scholarship on race and ethnicity into women's psychology, thus providing a psychology of *all* women. Women typically have been described collectively; but we are diverse.

4. Facilitating connections between readers' experiences and psychological theories and empirical research. The books in this series offer readers opportunities to challenge their views about women, feminism, sexual victimization, gender role socialization, education, and equal rights. These texts thus encourage women readers to value themselves and others. The accounts of women's experiences as reflected through research and personal stories in the texts in this series have been included for readers to derive strength from the efforts of others who have worked for social change on the interpersonal, organizational and societal levels.

A student in one of my courses on the psychology of women once stated:

> I learned so much about women. Women face many issues: discrimination, sexism, prejudices . . . by society. Women need to work together to change how society views us. I learned so much and talked about much of the issues brought up in class to my friends and family. My attitudes have changed toward a lot of things. I got to look at myself, my life, and what I see for the future. (Paludi, 2002, p. 378)

It is my hope that readers of the books in this series also reflect on the topics and look at themselves, their own lives, and what they see for the future.

I am honored to have *Bullies in the Workplace* included in this series on women's psychology. This volume offers suggestions for all of us who want to know more about prevention and responses to academic and workplace bullying. All of the contributors to this volume are deeply committed to ensuring the eradication of bullying and other forms of violence against students and employees. I am honored to have had the opportunity to work with them on this volume.

REFERENCE

Paludi, M. (2002). *The psychology of women* (2nd ed.). Upper Saddle River, NJ: Prentice Hall.

Foreword

Philip E. Poitier

When parents send their children to school, they have a very basic belief and expectation that their children will be given a quality education, that their children's needs will be met, and that they will be safe. Parents rightfully believe that educators, who have made the solemn promise to educate their children and to act *en loco parentis*, will do everything possible to ensure that those basic expectations are met, and that belief should suffice. However, given the current concerns about education costs and mandates, the common-core curriculum, and effective teaching evaluations in schools, can like-interested stakeholders, such as parents, teachers, and communities continue to provide the necessary attention and support to antibullying initiatives with so many other competing issues in education today?

The answer, of which we are all aware, is that we must. We as a society cannot allow our attention to waver until another national news tragedy causes us to refocus on the issue, not simply for bullying in schools, but also within our society, only to find that we have lost hard-won ground. Every day, the problem of bullying forces children to live with deep pain that for some may seem unendurable. It may not be until some inescapably overt act is committed or some critical piece of evidence emerges that the important adults in a child's life recognize the desperate feelings of loneliness and the emotional pain of the bullied child. What amount of irrevocable harm may have been caused during these collective and societal lapses of attention? How will it impact youth later in the workplace?

Many community stakeholders have become more aware that the harm of the recurring torment from direct and indirect harassment, of ostracism, or perhaps even physical harm all having lasting effects on targets well into adulthood, if not for a lifetime. However, do we also consider the possible negative implications for present and future productivity for the target, the offender, and society at large? It has been reported (by the Bureau of Justice Statistics (BJS) and the National Center for Educational Statistics Institute of Education Sciences (IES) Indicators of School Crime and Safety: 2013 Report) that most bullying occurs in school: about 28% of all students ages 12 to 18 have reported being bullied at school. According to the Centers for Disease Control and Prevention's Youth Risk Behavior Surveillance 2013 report, an average of 7.2% of students across the 39 states surveyed (range 3.6% to 13.1%), as many as 160,000 each day, admitted to being absent from school due to fears of being bullied, losing valuable class time in the process. The children who bully are not left unscathed in this either. The American Society for the Positive Care of Children (ASPCC) reports that the statistics for children who bully have remained fairly static for at least a decade: those children are as much as six times as likely as other children to have been arrested or incarcerated by the age of 24. Even among adults, the National Institute of Occupational Safety and Health reported a $19 billion loss of employment and a $3 billion reduction in productivity due to workplace bullying. The ASPCC has reported that as many as 20% of high school students have seriously considered suicide within the past 12 months.

I can remember many years ago, when I was a police officer and newly assigned as a school resource officer, that a young student had returned to my school after a failed suicide attempt. As we spoke during lunch upon the student's return to school, the student admitted to me that the prospect of returning to school at the end of the vacation break was so frightening due to the unending bullying that ending life was far preferable. The student felt no one could stop the harassment, because no one had seemed to try up to that point, and that the bullying students were far too strong to have been stopped even if anyone had tried to help. The student went on to say that no allies had presented themselves, and being of no real value to anyone, "Why would anyone miss me?" "At least," the student went on, "the torment would end." I remember trying to hide my surprise that such a wonderfully bright and talented young person could possibly have had such feelings of low self-esteem to feel driven to such action as to attempt suicide. Every child is precious and valuable to us all, and no child should feel such hopelessness. Every life lost is a loss of all of its potential to every other citizen. I also felt both anger and sorrow that none of us, not even that student's family members, had recognized the signs, as in those days, although well researched in academic circles, bullying was not well legislated nor was much a part of the curriculum in schools.

Every citizen, particularly a child, has a basic right to actual safety and also feeling safe, and many states have recently enacted legislation in schools, such as New York's Dignity for All Students Act, for initiatives in school to support such rights.

That the issues surrounding bullying come together at schools should not by itself surprise us, as the vast majority of homes in any given community are inextricably connected by that community's children's attendance in its public school. Much of the focus on the issue of bullying is placed on schools due to this nexus, but of equal partnership in the stakeholder relationship is the community in which the child resides for the remaining two-thirds of every school day. Schools and communities must continue to partner in the sharing of information regarding the effects of bullying, the local problem, and successful strategies to combat the harm. We should all consider that while the professionals who counsel our children, on both sides of the issue, may have precedence by way of the protected practice skills to counsel both offender and victim, every person in that child's community should consider having an interest in that child's well-being. Every parent and every person in each community can help put his or her "shoulder to the wheel" by learning to recognize the signs, learn supportive strategies, and improve the conditions in which a bully-free school, and more important, a bully-free community and society may flourish. These are things in which we must all take an active part.

So, how do school officials concerned with safety and security at schools help to foster both the climate and the culture that serve to mitigate the effects of bullying? First and foremost, erect a very, very large tent. If we are truly seeking to have a positive effect on the culture of bullying, as many stakeholders as possible, from student to parent and beyond should seek to thoroughly understand the issues and concepts. This continuing education is essential. Thanks to the work of many behavioral scientists, such as Dr. Dan Olweus as well as many others, there is a ready wealth of information on the topic of bullying. The body of work defining the problem and its concepts should be coupled with a local understanding of the problem, such as the picture gained by a school survey of student perspectives. The continuing education of all key stakeholders must be a critical component in a successful program.

Parents and educators should know how and where students are bullied. Knowledge of the forms of bullying are also important. Do all stakeholders know what to look for and how to recognize the warning signs of bullying behaviors? Successful schools also set clear behavioral expectations within the school's code of conduct, based on law, regulations, and school policies that are fairly enforced, and share this information with the community. Parental concerns and questions should be welcomed and swiftly acted upon. Although bullying behaviors have technical distinctions from ordinary poor behaviors, students must come to trust that the adults will understand the difference, listen to them, respond quickly and appropriately to bullying behaviors, and also help to allay their fears about reprisals.

I have observed that understanding the ethos of the community and developing methods of reporting that resonate well within it may help to ease the fears of those students who are reluctant to report and go against cultural norms. In my experience, this appears to have achieved the desired effect by seemingly increasing reports of bullying. In the schools where I've seen successful, research-based efforts, the students themselves were active in the attempts to positively change the school's culture and climate. My multidistrict experiences have informed me that when a school community, from administration to classroom teachers and support staff, students, and parents, achieves the essential critical mass of "buy-in" and are prepared to exhibit the endurance necessary for continued efforts, successful mitigation of bullying behaviors will be possible.

This is one of the reasons why I believe that this book, and the work and research therein, and particularly the work of Dr. Michele Paludi, is so very important. Dr. Paludi has been a tireless advocate of these children and employees and of the message that we can all work cooperatively to help stop this affliction to our children and adults by continuing the research and sharing the information that is needed by all of the stakeholders, be they teachers, parents, or community members. Thank you Michele for this, and I look forward to the day when every child will feel he or she is "bully-free" at school, because schools and workplaces really are the places where hopes and dreams are nurtured.

Acknowledgments

I thank my sisters, Rosalie and Lucille, for their support. Some friends also deserve my appreciation for their listening: Steven Earle, Dan Biladeau, Tony LoFrumento, Brad Fowler, Johanna Duncan-Poitier, and Philip Poitier. I also thank my colleagues at Siena College for their impact on my research, advocacy, and thinking about bullying.

Thanks also go to Debbie Carvalko and her colleagues at Praeger. And to Antoinette and Michael, who taught me to help others, to be their voice, to speak up when I see injustice: I say thank you.

Introduction

Michele A. Paludi

Knowing what's right doesn't mean much unless you do what's right.

Theodore Roosevelt[1]

In 2010, Kevin Morrissey committed suicide. He had been employed as the managing editor of the *Virginia Quarterly Review*. Coworkers had stated there was a pattern of workplace bullying on the part of his supervisor, Theodore Genoways, that pushed Morrissey to take his own life. A former employee stated that administrators at the University of Virginia had been aware of the corporate bullying of Morrissey for five years (McNair, 2010). Maria Morrissey, Kevin's sister, had stated that "our family is convinced by all that we have learned since Kevin's death that, were it not for Genoways' relentless bullying, Kevin would be alive today" (cited in McNair, 2010, p. 2). Wilson (2010) reported that Genoways would be "overheard screaming at Mr. Morrissey behind this office door" (p. 4). Genoways had described Morrissey as "prickly, mercurial, often brooding . . . his demeanor, to my mind, was often unacceptable for the workplace" (cited in McNair, 2010, p. 2). Human resource personnel informed the journal staff that they would have a mediator try to resolve the issues between Morrissey and Genoways. A coworker of Morrissey had alerted human resources that they "feared that Kevin was suicidal" (cited in McNair, 2010, p. 5).

It has been documented that Morrissey had confronted Genoways about excessive and lavish parties held at his home and large amounts of advances provided to contributing authors. Shortly following this conflict, Genoways portrayed Morrissey as being depressed and mentally ill. Morrissey had reported the behavior on the part of Genoways to human resources, the university ombudsperson, and the president's office. No assistance was ever provided; they most likely interpreted Morrissey's complaints in light of their being told he was "mentally ill." Wilson (2010) noted that Morrissey's cell phone records indicated that during the final two weeks of his life, Morrissey had made 17 calls to the human resources department, president's office, and "university officials responsible for employee assistance and faculty-staff relations" (p. 6).

As I was completing the editing of this volume, the United States celebrated National Bullying Prevention Month (October) and the United Kingdom honored Anti Bullying Week (November). The Workplace Bullying Institute celebrated "Freedom from Workplace Bullies" during October. The goals of these campaigns, much like this volume, were to promote awareness of the prevalence and impact of bullying on individuals and their loved ones and on schools, college campuses, and workplaces. The campaigns and this volume encourage employers, human resource departments, students, faculty, and employees to take action (e.g., discuss bullying in classes; develop an antibullying policy and training program for the organization; facilitate an "act of kindness day" for the entire campus). The theme for the United Kingdom's campaign was "Let's Stop Bullying Together"; the United States selected "Stomp Out Bullying."

During their weeklong celebration, the Workplace Bullying Institute (2014, p. 1) offered an instant poll for individuals to take online. The question was simple: *What training or education does (did) your employer provide related to workplace bullying?* The results were as follows:

None (88%)

Online slide show/video, bullying being taught with other forms of harassment (5%)

Mandatory in-person training, bullying taught along with other forms of harassment (4%)

Voluntary in-person training, bullying taught along with other forms of harassment (1%)

Mandatory in-person training, bullying taught as a separate topic (1%)

Online slide show/video, bullying being taught as separate topic (1%)

Voluntary in-person training, bullying taught as separate topic (0%)

The Workplace Bullying Institute (2014) reported that 27% of employees have current or past experiences with abusive conduct at work; that 72% of the individuals polled are aware of workplace bullying; bosses are still the majority of bullies; and 72% of employers deny, discount, encourage, rationalize, or defend workplace bullies and bullying.

Similar findings were reported by the Society for Human Resource Management in 2012. Approximately half of the organizations studied reported there were incidents of bullying experienced in the workplace. In addition, approximately 75% reported verbal abuse of employees. Other behaviors commonly experienced were malicious gossiping and spreading lies or rumors about employees. Half of the organizations indicated their workplace had experienced threats or intimidation of employees. Finally, this research reported that larger organizations (defined as having 500 to 2,499 employees) were more likely to have experienced an incident of bullying than smaller organizations.

Bullying is unwelcome or unreasonable behavior that demeans, intimidates, or humiliates people either as individuals or as a group (Namie & Namie, 2009, 2011). Bullying behavior is often persistent and part of a pattern, but it can also occur as a single incident. It is usually carried out by an individual but can also be an aspect of group behavior. Bullying can be direct (face-to-face) or indirect (via texting or e-mail). Furthermore, bullying can be physical (e.g., pushing, kicking, hitting), emotional (humiliating, tormenting, ostracism), or verbal (name calling, spreading rumors). Cyberbullying is defined as bullying an individual using any electronic form, including, but not limited to, the Internet, interactive and digital technologies, or mobile phones.

Mobbing is a particular type of bullying behavior carried out by a group rather than by an individual. Mobbing is the bullying or social isolation of a person through collective unjustified accusations, humiliation, general harassment, or emotional abuse. Although it is group behavior, specific incidents such as an insult or a practical joke may be carried out by an individual as part of mobbing behavior.

Corporate bullying involves an employer who bullies the staff, knowing that the employees will be afraid to speak up for fear of retaliation. Examples of corporate bullying include managers who force employees to work long workweek, who deny benefits, and who view stressed employees as week. Corporate bullies also encourage staff to "tell" on coworkers by using threats or rewards. Factors that contribute to corporate bullying include significant organizational change, workplace relationships, managerial styles, and leadership styles. For example, an authoritarian managerial or leadership style demands micromanagement of the employee, who is not provided an opportunity to ask questions or share ideas with the manager. Employees have no input into decision making (Hackman & Johnson, 2009).

Thus, corporate bullies provide false or misleading information, restrict staff's activities, threaten excessive harm for failure to comply with their requests, publically humiliate staff, use name calling, and abuse the organizational power invested in them. Although corporate bullying may include physical abuse, most bullying is psychological in nature. Corporate bullies manipulate targets into thinking they are misreading the situation—"it's all in their mind." The Workplace Bullying Institute (2014, pp. 1–2) offered examples of corporate bullying experiences:

> Everything your tormenter does to you is arbitrary and capricious, working a personal agenda that undermines the employer's legitimate business interests.
>
> You are constantly feeling agitated and anxious, experiencing a sense of doom, waiting for bad things to happen.
>
> People feel justified screaming or yelling at you in front of others, but you are punished if you scream back.
>
> You are shocked when accused of incompetence, despite a history of objective excellence, typically by someone who cannot do your job.

Hornstein (1996) characterized corporate bullies according to their "eight daily sins": Deceit, Constraint, Coercion, Selfishness, Inequity, Cruelty, Disregard, and Deification.

Namie and Namie (2003) identified three kinds of corporate bullies:

1. Chronic Bullies: bullying occurs because of their personality, which involves harming others.
2. Opportunistic Bullies: bullying occurs because of their involvement in office politics.
3. Accidental Bullies: bullying occurs but the bully is not cognizant of the impact of their behavior on others; when they are made aware of their behavior they cease engaging in the aggressiveness.

Leymann (1996) outlined a process of workplace or corporate bullying that is characterized by five phases:

1. Conflict: some critical incident occurs
2. Aggressive Acts: psychological assaults that establish bullying dynamics
3. Management Involvement: Supervisors misjudge the situation. Rather than supporting the survivor of bullying, management isolates and perhaps terminates the target of the bullying
4. Branding of the Target: Labels the target as difficult, mentally ill, troublemaker
5. Expulsion: Target of bullying leaves the organization voluntarily or forced resignation

INCIVILITY, DOMESTIC VIOLENCE, AND BULLYING

It is appropriate that October is associated with bullying awareness in the United States because it is also National Domestic Violence Awareness

Month. Several scholars have discussed workplace violence and campus violence along a continuum of aggressive behaviors that includes bullying (e.g., Paludi, Nydegger, & Paludi, 2006). These forms of violence are abuses of power and use of aggression with the intention of hurting another individual. This continuum has been characterized as follows:

INCIVILITY/MICROAGGRESSIONS
HARASSMENT AND DISCRIMINATION
INTIMATE PARTNER VIOLENCE
RAPE
STALKING
HAZING
CYBERVIOLENCE
BULLYING
ROBBERIES
HOMICIDE

Incidents of workplace violence, including homicide, have been precipitated by aggressive verbal and nonverbal behavior that went unreported by coworkers and managers. In recent years, research has documented a relation among incivility, bullying, and workplace violence (Cortina, Magley, Williams, & Langhout, 2001; Lim & Cortina, 2005; Nadal, 2010; Nydegger, Paludi, DeSouza, & Paludi, 2006). Incivility, a form of interpersonal mistreatment in the workplace, has been defined as "low intensity deviant behavior with ambiguous intent to harm the target, in violation of workplace norms for mutual respect . . . uncivil behaviors are characteristically rude and discourteous, displaying a lack of regard for others" (Andersson & Pearson, 1999, p. 457). Incivility thus includes (a) verbal aggression toward a coworker (e.g., swearing); (b) isolation of a coworker (e.g., not telling an employee of a department meeting); and (c) disrespect (e.g., public humiliation, interruption during meetings) (Lim & Cortina, 2005).

Respondents in research by Forni and colleagues (2003) indicated the following behaviors were examples of workplace incivility:

Taking, without asking, a coworker's food from the office refrigerator
Refusing to work hard on a team effort project
Shifting the blame for your mistake to a coworker
Reading someone else's mail
Neglecting to say please or thank you

Cortina and colleagues (2001) reported that 71% of their sample stated they had experienced at least one uncivil act during the five years prior to the study. Forni and colleagues (2003) reported more than one-third of their 130 research respondents indicated they had experienced incivility at their jobs. In addition, 33% reported the acts of incivility were frequent. Sixty-five percent indicated they had witnessed incivility frequently.

Daniel (2009) noted that workplace bullying closely resembles the experience of an individual who has been victimized by intimate partner violence. Similar to an abusive partner, the bully inflicts pain when he or she wants to and keeps targets wondering when bullying behaviors will occur and when there is a period of peace. Bullies, like individuals who batter, do not engage in the behavior continuously. Rather, a cyclical pattern of bullying is common. Walker (1979) identified a pattern of battering that may be applied to bullying as well. In the tension-building phase, there are battering (bullying) incidents. The individual attempts to avoid escalation of the battering (bullying) by trying to "calm" the partner (boss) and by staying out of his or her way. Tension builds too high to be controlled by these efforts and the batterer (bully) responds with an acute battering (bullying) incident in the second phase. In phase three, the tension from the first two phases is gone and the batterer (bully) becomes "charming" toward the individual. The batterer (bully) apologies and promises to never batter (bully) again. The duration of these phases varies. The level of violence tends to increase both in frequency and severity as the relationship continues over time.

IMPACT OF WORKPLACE OR CORPORATE BULLYING

There are high costs of bullying to employees. They include depression, feelings of helplessness, decreased productivity, headaches, anxiety, sleep disturbances, and disordered eating. Individuals commonly leave the workplace (or campus) as a consequence of being bullied. Individuals who are terminated have the emotional costs of bullying triggering post-traumatic stress disorder. The cost of bullying to organizations includes decreased productivity, deterioration of work, absenteeism, lack of communication and team work, mistrust of management, and decreased morale. The Workplace Bullying Institute (2014) identified some early warning signs that bullying is occurring (p. 1):

You feel like throwing up the night before the start of your workweek.
Your frustrated family demands that you stop obsessing about work at home.
Your doctor asks what could be causing your skyrocketing blood pressure and recent health problems, and tells you to change jobs.
You feel too ashamed of being controlled by another person at work to tell your spouse or partner.
All of your paid time off is used for "mental health breaks" from the misery.

Days off are spent exhausted and lifeless, your desire to do anything is
gone.
Your favorite activities and fun with family are no longer appealing or
enjoyable.
You begin to believe that you provoked the workplace cruelty.

The work performance of individuals who witness incidents of
bullying are also impacted. These bystanders suffer from feelings of guilt
that they did not intervene in the bullying incidents. They also become
intimidated and perform less efficiently, fearing that they may also be
bullied.

Employees who have witnessed workplace bullying experience a
greater fear and negative mood at work (Paludi et al., 2006). Job satisfaction is an excellent predictor of voluntary turnover in organizations
(DeCenzo & Robbins, 2007). Thus, the lower the employee's job satisfaction, the higher the turnover. Furthermore, there is a direct relationship
between (a) job satisfaction and employee engagement (e.g., wanting to
do more for their organization to make the organization succeed) and (b)
job satisfaction and job performance. Thus, bullying impacts the functioning of the entire organization (Society for Human Resource Management,
2012). In fact, bullying and other forms of workplace violence cost businesses in the United States approximately $4 billion annually from lost
work time; recruiting, hiring, and retraining of new employees; decreased
morale; increased stress; decreased trust; increased insurance premiums;
increased employee medical benefits payouts; and increased security costs
(Kelloway, Barling, & Hurrell, 2006; Miller, 2010).

THE PRESENT VOLUME

I invited colleagues to contribute chapters about the definition, cultural
meanings, impact of, and organizational changes needed with respect to
corporate or workplace bullying. The contributors are from a variety of
disciplines, including psychology, human resources, law enforcement,
education administration, and residence life on college campuses. Their
work greatly assists us in understanding bullying, especially the relation
between childhood or adolescent bullying and workplace bullying. They
share my belief that we need expertise from a variety of disciplines in order to understand workplace bullying and effect organizational change
with respect to prevention and responding to incidents of bullying. I am
honored to include their work in this volume.

I hope this volume provides answers to questions you are asking about
workplace bullying. I ask all of us to become active bystanders: speak up
when we see and hear bullying of children, teens, and adults. When we do
not intervene on individuals' behalf, they learn that no help is available;

they have to suffer in silence and that they are alone. They don't have to be alone. We must be there for them.

NOTE

1. From http://www.goodreads.com/quotes/90886-knowing-what-s-right -doesn-t-mean-much-unless-you-do-what-s.

REFERENCES

Andersson, L., & Pearson, C. (1999). Tit for tat? The spiraling effect of incivility in the workplace. *Academy of Management Review, 24,* 452–471.

Cortina, L., Magley, V., Williams, J., & Langhout, R. (2001). Incivility in the workplace: Incidence and impact. *Journal of Occupational Health Psychology, 6,* 64–80.

Davis, T. (2009). *Stop bullying at work.* Alexandria, VA: Society for Human Resource Management.

DeCenzo, D., & Robbins, S. (2007). *Fundamentals of human resource management* (9th ed.). New York: Wiley.

Forni, P., Buccino, D., Greene, R., Freedman, N., Stevens, D., & Stack, T. (2003). *The Baltimore workplace civility study.* Retrieved from http://www.U.balt.edu /jfi/jfi/reports/civilty.

Hackman, M., & Johnson, C. (2009). *Leadership: A communications perspective* (5th ed.). Long Grove, IL: Waveland Press.

Hornstein, H. (1996). *Brutal bosses and their prey: How to identify and overcome abuse in the workplace.* New York: Riverhead Books.

Kelloway, E., Barling, J., & Hurrell, J. (2006). *Handbook of workplace violence.* New York: Sage.

Leymann, H. (1996). The content and development of mobbing at work. *European Journal of Work and Organizational Psychology, 5,* 165–184.

Lim, S., & Cortina, L. (2005). Interpersonal mistreatment in the workplace: The interface and impact of general incivility and sexual harassment. *Journal of Applied Psychology, 90,* 483–496.

McNair, D. (2010). *Tale of woe: The death of the VQR's Kevin Morrissey.* Retrieved on from http://www.readthehook.com/66869/cover-tale-death-vqrs-kevin -morrissey.

Miller, L. (2010). *Workplace violence: A preventable trauma.* Retrieved from http:// www.doereport.com/article_workplaceviolence.php.

Nadal, K. (2010). Gender microaggressions: Implications for mental health. In M. Paludi (Ed.), *Feminism and women's rights worldwide* (pp. 155–175). Westport, CT: Praeger.

Namie, G., & Namie, R. (2009). *The bully at work: What you can do to stop the hurt and reclaim your dignity on the job.* Naperville, IL: Sourcebooks.

Namie, G., & Namie, R. (2011). *The bully-free workplace: Stop jerks, weasels and snakes from killing your organization.* Hoboken, NJ: Wiley.

Nydegger, R., Paludi, M., DeSouza, E., & Paludi, C. (2006). Incivility, sexual harassment and violence in the workplace. In M. Karsten (Ed.), *Gender, race and ethnicity in the workplace* (pp. 52–81). Westport, CT: Praeger.

Paludi, M., Nydegger, R., & Paludi, C. (2006). *Understanding workplace violence: A guide for managers and employees.* Westport, CT: Praeger.

Society for Human Resource Management. (2012). *SHRM survey findings: Workplace bullying.* Retrieved from http://www.shrm.org/research/surveyfindings/articles/pages/workplacebullying.aspx.

Walker, L. (1979). *The battered woman.* New York: Harper.

Wilson, R. (2010). *What killed Kevin Morrissey?* Retrieved from http://chronicle.com/article/What-Killed-Kevin-Morrissey-/123902/.

Workplace Bullying Institute. (2014). *WBI U.S. workplace bullying survey.* Retrieved from http://www.workplacebullying.org/wbiresearch/wbi-2014-us-survey/.

Part I

Workplace Bullying: Personal Reflections, Definitions, and Impact on Individuals and Organizations

Chapter 1

Toppling the Ivory Tower: Bullying in Higher Education: An Interview with the Researchers

Martina L. Sharp-Grier and Jennifer L. Martin

In October 2014, Dr. Michele Paludi, editor of this volume, invited us to discuss how researchers can educate the college and university campus communities to prevent campus bullying. Her question was: "In what ways can researchers inform college/university campuses about scholarly work on bullying on campus?" After considering the obvious answers— researchers can operationalize and identify types of bullying; identify those most at risk for being bullied, and report the frequency at which they are tormented; posit methods by which to analyze bullying performance; and identify effective methodologies to interrupt bullying behavior—we agreed that the principal way in which researchers can inform the academy about bullying is by giving a voice to those who are often voiceless: persons who have experienced and overcome bullying within a venue presumed impervious to bullying influences. Involving experts who possess empirical knowledge can be invaluable to the analysis and interpretation of bullying. Because we have both experienced bullying in higher education, we decided to start with ourselves, to share some of our own stories and insights that have helped us. Our method for this chapter involves interviewing one another in order to share our personal experiences and how we have translated them within our current institutional homes.

Q: Dr. Martin: What have you done to communicate your years of research and advocacy on the topic of bullying within your institution?

First, I must say that it is difficult to stand up and to vocalize issues around bullying, especially as a new faculty member seeking tenure. We must first do everything we can to keep ourselves safe as well as sane. In order to do this, we must cultivate supportive networks, both inside and outside of our institutions. Our aggressors, or those who seek to preserve the status quo, may attempt to paint us as "crazy" or "angry," or even "aggressive." I was recently called a bully because I questioned my departmental norm of acquiescing to perform additional work based upon gender status. Because I disagreed and refused to do additional work, and made this known, I alienated other women who had accepted this expectation for years. Some women were grateful that I attempted to put an end to this inequitable practice, but others painted me as aggressive for stirring up trouble and making them feel uncomfortable. The lesson here is that any time one attempts to challenge the status quo, there will be consequences. These consequences are not always pleasant for the whistle-blower; this is why it is crucial for us to have mentors who can provide guidance through this difficult and unsafe work. Second, when attempting to challenge, and, ultimately change, inequitable institutional norms and practices, we must not only highlight the inequitable, unethical, and perhaps, illegal practices, but we must also make known what equitable workplaces should look like. We must point to models of best practice for leadership, communication practices, evaluation procedures, division of labor, and safe ways to report microaggressions, bullying, and civil rights violations.

Q: Professor Sharp-Grier: What are some practices that have kept you both safe and sane when dealing with institutional and collegial bullying, particularly pertaining to multiple minority identity status inequities and microaggressions?

First and foremost, I keep in mind that try as I might not to, I always have a target on my back. My blackness, my sexual identity, and my sex itself are ripe for scrutiny and are (in the "right" hands) perfect fodder for hostile critique and action. This is especially true in a venue where there are so few full-time African American faculty and fewer "out" gay faculty. My acceptance of what I call "the inevitable reality" frees me to be a vocal advocate for the disenfranchised and against behavior (and attitudes) which reinforces the structural inequalities inherent in the institution. To be sure, it's completely frightening to acknowledge that you are the moving target in a professional game of skeet; however, it is simultaneously liberating. The fear of stereotype threat is negated when one realizes that one will *always* be seen as the stereotype. Second, I try not to allow bullying—in any of its forms—to go unchecked. Particularly in my most recent experience, I was not content to simply "take it" and walk away licking my proverbial wounds. I stood up to the structural forces and demanded answers. It's important for those who are marginalized to understand that they absolutely have the power (and a fiduciary responsibility to self and colleagues) to illuminate bullying, mobbing, and other tactics and to demand action. Third, as a sociologist, I am keenly aware of the power structure inherent in formal institutions. Unfortunately, academe is not immune to the posturing and jockeying of those who hold power, as they struggle to illuminate their status and maintain their privilege. That knowledge is well considered when the jabs begin to feel personal. My mantra: "It's only a game, Martina."

Q: Dr. Martin: What advice would you give to other scholars regarding the effective navigation of workplace bullying?

It is very important that we are aware of our rights. Civil rights guidelines are not made readily known to stakeholders in general. This is a practice that must be changed if we are ever to facilitate our institutions evolving into more equitable places. To start, I recommend familiarizing ourselves with federal guidelines,[1] sharing them with our colleagues, and advocating for their inclusion in faculty, staff, and student handbooks. We must also make ourselves aware of what to do if our institutions do not work to put an end to illegal practices. If you feel you have been subject to harassment in the workplace, please watch the following video.[2]

Q: Professor Sharp-Grier: How have you taken these lessons, both from practice and research, and communicated them within your institution with the goal of creating more equitable institutional policies and practices?

As I am able, I routinely involve myself in social justice work within the institution. I am a Safe Space trainer and ally, and I am a vocal advocate for the LGBTQ QIAAP community.[3] Moreover, I routinely monitor the Affirmative Action plan of my institution. I gather data from administration regarding the goals and benchmarks that they have created for themselves concerning faculty of color and women, and I have illuminated inconsistencies to administration when necessary. Lastly, I have aligned myself with an independent faculty advocacy organization, which adds another layer of checks and balances regarding, knowledge of, and ability to act against, inequitable behavior—both on the individual level, and at the institutional scale. My goal is not to be adversarial (unless it becomes necessary); rather, I seek to illuminate problems and advocate for change.

Q: Dr. Martin: What advice would you give to administrators who seek to interrupt the frequency with which workplace bullying takes place within their institutions?

The advice I would give to administrators is as follows: do not fear transparency. Place civil rights guidelines in faculty, staff, and student handbooks. Make all stakeholders aware of their rights as well as the consequences for those who violate the rights of others. Make contact information of Title IX coordinators and other civil rights officers readily available to faculty, staff, and students. Train faculty, staff, and students in civil rights guidelines, and make it explicit that the college or university expects strict adherence to the aforementioned guidelines. Stress that you not only value but require an equitable workplace.

Q: Professor Sharp-Grier: Do you have any closing words regarding workplace bullying in general or microaggressive, identity-based bullying, specifically?

Systems of power and control are brutal, and their effects on both individuals and institutional structure are oftentimes debilitating, to say the least. As a sociologist, I absolutely understand the dynamic of workplace bullying performance as it relates to the maintenance of power, supremacy, and occupational leverage; yet, I am dumbfounded at the level to which it has been accepted in the academic reserve—a space where, ostensibly, we should "know better"—especially when the oppression takes form as identity-based intimidation and maltreatment. That being said, I believe that the structural implementation of a Procedural Justice/Restorative Justice based response to the phenomenon will, in the short term, alleviate the effects of both power-driven and identity-based bullying, and in the long term, curtail and eradicate their use in academe. As I noted earlier, we have a fiduciary responsibility to each other, as members of our respective organizations, to ensure that we provide a safe, nondiscriminatory, and—as much as can be done in a hierarchical venue—a mutually deferential space within which to pursue our academic passions and career goals.

We wish the reader equity in the workplace and courage when equity is absent.

> Don't be afraid of your fears. They're not there to scare you.
> They're there to let you know that something is worth it.
>
> C. JoyBell

NOTES

1. See the following Letter to Colleagues: http://www2.ed.gov/about/offices/list/ocr/letters/colleague-201010.pdf.

2. And the following bullying, harassment, and civil rights guidance video: http://www.stopbullying.gov/videos/2014/02/civil-rights.html.

3. For more information, see Safe Space material available through GLSEN at http://safespace.glsen.org/.

Chapter 2

Workplace Bullying: Concerted Activity as a Viable Solution

Jerry Carbo

In the course of my career as a human resource professional, attorney, researcher, union leader, and advocate, I have witnessed, studied, and taken steps to eliminate workplace bullying from various directions. I have seen more workplace bullying in that time than I would hope to over an entire career, and I have seen the terrible effects it can have on its targets. In fact, I have been the target of workplace bullying on at least two occasions and have felt how the bullying can impact even a researcher who has a fairly deep understanding of the phenomenon. I have spent a large part of my career attempting to eliminate workplace harassment and bullying and have a deep devotion to eliminating as many acts of workplace bullying as possible. Although I have experienced more bullying than I would care to see, these experiences have also played a big part in my research of the phenomenon, often as a participant observer. Over the course of this time, I have found that concerted activity does indeed present a possible solution to workplace bullying, and I have developed this position over the course of my research and experience. The research has included in-depth discussions and focus groups with targets of workplace bullying and a comparative case study of union reactions to workplace bullying that I have accumulated over nearly two decades. This comparative case study often entailed my engagement as a participant observer, in one case as an employee relations manager and in the other two as a union member and even leader. I have also come across other examples of concerted activity responses to workplace bullying through training sessions, conferences, and informal discussions with union members and leaders.

The aim of this chapter is present as many of these experiences as possible. I will share my position as to why concerted activity can indeed help to eliminate workplace bullying, while at the same time ineffective action by unions can exacerbate the problem of workplace bullying. It is my desire that this chapter will present hope and ideas to targets of workplace bullying. Further, this chapter will present ideas and lessons for worker advocates, including union organizers, shop stewards, and leaders. Finally, this chapter should also spur further research into possible solutions to workplace bullying as well as other potential solutions.

WORKPLACE BULLYING AND ITS OUTCOMES

There are many different definitions of workplace bullying. The most basic starting point to gain some insight is to turn to the dictionary definition of the topic. *Merriam-Webster's Dictionary* defines the verb "bully" as: "to behave as a bully toward: DOMINEER, syn. Browbeat, intimidate." "Domineer" is further defined as "to rule in an arrogant manner, to be overbearing, intimidate as to make timid or fearful, to compel or deter by or as if by threat." However, to understand workplace bullying, we need to go further than this basic definition. Based on the narratives, interviews, and focus groups with targets of workplace bullying, Carbo and Hughes (2010) developed the following definition of workplace bullying: Workplace bullying is defined as the unwanted, unwelcome abuse of any source of power that has the effect of or intent to intimidate, control, or otherwise strip a target of their right to esteem, growth, dignity, voice, or other human rights in the workplace.

However, no matter which definition of bullying is used, workplace bullying is a severe and pervasive problem. For targets of bullying, the outcomes of workplace bullying can be devastating. Bullying studies have shown a clear connection between health and bullying. Health outcomes for the victims have included anxiety, depression, insomnia, nervous symptoms, melancholy, apathy, sociophobia, and post-traumatic stress disorder symptoms (Rayner, Hoel, & Cooper, 2002). Further, these health effects can be very pronounced, even early on in a bullying scenario.

According to Gardner and Johnson (2001, p. 28), "bullying causes stress-related illnesses that shatter many careers. Anxiety, stress and excessive worry head the list of health consequences for targets, thereby interfering with their ability to be productive at work." Keashley and Neuman (2004, p. 346) found that "exposure to bullying is associated with heightened levels of anxiety, depression, burnout, frustration, helplessness, negative emotions such as anger, resentment, and fear, difficulty concentrating, and lowered self-esteem and self-efficacy." Bullying has also has been linked to symptoms consistent with post-traumatic stress syndrome, suicidal thoughts, and attempts. There is also clear evidence that some victims of bullying end up committing suicide (Rayner et al., 2002). According to Davenport, Schwartz, and Elliot (2002, p. 33), "For the victim, death—through illness or suicide—may be the final chapter in the mobbing story." According to Einarsen (1999, p. 16), bullying may be "a more crippling and devastating problem for employees than all other work-related stress put together."

Not only is workplace bullying a severe problem, it is also pervasive. A Michigan study by Keashley and Jagatic (2003) found 59% of respondents had "experienced at least one type of emotionally abusive behavior at the hands of fellow workers." Swedish research in the 1990s found that 3.5% of the labor force fell victim to mobbing at any one time (Davenport et al., 2002, p. 25). Hornstein (1996, p. 5) suggested that 20% of the American workforce faces workplace abuse on a daily basis, and 90% will face it at some point in their careers. The problem of workplace bullying is also a growing phenomena, "the incidence and the severity of occupational violence are increasing across industrialized countries, particularly for workers who have significant levels of face to face contact with their clients or customers" (McCarthy & Mayhew, 2004, p. 148).

FEW VIABLE SOLUTIONS FOR TARGETS

Although steps have been taken to combat workplace bullying in many countries, through legislation (i.e., France, Canada, Sweden) and the common law (United Kingdom, Australia, Canada, and Germany), little has been done in the United States to address workplace bullying. The only two potential legal avenues of redress in the United States fail to protect the majority of targets of workplace bullying. First, under Title VII, the Americans with Disabilities Act, Age Discrimination in Employment, and under most state human rights laws, harassment based on protected status such as race or gender is unlawful. However, the reality is that only one in four cases of workplace bullying are based on a protected class (Namie & Namie, 2009). The protections against harassment under these Equal Employment Opportunity (EEO) laws is based on preventing discrimination against protected classes, not protecting worker dignity. The Supreme Court was clear in this position in *Harris v. Forklift*, 510 U.S. 17 (1993): "The critical issue, Title VII's text indicates, is whether members of one sex are exposed to disadvantageous terms or conditions of employment to which members of the other sex are not opposed." This alone makes the EEO laws an unviable remedy for 75% of targets of workplace bullying. Further, heightened standards for proving the severity and pervasiveness under EEO laws leave many cases of bullying that strip the targets of their dignity, voice, and other human rights in the workplace with no avenue for relief, even if the bullying is based on a protected status (Carbo, 2009). This lack of relief is further evidenced by the severe uphill battle that plaintiffs in employment discrimination cases face (Clermont & Schwab, 2004).

The second protection against these types of behaviors is the common law tort claim of intentional infliction of emotional distress (IIED). This claim also leaves little hope for most targets of workplace bullying. IIED claims are even a weaker remedy as they cover only the most atrocious acts of bullying with the most severe of outcomes. In one case, the West Virginia Supreme Court ruled that "the first element of the cause of action is a showing by the plaintiff that the defendant's actions towards the plaintiff were atrocious, intolerable, and so extreme and outrageous as to exceed the bounds of decency. The defendant's conduct must be more than unreasonable, unkind or unfair; it must truly offend community notions of acceptable conduct" (*Travis v. Alcon*, 1998). The Third Circuit Court of Appeals suggested in *Cox v. Keystone Carbon Co.* (1998), "[I]t is extremely rare to find conduct in the employment context that will rise to the level of outrageousness necessary to provide a basis for recovery for the tort of intentional infliction of emotional distress."

Second, by its very definition, an IIED claim requires the plaintiff to prove the defendant's intent: "A plaintiff must show that the defendant acted with an intent to inflict emotional distress upon the plaintiff, or acted in a reckless manner such that it was certain or substantially certain that emotional distress would result from the defendant's actions" (*Travis v. Alcon*, 1998). Proving intent in workplace bullying claims presents a nearly impossible hurdle for targets (Carbo, 2009).

To sustain a claim under the tort of outrage or IIED, a plaintiff must show a third element of an IIED claim—severe emotional distress. Although not every jurisdiction will require testimony from an expert witness to prove severe emotional distress (*Travis v. Alcon*, 1998), many others go even further. For instance, the Pennsylvania Supreme Court has ruled that the plaintiff's own testimony regarding his or her severe emotional distress is not enough proof to meet his or her burden of proving this element of the claim (*Kazatsky v. King David Memorial Park, Inc.*, PA 1987). In *Love v. Georgia Pacific Corporation* (WV, 2001), the Supreme Court of West Virginia mentioned that emotional distress may not be enough to sustain a claim even when there is expert testimony and the plaintiff is receiving treatment and has been prescribed an antidepressant. This standard suggests that perhaps the courts are looking for some type of severe emotional breakdown in order to sustain a claim for IIED. The Western District Court of Virginia made it very clear that claims of IIED will most often fail because the harm is not severe enough (*Glover v. Oppleman*, W.D. Va., 2001).

Although the U.S. legal system offers very little hope for targets, employer human resource (HR) systems often exacerbate rather than solve the bullying problem (Namie & Namie, 2009). Fox and Stallworth (2004) have found tepid support at best for alternative dispute resolution systems as a viable solution. The qualitative interviews that I conducted during my dissertation research, together with the focus groups that followed, suggest that the support for concerted activity among these research participants grew out of a growing consciousness of being a class of targets (Carbo, 2009). This is of particular importance because if any possible solution to workplace bullying is to be effective, targets must be willing to engage in that solution.

CONCERTED ACTIVITY AND UNION ACTION PROVIDES A GLIMMER OF HOPE

The purpose of a union is to make the lives of workers better (Moody, 2007). This is the very heart of unionism and concerted activity. According to Yates (2009), it is this concerted activity that can and often does protect the dignity of workers. This same dignity is stripped from workers who are targets of workplace bullying (Carbo & Hughes, 2010). Further, the workplace bully requires a power imbalance in order to be able to torment their targets (Carbo, 2009). This is the very type of imbalance that concerted activity is meant to eliminate (Budd, 2013). Targets of bullying are also stripped of their voice in the workplace (Carbo & Hughes, 2010), a voice that again is protected and secured through the labor relations process of concerted activity (Budd, 2013; Yates, 2009). When we simply consider the outcomes of bullying—the loss of voice and dignity for the target as well as the necessitating factor of a power imbalance, coupled with the outcomes of concerted activity, and more power for workers, and protection of voice and dignity—in theory, concerted activity seems to be a viable solution to workplace bullying.

However, in order for any solution to be viable, targets must also support the potential solution. This lack of support was one of the potential problems with alternative dispute resolution as a solution. Further, in the course of both interviews and focus groups, targets of bullying were supportive of the idea of concerted activity as a solution to workplace bullying. One target stated that if his state had collective bargaining rights for state employees such as himself, he would immediately join a union to address his issues with workplace bullying (Carbo, 2009). Other targets felt that concerted activity in the absence of direct collective bargaining rights presented a strong option to deal with workplace bullies, and of all of the options presented and discussed in a series of focus groups (HR departments, litigation, legislation), targets of bullying were clear that concerted activity presented the most viable solution for current targets. However, for concerted activity to be effective, there must be a sense of class consciousness (a love and saliency) that must occur (Wheeler, 2002). In the course of focus group discussions with targets of workplace bullying, a sense of class consciousness developed among the targets. Targets expressed that their experiences had much in common (saliency), and they often became more concerned for other targets in the focus group than they were even for themselves (love) (Carbo, 2009).

Although concerted activity and union involvement present a potential path to address workplace bullying, we must turn to exploring the specific tactics and methods of concerted activity that can be effective in addressing workplace bullying. Yamada (2004) presents three ways that collective bargaining can be used as a tool to combat workplace bullying.

> First unions can and should bargain for collective bargaining provisions that protect their members against abusive supervision. Second, even in the absence of specific protections against abusive supervision, the general substantive and procedural rights in an agreement may provide legal protections for a bullied union member. Third, effective shop stewards can serve as valuable mediators when bullying situations occur, including those between union
> • members. (Yamada, 2004, p. 494)

The next section of this chapter will explore how concerted activity at each of the phases of the labor relations process—the organizing or strategic phase, the collective bargaining phase, and the day-to-day management of the collective bargaining agreement (CBA)—can address and help to eliminate workplace bullying. I will explore the specific tactics that have been used to address workplace bullying at all phases of the labor relations process. A review of these experiences leads to the conclusion that concerted activity can indeed present a path to eliminating workplace bullying. Where workers are represented, unions can indeed address the bullying and thus condemn the bullying through strong responses. Unions might also simply ignore bullying, viewing it as something outside their realm of collective bargaining and something that is merely a management problem. Unions can even reward bullying by easing their tactics toward bullies or by being intimidated by the bullying and backing away from the bully on other issues. This type of tacit approval in essence cedes control to the bully and is a reward for his or her behavior. Whether or not they do and how unions respond oftentimes will impact not only the bullying situation, but also the view of union efficacy by the target and those who know of the situation.

ADDRESSING WORKPLACE BULLYING IN THE ORGANIZING PHASE

The organizing phase or strategic phase of the labor relations process entails the formation of a union in a workplace, either by the employees deciding to organize themselves or by an external union attempting to organize workers. These organizing drives are defined as either being strategic or opportunistic, but the reality is, in either case, there is always a level of opportunism (Budd, 2013). In every organizing drive, in order to be successful, the workers must perceive there to be some level of detriment that is shared among the workers that could be addressed via concerted activity. In order to be successful, an organizing drive must indeed address issues that are salient or important to the members being organized (Wheeler, 2002). Workplace bullying presents an opportunity in all three regards. First, workplace bullying is clearly pervasive in the American workplace. Further, once bullying is introduced into a workplace, it quickly spreads both in terms of the specific target (a progression from bullying to mobbing) and from a cultural perspective of the spread of bullying to other targets. Second, as evidenced in the course of my research, when targets discuss their experiences, they tend to become concerned about the experiences of other targets and develop a form of class consciousness. In fact, listening to others' experiences seems to heighten the perception of their own detriment as well. Finally, targets of workplace bullying were overwhelmingly supportive of concerted activity as a potential solution. Further, a case study at a university shows that an organizing drive at least focused in part on bullying can indeed eliminate at least a bully from the workplace, if not the bullying culture.

This organizing drive was a bit out of the norm. First, joining the union was completely voluntary even if the drive were successful. Public workers in this state did not have collective bargaining rights, and, therefore, there was no certification process. Thus, there were very few official actions the union could take other than to represent employees in a state-mandated but limited grievance process. Second, the organizing drive at this facility had really developed in response to comments from state legislators. These legislators indicated that faculty were lazy and should be teaching more courses. So the advent of the union drive centered around what could be termed bullying, but bullying that was outside the workplace. However, the drive also shifted toward addressing internal workplace bullying by the president of this university.

The union leadership readily recognized the bullying environment in the workplace, as well as the bullying nature of the president of the university. In this case, the organizers for the union were truly internal members, with support from an external union (another key to organizing success). The union organizers also began to see that the university president did little to address their concerns with legislators. The union did try to get the president to engage in meetings and discussions, but he refused. The union held union day events, appeared at trustee meetings, wrote op-eds and letters to the editor, and represented faculty members in disputes with the president where they were able to fit the dispute under the state employee grievance process. As part of an organizing drive, unions are also more successful in organizing workers when they act as a union from day one (Brofenbrenner & Hickey, 2003). They in essence took steps to address workplace issues, whether it is offering legal support, direct action, or helping workers utilize internal conflict resolution processes. In this case, the members were availed of a state worker grievance process via a state statute. At first, the union was hesitant to use this grievance process because they viewed it as a process to be used only when one feels they are going to win. However, eventually the process was used as more of a signaling and nuisance process. The pressure placed on the bully in this case entailed a bit of a community or pressure campaign. In addition, internally there was a campaign of, in essence, pestering the bully, ensuring that they would be there at every opportunity to address his iron-fisted control over the university. Eventually the bully left the organization.

By placing attention and a light on the bullying behavior in this organization as part of an organizing drive, the union organizers at least in part were able to address the workplace bullying. They provided a support system for targets, via direct action, the formal grievance process, and moral support. They also continued to focus on the bully until such time as the bully decided to leave the organization. The bully, of course, never indicated that he was leaving due to these actions, but at the least, the strong position of this union against this workplace bully would have made the bully's decision to leave a bit easier.

COLLECTIVE BARGAINING AND WORKPLACE BULLYING

Once a union has successfully organized a workplace, the next phase of the labor relations process is to negotiate a contract. In this phase of the labor relations process, unions can address workplace bullying in three ways. First, the union could indeed negotiate a direct antibullying clause. Second, the union could make bullying in the organization or even a specific bully the focus of negotiations and their willingness to engage in the process in a productive manner. An example of this tactic will be shared below. Finally, a union can look to understand bullying prior to negotiations, identify the tactics of a bully, and eliminate the potential bully's control over these tactics by negotiating clauses that address these specific tactics or take this tactic out of the hands of potential bullies.

The first route, at least in theory, would be the most effective: negotiate a specific antibullying clause via negotiations. Employers are mandated under the National Labor Relations Act and under many state labor laws to negotiate with the union over wages, benefits, and other terms and conditions of employment. Workplace bullying would seem to clearly fall under these mandatory topics. Workplace bullying has a dramatic impact on workers' terms and conditions of employment. Bullying in the workplace leads to increased stress, depression, physiological illnesses, and even violence and death as well as increased absenteeism, workplace injuries, and turnover. Targets are often forced to abandon their jobs or to suffer great levels of psychological or even physical harm.

Unions can and should address workplace bullying directly in collective bargaining by negotiating direct antibullying clauses and protections for their members. Although such bargaining is definitely viable, it appears at best to be in its infancy. Further, even if the union negotiates this type of clause, it must be aware of the potential pitfalls of bullying clauses such as those identified in potential legislation. These would include requirement of intent, a heightened requirement of severity and pervasiveness, a focus on protected statuses or even bullying tactics rather than employee rights, and the outcomes to the targets such as stripping the employee of his or her rights to dignity and voice.

Although direct antibullying clauses might present the ideal, there are indeed other ways that workplace bullying and workplace bullies can be addressed in the course of collective bargaining. One way is to make bullying or bullies (or even a single bully) the focus of negotiations or to make addressing these behaviors by management a prerequisite to good faith bargaining. One such example of this topic came via a union in the manufacturing sector in the Deep South. This facility had a firmly entrenched division between supervisors and line workers (even though most supervisors had first been line workers). The supervisors had a history of management through intimidation, but one supervisor in particular was considered the worst of the workplace bullies in the plant, and he, in essence, became a big part of the focus of the upcoming negotiations.

This facility had experienced a strike during the prior CBA negotiations, and there was a clear statement by corporate leadership that if there was another strike, the work would be moved out of the plant. On many occasions, including my first week as employee relations manager, the president of the local union and the chief steward both made it clear that Jim[1] would be the number one bargaining issue if nothing was done to change his behavior. This was also communicated to the human resources and plant managers. At first his statements were friendly in nature and seemed to be more of informing me there was a problem. However, as Jim's behaviors continued, the threats became greater and greater. This union, over the course of the three years, found ways to address Jim's behavior during the day-to-day management of the CBA. As a result, on the first day of negotiations, when the union's lead negotiator from the national branch suggested it would not engage in negotiations until the management had a plan to deal with Jim, the local leaders intervened and stated that the issues with Jim had been addressed. However, the point here was that the union was indeed willing to make this workplace bully a bargaining issue.

A third method of addressing workplace bullying indirectly during the collective bargaining phase is to take away the tactics that bullies use to bully. This method would require the union negotiators to understand both common forms of bullying as well as the specific tactics of bullying in their organization. For instance, in one case of bullying in academia, the workplace bully used committee assignments as one of his tactics of bullying. If he disagreed with a faculty member, he would have him or her removed from a committee or in one case even disband the entire committee. If the formation and purpose of the committee work would have been a part of a CBA, this would have eliminated at least one tactic of this bully. In another situation, the bully used periodic seat checks to control his targets and to punish those whom he chose to punish. In this case, a just cause clause could have addressed the bullying, and more control over the work requirements could have taken the seat check out of the hands of the bully. Bullies are also known for engaging in tactics such as blaming targets for errors, making unreasonable job demands, inconsistent application of work rules, and threatening job loss (Namie & Namie, 2009). With each of these tactics, CBA clauses can indeed take these tactics away from the bully.

The bargaining phase of the labor relations process presents opportunities for labor unions to address workplace bullying. Unions should be willing to address bullying as a mandatory topic and to negotiate specific antibullying clauses. However, in the alternative, the collective bargaining phase presents union leaders with the whip to force management to address workplace bullies. As the southern manufacturing union demonstrated, the threat of a bully's behavior holding up negotiations will at least give management negotiators pause.

SUPPORTING TARGETS OF WORKPLACE BULLYING DURING THE DAY-TO-DAY MANAGEMENT OF THE CBA

Moody (2007, p. 177) stated: "The workplace is where union members have power—real and potential." This power comes through in the day-to-day work and the support the union leadership provides to members to protect their working conditions and their dignity on the job. This phase of the labor relations process provides union leadership with the most opportunities to address the workplace bully and to address them on their own stomping grounds—the day-to-day work environment. This phase of dealing with the bully, like all true union power, is the key to making members' lives better by eliminating the bullying. Unions, shop stewards, union leaders, and even union activists can help to eliminate bullying at this phase in three ways. First, unions can indeed enforce with vigor direct antibullying clauses. Second, unions can make sure to enforce indirect clauses, especially where enforcement will eliminate workplace bullying. Third, unions, stewards, and even activist members can create disincentives for specific bullies to continue their bullying behavior. In other words, they can eliminate bullying behavior via punishment (the behavior being followed by a negative stimuli) or negative reinforcement (only taking away a negative stimuli when the behavior truly stops). However, perhaps more than any other, this phase also presents the opportunity for the pitfalls, where unions can actually cause the bullying in workplaces to become worse.

Direct Clauses—Ensuring Enforcement

Enforcing a direct clause that deals with workplace bullying should seem to be an automatic. However, just like any other clause in a CBA, this does not always happen. Unions have often ceded control over day-to-day issues to management and may even cede enforcement of CBA clauses to protect a focus on partnership with management (Moody, 2007). Union leaders, in the guise of protecting the partnering relationship with management, will often dissuade union members from filing grievances, the very mechanism that is used to enforce clauses (Moody, 2007). However, union leaders and activists who focus on members' needs and rights can indeed ensure strong enforcement of CBA clauses (Moody, 2007).

Indirect Clauses—An Alternative Route

Workplace bullying can be addressed on a day-to-day basis by focusing on the outcomes of workplace bullying and clauses that would protect against these types of outcomes. For instance, many CBAs have safety clauses that require employers to provide a safe working environment. One union in the Midwest indicated that it had success addressing bullying through the general duty safety clause in its CBA. For another Mid-Atlantic union, a dignity clause has been used to address abusive behaviors by supervisors. Actions that strip employees of their rights under a CBA should also be addressed by stewards and activists to deal with workplace bullying. For example, in one faculty union CBA, members were ensured academic freedom in the classroom. This is generally viewed to include the right to select content, but also most clearly the right to select teaching methods. One bullying supervisor in this union decided to exert control over a target's classroom. In this case, the tactic could be taken away through a vigorous pursuit of a grievance for this impingement. However, a weak or less aggressive pursuit would indicate acceptance of this behavior, as discussed below.

Union leaders, stewards, and activists can also address workplace bullying in the day-to-day environment by addressing the tactics used by bullies. A general understanding of workplace bullying can help union leaders to identify the sources and tactics of bullying in general, such as those mentioned in the collective bargaining section, but also unions that pay attention to the day-to-day environment will be able to identify a bully's specific preferred tactics. Union representatives can gain an understanding of specific tactics used in their workplaces by listening to members' concerns and ensuring activism at the most basic level of the workplace via active stewards.

CBA clauses that take these tactics away from bullying supervisors by granting these powers and rights to workers should be aggressively enforced. For instance, if a supervisor tries to take duties away that are specifically listed in the purview of an employee's job under the CBA, a union should enforce such a clause to eliminate the bullying. Bullies often use reward and punishment power as a tactic. However, most CBAs contain just cause clauses for disciplinary actions. Union leaders and stewards should be very skeptical of *all* disciplinary actions (even minor steps and so-called informal steps) and ensure that the supervisor has indeed disciplined employees only where there has been just cause. Further, the use of rewards, particularly if they are used to persuade employees to forego their Section 7 or state-level concerted activity rights, would amount to an unfair labor practice (ULP) that union leaders can and should address. Many of the other behaviors that bullies utilized are also often addressed in CBAs, including promotion policies, performance reviews, hours of work, and training assignments. By enforcing these clauses, union leaders can eliminate the ability of bullies to use these policies against their targets.

Even where the bullying behavior does not fall under a direct or indirect CBA clause, assertive union leaders, stewards, and activists can indeed play a role in ending the bullying behavior by addressing the bully directly via punishment or negative reinforcement of the behavior. One such possible method is sometimes referred to as the nuisance grievance. In this case, the union steward can force the bully to have to deal with a series of grievances that are filed, not necessarily in the hope of winning the grievances, but in the hope of forcing the supervisor to change his or her behavior. One Mid-Atlantic union referred to the use of this practice as "blue storm" because their grievance forms were blue in color. In a similar vein the union leadership can hold the bullying supervisor to the letter of the law of the CBA. In this case, each time the supervisor violates even the most minor detail of the CBA, a grievance would be filed. The southern manufacturing union engaged in both of these processes in order to deal with Jim, the bullying supervisor in the earlier example. In this plant, there were over 300 grievances in backlog, and among these there were many the union simply refused to settle. Many of these were in Jim's areas, and grievances were filed every week against Jim. Many of these grievances fell outside the CBA's clause coverage, and Jim and his immediate supervisor would typically provide the answer that this was not a CBA violation. However, the union refused to resolve these issues until the underlying behavior was addressed. For the plant, this backlog looked bad to higher levels of management, and it became a potential impediment to negotiations. It was not until the bullying behavior was addressed and had subsided that these grievances were resolved en masse. Under either tactic here, the bullying supervisor would in essence be presented with the negative stimuli of the grievances in response to the bullying behavior. Similarly, as the bullying behavior subsides, this can be followed by the union backing off the nuisance grievances or letter of the law grievances (i.e., a form of negative reinforcement).

There are also other ways that union leaders and activists can address the bully via means outside the grievance process. In *A Trouble Maker's Handbook*, Michael Ames Connor (2005) presents an example where union members engage in concerted activity in response to supervisory behavior that could be considered bullying. In this case, when a supervisor steps out of line, an announcement is made calling "Harry Bridges," legendary International Longshore and Warehouse Union leader of the past, to the area of concern. Thirty to 40 coworkers arrived in the area to challenge the supervisor's decision or action. It is this "movement" that put an end to the bullying behavior.

Unions can also exert pressure on bullies through the use of other laws and policies. For instance, the southern manufacturing union helped workers in the bully's area to utilize their rights to bid out of the area and even influenced other members to refrain from bidding on jobs where members in the bully's area were bidding. The union also pushed members not to bid into the area or to refuse voluntary overtime. Further, stewards trained employees in the area concerning their rights under the Family Medical Leave Act and the limitations of the company's attendance policy. As a result, the supervisor's bullying behavior led to workers bidding out of his area, high levels of absenteeism in his area, and an inability to adequately staff his area. These negative stimuli were meant to punish and stop the bullying behavior. The bullying behavior did eventually subside and the union backed off.

THE DANGERS OF THE WEAK RESPONSE

Unions can indeed address workplace bullying in all three phases of the labor relations process. To truly end bullying in the workplace, the enforcement must exist at the day-to-day level. The power and impact of an organizing drive subside over time. CBA clauses have little meaning if they are not enforced. Bullying occurs in the day-to-day world of workers' lives and it must be addressed there. However, it is not enough to merely address it. Weak, absent, or ineffective responses can also exacerbate the bullying behavior. This was particularly the case with one union in a professional academic setting.

In this case, the union response to a bully was disjointed, often weak, and even absent. Initially, a local union president met with the bully when she was informed of the bully's seemingly indifference to the CBA. She met with him to explain that this facility was an organized facility, and that employees had rights and the manager had responsibilities as set out in the CBA. However, this meeting was not really to address any specific bullying action, but was in response to the bully's initial steamrolling style of control and implementation of changes in his department.

Union representatives also intervened in a couple of potential disciplinary procedures against employees in the manager's department and ensured that no discipline was taken. However, in one case the bully made it clear that while no formal discipline had occurred, he in essence kept his own file of "written warnings." This was clearly a violation of the CBA, but no grievance was filed. There were never any steps taken to suggest that if the manager continued these behaviors there would be a negative outcome toward him. In fact, this union was extremely hesitant to use the grievance process, and each grievance filed was viewed as being a very big deal and having the potential to harm its partnership relationship with the administration—a position not atypical of cooperationist business unionism, but one that has been shown to weaken union power and fail to address member concerns. This union had a tradition of relying on more informal processes, and, in the words of some, relying on a former "benevolent dictator" that led the institution. This same attitude toward the benevolent dictator seemed to permeate the interaction with managers and the dictator's successors, even where it was clear they were far from benevolent. As a result, in this case, there was an absence of a formal intervention.

In yet another specific case of bullying by this same supervisor, bullying had become much more common as a result of the weak union response and lack of management response. The union leadership's focus appeared to be more concerned with policing their members than they were with addressing the bullying. In this case, the bully had engaged in one of his usual practices of calling the union member to his office for a meeting without any details about the purpose or content of the meeting. Union leaders had been informed of this practice on several occasions. When the union member asked her department representative to represent her at the meeting, the union representative sent a formal notice to the union president requesting the union's formal authority. Rather than granting authority several weeks later, the day *after* the meeting the union leader sent a cease-and-desist order to the union representative, stating he had no authority to represent the union member, despite the union member's request. The union president then requested that the union's outside attorney look into the matter to prevent the representative from representing the member. The union was more concerned with centralizing control of representing members and the grievance process. This became clearer as the union leadership took control of the grievance resulting from this meeting, but took no real action to address the supervisor's bullying behavior. Not only was the union representative stripped of power, but the target of the bullying was seen as weak as well. The message was clear that the union would not allow concerted activity to be used to address supervisory bullying. Clearly this supervisor as well as others in that workplace would not have to fear "Harry Bridges" showing up at their door.

In numerous cases, the union leaders decided to in essence allow the bully's behavior to slide by signaling a weak or even accepting approach to the bully's behavior. In one case, the bully's tactic of using project funds and awards to target specific employees, reward his selected few, and to turn union members against each other was an issue in the more informal meet-and-discuss process. The bully himself never attended the process to address these issues. Although this funding was discussed, the result was that the union's position was that departments could in essence spend discretionary funds any way they wanted. What was potentially a ULP (changes in wages) became an accepted practice, even though there was strong evidence it was used to bully union members. In another situation, the bully had targeted a group of individuals who had volunteered to engage in an employee search process. In this search, the bully had called search members to his office, had used the EEO department to threaten the search members, called the search members liars, and had sent many of his threats and insults in e-mails. Although the union leadership did get involved in essence to remove the manager from the search process so that it could move forward, no grievance was filed and no threat was made about a future grievance if the manager engaged in these same actions. Instead, the committee was actually left with the feeling that the only way to resolve this issue was to work out a compromise with the manager. The nonmandatory meetings the manager decided to take attendance at were handled in an even more absent fashion as the union leadership simply stayed out of any discussion of these issues. Finally, where another faculty member was called to one of the manager's favored secretive meetings, the union representative did show up to ensure no discipline was taken, but then actually thanked the manager for having a meeting and suggested that if his reasons had proven valid he would have a right to call such a meeting (in essence, if an employee disagreed with the way he had spent funds and discussed this with others, he would have a right to investigate these employees). On other occasions, the bully was allowed in essence to violate CBA clauses such as academic freedom clauses and member investigation clauses with only one formal grievance filed during this entire process.

This union had many paths available to address this bullying supervisor. It could have taken the path of the southern manufacturing union and made these issues part of the collective bargaining process. It could have also followed the lead of this union and made sure that at every chance it filed a grievance against this supervisor. Instead, only one grievance was filed, and this was at the initiation of the department representative after the union president was informed by outside counsel that his position in terms of Weingarten representation[2] was wrong and the representative was in essence correct. However, even with this grievance, the representation was tepid at best, with no real investigation and failure to address the bullying behavior and patterns of bullying. The union clearly could have taken the route to ensure taking the bullying tactics away from the supervisor via the grievance process over specific clauses and even ULPs. The use of rewards for those who would not engage in their concerted activity rights by this supervisor was brought to the leadership's attention on many occasions and simply brushed aside as acceptable. The pattern of calling meetings with faculty that was clearly covered by a clause in the CBA was ignored on numerous occasions with no formal grievance filed. Finally, the union clearly shied away from any sort of direct action.

Much like the results of ineffective responses to workplace bullying by management, the weak and ineffective response by this union leadership exacerbated, rather than abated, the workplace bullying by this supervisor and for their members. The weak response not only indicated a lack of potential penalty to the bully, but also represented tacit approval of all tactics and even direct approval of others, such as through the use of funds and the calling of meetings outside of the CBA requirements. This response not only led to an increase in bullying behavior, but also led to numerous targets losing faith in the union, leaving the union, and even leaving the organization. In fact, three of the specific targets of workplace bullying left the organization and others disengaged from union activity.

The culture of this department has also clearly changed. There are many more closed-door meetings, employees leave the office as quickly as possible, and departmental meetings and events that were once much more collegial and even celebratory have become burdens that more and more employees avoid. Many employees continue to state they are in constant fear of what might happen next. The manager's selected few employees also seem to have become emboldened and more likely to engage in similar bullying behavior, leaving other employees and targets even more isolated. Finally, this department has experienced nearly unheard of levels of turnover in the past several years.

This weak response to the workplace bullying also has an additional drawback to the union. At least in part due to the ineffective response to the workplace bullying, there has been a clear response to union efficacy. Several employees who were active in past union events have withdrawn. Several targets have stated they no longer want to involve the union in their disputes and will just hold off on dealing with them until later in their careers. Some targets have stated a desire to run for union office in order to change the way these issues are addressed. Overall, it is clear that the support for union leadership and perhaps the union as a whole has begun to wane.

BENEFITS TO UNIONS OF ADDRESSING WORKPLACE BULLYING IN ALL THREE PHASES

Not only does concerted activity present a potential path for targets, but bullying also presents a potential path for union revitalization. Addressing workplace bullying can be a benefit to specific unions and to the labor movement in general. Addressing workplace bullying can lead to increased union power and increased perception of union efficacy by members, and it presents a potential path to organizing success and potentially labor revitalization.

In the United States, current union density stands at around 12% overall and 7% in the private sector (Budd, 2013). No serious labor researcher, advocate, or leader can deny that labor is in trouble of becoming what is often phrased too small to matter (Brofenbrenner, 2005). However, according to Namie and Namie (2009), the density rate of bullying (i.e., percentage of American workers who are bullied) stands at 37%. Further, as mentioned earlier, Hornstein (1996) suggested that nearly all U.S. workers will suffer abuse on the job at some point. Unions that address or propose that they will address workplace bullying can achieve the love, hope, and saliency that has been critical to successful organizing (Weikle, Wheeler, & McClendon, 1998). The love and concern that is a form of class consciousness come through in discussions with targets of workplace bullying. As mentioned earlier, throughout the qualitative interviews and focus groups of targets of workplace bullying, targets showed a high level of concern for one another (as one target put it, he wanted to go and beat up another target's bully). They showed a growing level of perceived commonality of their experiences and also shared a belief that by coming together concerted activity could help to eliminate their workplace bullying. The professional academic union's organizing drive in a state without collective bargaining rights for state workers is also an indicator of how bullying and addressing a bully can at least be a part of a successful organizing drive. Brofenbrenner (2003, p. 10) found a key to successful organizing is focusing on "issues that resonate in the workplace . . . focusing on two or more of the following during the campaign: dignity, fairness, quality of service, power, voice or collective representation." The reality is that a focus on bullying addresses all of these issues.

Addressing workplace bullying can also lead to greater satisfaction, union commitment, and mobilization of already organized workers. Kelly (1998) found that the key to mobilizing members was that they must attribute an injustice to one party and the ability to deal with that injustice to another. With bullying, this would mean that if the target sees the injustice as coming from the bully (a very clear outcome) and the union as addressing or ending the bullying, he or she will be more likely to support the union and to be an active and mobilized member. Kelly's mobilization theory (Brown Johnson, & Jarley (2004, pp. 543–562) states that "in order to participate, members must believe that their union is just and is seeking redress for an unjust act." Clearly, targets of bullying will see their bully as acting in an unjust way, and, as has been shown above, it is clear that unions can indeed address and end workplace bullying. The increased perception of union efficacy that can be achieved by addressing workplace bullying will in turn lead to an increase in union solidarity and activism (Fiorito, Tope, Steinberg, Padavic, & Murphy, 2011).

Union leaders, organizers, activists, and those who support the idea of a revitalized labor movement should realize that they can indeed help targets to address bullying in their workplace. However, they should also be aware that addressing workplace bullying will be a mutually beneficial undertaking, as it will not only help to achieve the primary goal of the labor movement—improving the day-to-day lives of workers—but it will also lead to other related goals including more successful organizing of the unorganized, more satisfaction, activism, and mobilization of organized members; and these outcomes will lead to a stronger, more vibrant labor movement.

CONCLUSION

Targets of workplace bullying have few avenues available to them to address workplace bullying and to end their suffering. Concerted activity presents a potential path to address workplace bullying, and there have been clear specific examples where concerted activity at the various phases of the labor relations process has indeed successfully addressed workplace bullies or bullying behavior. Concerted activity in the workplace and union activity specifically present a path to address and eliminate workplace bullying. By addressing workplace bullying in all three phases of the labor relations process, union leaders, activists, stewards, and members can help to eliminate workplace bullying.

However, the effectiveness of the concerted activity will depend on the strength of the reaction to the bully by the union. In the case of the southern manufacturing union, the reaction was strong and consistent and addressed the bully on a day-to-day basis as well as part of the collective bargaining phase. The professional academic union in the organizing drive was also strong and direct, and in both cases presented here, the bullying behavior ceased (in one case the bully left the organization). On the other end of the spectrum, the second professional academic union did not engage in a strong response and even attempted to prevent union representatives and members from engaging in a strong and direct response. As a result, the bullying became worse. The implications should be clear. The chance to address the bully is available, but the response must be strong.

Finally, for the unions that are willing to address workplace bullying, not only will they achieve their primary goal of making the working lives of their members and workers in general better, but they will also strengthen their union and the labor movement. By addressing the injustice of workplace bullying, unions can be more successful in organizing members, and they will be able to drive satisfaction, union commitment, activism, and mobilization of their members and thus further spur the energy needed for a vibrant and strong labor movement.

NOTES

1. Pseudonym has been used.
2. Guaranteeing an employee the right to union representation during an investigation review.

REFERENCES

Brofenbrenner, K. (2005). What is labor's true purpose: The implications of SEIU's unite to win proposals for organizing. *New Labor Forum, 14*, 19–26.

Brofenbrenner, K., & Hickey, R. (2003, June). Winning is possible: Successful union organizing in the United States—Clear lessons, too few examples. *Multinational Monitor*, 9–14.

Brown Johnson, N., & Jarley, P. (2004). Justice and union participation: An extension and test of mobilization theory. *British Journal of Industrial Relations, 42*, 543–562.

Budd, J. W. (2013). *Labor relations: Striking a balance* (4th ed.). New York: McGraw Hill Irwin.

Carbo, J. (2009). Strengthening the healthy workplace act—Lessons from Title VII and IIED litigation and stories of targets' experiences. *Journal of Workplace Rights, 14*, 97–120.

Carbo, J., & Hughes, A. (2010). Workplace bullying: Developing a human rights based definition from the perspective and experiences of targets. *Working USA, 13*, 387–403.

Clermont, K. M., & Schwab, S. J. (2004). How employment discrimination plaintiffs fare in federal court. *Journal of Empirical Legal Studies, 1*, 429–458.

Connor, M. A. (2005). Harry Bridges prowls the stacks at Powell's. In J. Slaughter (Ed.), *A troublemaker's handbook*. Detroit: Labor Notes.

Cox v. Keystone Carbon Co. 861 F.2d 390, 395 (3d Cir. 1988).

Davenport, N., Schwartz, R. D., & Elliot, G. P. (2002). *Mobbing: Emotional abuse in the American workplace*. Ames, IA: Civil Society Publishing.

Einarsen, S. (1999). The nature and causes of bullying at work. *International Journal of Manpower, 20*, 16–27.

Fiorito, J., Tope, D., Steinberg, P. E., Padavic, I., & Murphy, C. (2011). Lay activism and activism intentions in a faculty union: An exploratory study. *Labor Studies Journal, 36*, 483–507.

Fox, S., & Stallworth, L. E. (2004). Employee perceptions of internal conflict management programs and ADR processes for preventing and resolving incidents of workplace bullying: Ethical challenges for decision-makers in organizations. *Employee Rights and Employment Policy Journal, 8*, 375–523.

Gardner, S., & Johnson, P. (2001, Summer). The leaner, meaner workplace: Strategies for handling bullies at work. *Employment Relations Today*, 23–36.

Glover v. Oppleman. 178 F. Supp. 2d 622, 642 (W.D. Va. 2001).

Harris v. Forklift. 510 U.S. 17 (1993).

Hornstein, H. A. (1996). *Brutal bosses and their prey: How to identify and overcome abuse in the workplace*. New York: Riverhead Books.

Kazatsky v. King David Mem'l Park, Inc. 515 Pa. 183, 527 A.2d 988, 995 (Pa. 1987).

Keashley, L., & Jagatic, K. (2003). By any other name: American perspectives on workplace bullying. In S. Einarsen, H. Hoel, D. Zapf, & C. Cooper (Eds.), *Bullying and emotional abuse in the workplace* (pp. 31–61). New York: Taylor and Francis.

Keashley, L., & Neuman, J. H. (2004). Bullying in the workplace: Its impact and management. *Employee Rights and Employment Policy Journal, 8*, 335–373.

Kelly, J. (1998). *Rethinking industrial relations: Mobilization, collectivism and long waves*. London: Routledge.

Love v. Georgia Pacific Corp. 209 W.Va. 515, 516 (2001).

McCarthy, P., & Mayhew, C. (2004). *Safeguarding the organization against violence and bullying*. New York: Palgrave MacMillan.

Moody, K. (2007). *US labor in trouble and transition: The failure of reform from above, the promise of revival from below*. London: Verso.

Namie, G., & Namie, R. (2009). *The bully at work: What you can do to stop the hurt and reclaim your dignity on the job* (2nd ed.). Naperville, IL: Sourcebooks.

Rayner, C., Hoel, H., & Cooper, C. (2002). *Workplace bullying: What we know, who is to blame, and what we can do*. London: Taylor and Francis.

Travis v. Alcon. 202 W.Va. 369 (1998).

Weikle, R., Wheeler, H., & McClendon, J. (1998). A comparative case study of union organizing success and failure: Implications for practical strategy. In K. Brofenbrenner, S. Friedman, R. Hurd, R. Oswald, & R. Seeber (Eds.), *Organizing to win* (pp. 38–54). Ithaca, NY: Cornell University Press.

Wheeler, H. N. (2002). *The future of the American labor movement.* Cambridge: Cambridge University Press.

Yamada, D. (2004). Crafting a legislative response to workplace bullying. *Employee Rights and Employment Policy Journal, 8,* 475–521.

Yates, M. D. (2009). *Why unions matter* (2nd ed.). New York: Monthly Review Press.

Chapter 3

Toward an Understanding of Bullying in the Workplace to Mitigate Deleterious Effects

Wesley S. Parks, Paula K. Lundberg-Love,
Aimee Stewart, Ceselie McFarland, and
Katherine Ann Scott

Bullying is not a new problem. As long as there have been people living and working in close proximity to one another, bullying has likely occurred. What has traditionally been thought of as a problem for children on the playground has garnered more attention in recent years regarding how adults are impacted. From political speeches achieving "viral" status on social media to daytime talk shows to conversations at the dog park, bullying in adulthood is now a part of the collective conscious. To that end, it was only a matter of time before aggressive and hostile behaviors in the workplace were examined by social psychologists and found to be congruent with bullying behaviors. Indeed, in a global economy with more and more workers competing for fewer of the "better" jobs, it might be expected that bullying of coworkers might be seen as a way to eliminate competition and further career aspirations. Even when not about competitive edge, bullying still manages to find its way into the workplace as a function of interpersonal dynamics that fulfills a need to highlight differentiation.

This chapter focuses on understanding how bullying manifests in the workplace and how mental health professionals can best understand this global phenomenon in order to mitigate its deleterious effects and better assist in creating a positive work environment.

UNDERSTANDING THE CONSTRUCTS

To understand any problem, we first need an operationalized understanding of the phenomenon that we are studying. With respect to bullying, this can be a daunting challenge. Ask any six people to define bullying and you might get as many as seven answers, and all of them could have partial validity. Many people believe wholeheartedly in their respective definitions of what constitutes bullying based on what has been portrayed in the media, what we ourselves have observed or suffered, or even what intuitively makes sense. Even mental health professionals may not always agree on what constitutes bullying depending on their levels of training, their occupational roles, or their theoretical framework. For example, a professional counselor may conceptualize a client's experiences in a clinical setting in a manner different from an industrial-organizational psychologist consulting on a human resource initiative for a large retailer. Perhaps, given the variability inherent in training and the milieus and agendas, it is better, in general, to have a global understanding of bullying, and in particular, how it can manifest itself in the workplace.

OPERATIONALIZATION—WORKPLACE BULLYING

In a commentary dating back to 1997, Spurgeon (1997) wisely noted that a core problem in understanding the effects of bullying in the workplace lies in the nomenclature itself. She notes there has been no consensus on how to define bullying, be it a discreet event or a range of aggressive behaviors. Indeed, when reviewing myriad published works for this chapter, one of the most troubling aspects of the research was a lack of consensus on the definition. Each article and each researcher seemed to craft a new definition, sometimes even the same researchers differed from one article to the next.

One reason why there is no single agreed-upon definition of workplace bullying is that research has been inconsistent as a function of who is doing the research. Agervold (2007) wrote that bullying and interest in workplace bullying have been around for many decades, but "modern" research into this phenomenon began in the late 1980s. Agervold cited prior work by Swedish researcher Henrik Leymann (1996) that characterized it as an extension of childhood bullying that had permeated into adult roles. Rayner and Hoel (1997) wrote that most American research into bullying has been focused on bullying in the schools, and even that research has been about reducing weapons in the schools rather than understanding the etiology of bullying. They note that most research regarding adult bullying in the workplace has been conducted in Europe, particularly in Scandinavia, where there is a scientific interest that is well aligned with public awareness.

"Mobbing" is a term that frequently emerges in European literature. According to Leymann (1996), it was originally used by Konrad Lorenz to describe animal group behavior and more recently has been used to describe aggressive group behavior in children wherein one child is singled out or "mobbed" by a group of peers. Leymann writes that he decided to apply this term to the workplace in the early 1980s and consciously chose to avoid the more American term of "bullying" because he felt bullying did not adequately capture the most accurate underlying mindset of the behavior. Specifically, he felt bullying was, at least in the 1980s, more about physical aggression rather than the more sophisticated behaviors involved in social isolation. Put another way, Leymann likened bullying to the prototypical playground bully, and he believed this was not a sufficient schema for the adult variant that focuses on social stigmatization rather than just a punch to the face or stealing of lunch money.

For this chapter, we will relabel mobbing as bullying because the nomenclature can be cumbersome when trying to account for the results of prior studies. As Salin (2003) noted, earlier research into workplace bullying has used labels such as bullying, mobbing, employee abuse, workplace aggression, victimization, social undermining, and workplace incivility. It is conceivable from a methodological standpoint that various researchers chose terms based on the intended outcomes of their studies, cultural commonalities, popular vernacular, or even a simple lack of foresight. Whatever the reality, for the sake of this chapter's readability, as well as the wish not to contribute to the already confusing naming conventions in place, we will simply use the label "bullying" going forward.

Because European scientists were at the forefront of workplace bullying research before Americans developed a theoretical or practical interest, the conceptualization suggested by Hoel and Cooper (2000) has been frequently referenced (Agervold, 2007; Ferris, 2009; Leymann, 1996; Saunders, Huynh, & Goodman-Delahunty, 2007). They defined bullying as an action by one individual or by a group of individuals (mobbing) that that can be overt or covert and is an abuse of power and control. This definition emphasizes the persistent nature of the negative experience. Agervold (2007) further noted that bullying definitions require a subjective reaction insomuch as the victim feels unable to mount an effective defense. Thus, the definition of bullying really does need to reflect the outcome as well as the initiation and process itself.

Another definition describes bullying as repeated or persistent negative acts toward one or more individuals involving a perceived power imbalance and creating a hostile work environment. Salin crafted this definition from prior work by Einarsen, Hoel, and others. The beauty of her definition is that it succinctly incorporates the subjective feelings, power differential, and persistent nature of any misbehavior that creates hostility in the workplace. It is a relatively simplistic yet holistic definition that is not complicated by semantics and includes the often overlooked legally crafted human resources construct of a "hostile work environment." This last point should be emphasized, as Rayner and Hoel (1997) advised that the definition of bullying is many times influenced by a legal or psycholegal perspective.

Leymann (1996) distinguishes true bullying from discrete conflict by focusing on the psychological repercussions stemming from the frequency and duration rather than what is done or how it is done. According to Leymann, with agreement from Salin (2003), the greater the frequency of bullying over a longer period of time, the more likely a person will function in "psychological terror." Olmstead (2013) suggested a rule of thumb to help decide if actions are anecdotal mishaps versus true patterns of perpetration. He recommended looking at one violation as a bad day, two as a very bad day, and anything more than three as a pattern that needs to be addressed immediately. Thus, it is possible to conceptualize the impact, and therefore the lasting effects, based on duration. Intuitively this makes sense, but from a practical standpoint, which we will explore later in this chapter, this concept will be critical from a diagnostic perspective.

Ultimately, the definition we like best comes from Vega and Comer (2005, p. 101), which describes workplace bullying as "a pattern of generally deliberate demeaning of co-workers or subordinates that reminds us of the activities of the schoolyard bully." Key to that conceptualization is the reminder that an imbalance in the power differential is necessary in the definition (Salin, 2003). MacIntosh's (2005) participants perceived that a bully could be any person who asserted power over others. Sometimes this power was a legitimate function of the job in supervisory or management capacities. Other times those without implicit authority gained power through the bullying. Clearly, without a perceived power imbalance, one would not feel particularly defenseless or powerless and thus susceptible to being bullied. This could theoretically be an imagined power differential if a hierarchically established one is absent. With this characterization in mind, there is no doubt that almost anyone can close his or her eyes for just a second and create a schema of workplace bullying based on that simply crafted definition.

TYPES OF WORKPLACE BULLYING

Agreeing on a definition of workplace bullying is but one part of the nomenclature issue. Another concern is delineating the actual observable behaviors that might fall within the realm of bullying. When considering the actual content of bullying, Salin (2003) once again seems to have a good conceptualization of the constructs. She provides a working under-standing based on prior publications that conceptualize the content in terms of negative behaviors beyond outright verbal aggression that in-clude social isolation, avoidance, gossip, personal attacks, excessive criti-cism, excessive monitoring, withholding information, and withholding or removing responsibility. We can quickly see that almost any behavior could fall into the realm of bullying depending on how that behavior is applied. We could easily examine all of the subtypes and subcategories of bullying, but that would fill an entire volume rather than a solitary chap-ter. Instead, for this chapter, we have opted to discuss two broad catego-ries: direct bullying and cyberbullying (a prominent example of indirect bullying).

Direct Bullying

In terms of classifying in-person or "in real life" behaviors, Ayoko, Callan, and Härtel (2003) crafted a simple yet fairly comprehensive list of specific bullying actions that occur in the workplace. Specifically, they list intimidation, public humiliation, verbal isolation, unrealistic expectations, meaningless tasks, excessive work monitoring, and information with-holding. This is similar to Salin's aforementioned constructs. Lewis, Coursol, and Wahl (2002) suggested that there may be a preference for passive-aggressive forms of harassment because it is more difficult to identify those sources. These include withholding crucial information, not contradicting rumors or false information, withholding support to vic-tims, or any other indirect behavior that implicitly condones what is occurring.

Cyberbullying

It is hard to imagine any modern workplace without technology. From e-mail to word processing to social media, technology is ubiquitous in most employment in the United States. Employees and management in the United States today frequently rely on technology as their primary means of communication (Hall & Lewis, 2014). Even traditional blue-collar jobs incorporate technology into the milieu. The result of this reli-ance on electronic communication and social media has created new ways of bullying in the workplace. The reality is, at least in our collective opin-ions, that cyberbullying is the new frontier in this field of research given the importance of the pressing area of modern technology.

Cyberbullying uses modern communication technology to send derog-atory or threatening messages, directly or indirectly, to publicly post deni-grating messages, share private and confidential information, share humiliating information or stories, and otherwise serve as a source of humiliation or objectification (Privitera & Campbell, 2009). Langos (2012) further divided cyberbullying into two main categories: direct and indirect. Direct bullying occurs in the private domain and the communication is sent directly to the victim from the bully. This can be accomplished via e-mail, instant messaging (IM), short message service (SMS) texting, multimedia message service (MMS) texting, video chat, among others. Indirect bullying occurs publicly and the communication is delivered en masse via social media platforms like Facebook, Twitter, blogs, websites, group chats, Listservs, bulletin boards, or other public media outlets.

D'Cruz and Noronha (2013) observed that the literature is sparse on cyberbullying. Much research into technology in the workplace has been focused on efficiency and advancement as well as quelling "cyberloafing" or time drains of using social media during working hours. They note that most of what has been studied has focused on the cyberbullying of children and adolescents. More research in adults has focused on face-to-face interactions. Still, there is growing anecdotal evidence that suggests that incidence rates of adult cyberbullying have increased to the point of becoming almost commonplace. Hall and Lewis (2014) aptly described how bullies have used Facebook, Twitter, and other social media to bully and harass coworkers and subordinates. With social media expanding at a rapid rate, and some platforms having in excess of a billion users worldwide, they expect this avenue of bullying to grow in the workplace without some form of organizational guidance and oversight.

There are numerous parallels between cyberbullying and direct bullying. According to D'Cruz and Noronha (2013), there is significant overlap in terms of observed behaviors, outcomes, levels of organization involved, sources of bullying (perpetrators), as well as individual and group targets. Their study revealed how the combination of cyberbullying with traditional face-to-face bullying encroaches on personal, spatial, temporal, and social boundaries. Indeed, what we do see is that cyberbullying adds a new weapon to the arsenal and in fact may simply be a more efficient and far-reaching method of bullying than face-to-face interaction.

MODELS OF WORKPLACE BULLYING

After reviewing dozens of resources for this chapter, it appears that researchers have identified individual and work-related factors that are associated with bullying. In fact, all of the articles reviewed had a focus on both personality features or traits of bullies and the workplace itself. Some were more focused on the personality factors, and surprisingly one even related personality to the workplace and reactions to the workplace rather than an independent factor. This suggests that personality traits are important, but also important is how personality develops in the workplace and in response to workplace assaults and trauma. Looking at a systems theory approach might be useful. Regardless, all of the research reviewed for this chapter provided some evidence that personality is, indeed, a factor in workplace bullying.

One model of bullying that we considered is the three-way approach proposed by Baillien, Neyens, De Witte, and De Cuyper (2009). Though their diagramming of the model was complex, it can be divided into three constructs: intrapersonal, interpersonal, and intragroup levels. Intrapersonal bullying is concerned with job frustration and coping mechanisms. Examples could include low job satisfaction, changes in work environment, and personal problems outside of work. Think of this as one worker's internal reality. Interpersonal bullying arises from conflicts between the worker and others and how those conflicts are managed. These conflicts can stem from work-related problems or personal conflicts between workers. Lastly, intragroup bullying is all about the workplace as an organization. This is not so much focused on the actual management or characteristics of the organization as it is on the "culture" present in the workplace. The authors referred to a "culture of gossip" and a workplace where backbiting and mockery are commonplace. The importance of this model is that it does incorporate two dimensions of personality—self-conceptualization and interpersonal functioning—when looking at the bully and the target. The limitation, however, seems to be an oversimplification of the organization itself by considering only a broad cultural point of view rather than quantifiable specifics about individual operations.

Another interesting approach was suggested by Balducci, Fraccaroli, and Schauefil (2011). These authors sought to integrate personality factors and work environment into a comprehensive model, noting that prior research tended to be divergent rather than integrative. Six factors were considered: job demands, job resources, neuroticism, focused interaction of the prior three items, bullying, and post-traumatic stress disorder (PTSD) symptoms. Job demands, job resources, neuroticism, and focused interactions were all related to bullying. Furthermore, they found that bullying was related to PTSD symptoms. Ultimately, they concluded that personality and work-related factors were independently related to bullying, which suggests two different paths to workplace bullying.

A third interesting model of workplace bullying focused more on the company and less on the individual personality (Samnani & Sing, 2014). That is not to say that personality is not a factor, but rather they viewed the compensation structure and productivity as primary antecedents of bullying. They proposed that the behavior of the employees is guided by the organization's reward system, and that bullying occurs because of competition for rewards. Those who are more motivated for reward will engage in bullying behaviors in order to maximize earnings. They also suggested that stress in the workplace may induce aggressive behaviors. This extended previous research conducted by Hauge, Skogstad, and

Einarsen (2007) who found stressful work environments to be a breeding ground for workplace bullying.

Though we are fond of operationalization and clearly defined concepts, we are forced to admit that our review of the literature has not identified one clear model for workplace bullying. Perhaps this is because aspects of the human condition cannot always be reduced to clear causalities. Workplace bullying is a complex concept and such that any given model may be able to explain any given situation.

WHO IS AFFECTED?

Citing an unpublished dissertation about workplace bullying, D'Cruz and Noronha (2013) observed that it is hard to tease out bullying from other forms of harassment categories such as age, gender, race, and sexuality. Their point is that some researchers argue these forms of harassment are closely linked and cannot be differentiated with any certainty. This fact can really blur the lines when investigating abuses in the workplace. For example, do researchers code sexual harassment as such, or is it bullying? What about ageism or gender discrimination? There are multiple variables, and with the ambiguity about what actually constitutes bullying in the workplace, it may not be possible to identify the best data points for the identification of victim populations.

There have been a variety of findings regarding gender influences. Rayner and Hoel (1997) found no significant difference between men and women as perpetrators of bullying. That is, equal numbers of both genders admitted to bullying. With respect to being a victim, however, they cited several studies where men rarely felt victimized by women, while women felt equally bullied by men or by fellow women. Perhaps this can be explained by the perception of the victim, and men may not perceive being bullied as adeptly as women. Alternatively, there could be a gender bias at play. It is conceivable that men are less willing to admit to being bullied. It is also possible that some men do not perceive the behavior as bullying when it comes from a woman.

Another study showed higher rates of bullying among male workers and supervisors (Hoel, Cooper, & Faragher, 2001). It was suggested by those authors that perhaps male-dominated work environments foster a hostile and authoritarian culture that is conducive to bullying. Although this study was conducted in Great Britain, it could be perceived as the American equivalent of the "good ol' boy" network imploding. In terms of the personality factors considered in some models of bullying, this might be considered an extension of the "frat boy" mentality that can actually begin in males via sports or other male-dominated interests in childhood and be fostered by repeated social learning in adulthood.

Age

Rayner and Hoel (1997) found no significant discrepancies in age as a bullying factor. They noted a prior study did find that older workers were targeted more than younger workers. However, they cited additional work by Leymann (1990) that also found a lack of statistical significance among age groups.

Culture

Rayner and Hoel (1997) reviewed several works that noted that culture can play a role in how we interpret perceived bullying behavior. This culture may be as specific as workplace culture of a *Fortune* 500 company or as generalized as a geographic culture. Furthermore, cultural norms of any culture may impact the threshold at which someone feels harassed or bullied.

Occupation

A review of the literature revealed inconclusive findings regarding workplace bullying with respect to particular job type. Rayner and Hoel (1997) noted that many of the authors they reviewed relied on anecdotal data, and those mostly likely to appear in anecdotal texts would be white-collar workers who may be better able to recognize and articulate bullying and have access to workplace support. Thus, they believe there is a lack of data regarding a relationship between workplace bullying and job type. Salin (2003), however, did find that bullying was more frequently reported or endorsed in large and bureaucratic organizations. The more complex the decision-making structure or hierarchy, the more likely the concern for individuals is lost in the process, and thus it is less risky for the perpetrator to bully. This does beg a specific question about whether or not more human resource "hoops and hurdles" in the forms of steps and processes actually decrease the likelihood of a positive outcome.

Witnesses

In an exploratory study, Einarsen, Raknes, and Matthiesen (1994) found that victims were not the only ones reporting consequences associated with bullying. Observers of bullying also reported elevated levels of role conflict, dissatisfaction with the work environment, and displeasure with organizational leadership. Granted, the nature of the exploratory study did not clearly conclude that the similarly reported experience and symptoms were directly related to observing bullying, but it was an interesting finding nonetheless. A more recent literature review by Lewis and colleagues (2002) cited prior work where nearly 10% of workers reported witnessing bullying. Though they were not as severely impacted as the victims, they nonetheless reported feelings of distress similar to the actual victims. These are good indicators that when we consider who is impacted by bullying, we must think globally and systemically.

HOW DOES IT HAPPEN?

Theoretical models are good for understanding the abstract underpinnings of a phenomenon. Unfortunately, we do not live and work in a vacuum and we need more of a real-world understanding of how bullying occurs in the workplace. Salin (2003) noted that bullying is rarely explained by one solitary factor. Rather, it usually has multiple causes that combine to create a specific situational environment where bullying can occur and self-sustain. A surprising finding by MacIntosh (2005) was that victims of bullying were able to identify impediments to their own understanding of the bullying they suffered. Her participants reported that bullying sometimes began covertly and subtly, escalating over time from private attacks to more public displays. Given the gradual escalation, even when the bullying started from the onset of employment, it took time for the victims to accurately conceptualize what had occurred.

The Workplace Bullying Institute (WBI) is an American research group that has studied bullying in the workplace since the late 1990s. Their recent website-based poll of 658 respondents (WBI, 2012) suggests why employees believe bullying occurs. Top responses were that bullies are not punished and then thrive (21%), absence of laws or protections are too weak (15%), lack of company desire to address the problem (13%), coworkers stand idly by (13%), and the workplace culture rewards bullying behaviors (10%). Gary Namie, writing for the WBI, observed that the top three reasons listed were employer focused. Although we cannot possibly explore all the myriad ways bullying can develop in the workplace, we are able to consider some of the more frequently cited factors in the literature.

Social Learning

Social learning integrates cognitive and behavioral processes to account for real-world learning based on observation and the abstraction of meaning from others' reactions (Grusec, 1992). We engage in behavior based on observation of rewards and punishment. Certainly this can be applied to the workplace when workers engage in behavior that produces a result whereby they are rewarded (praise, promotion, increased pay), or perhaps the result is maintaining the status quo in the face of competition. Workers could potentially engage in deleterious behaviors to keep a job or to move up the workplace ladder.

Salin (2003) noted that modeling and imitation may influence the prevalence of bullying. When new workers, and especially management, are socialized into a workplace culture where bullying is normalized, they perpetuate the cycle. Social learning theory suggests that we will engage in the same activities of those around us when we see they are rewarded, or at least not punished. Indeed, Vega and Comer (2005) noted that unlike schoolyard bullies, adults are generally aware of the impact of their behavior on others.

Organizational Roles

Sometimes the workplace itself is the bully. Leymann (1996) cited 800 case studies that showed that poorly organized production and work methods, as well as helpless or disinterested management, contributed to bullying behavior. Similarly, the pressure to perform, the need to meet shareholder expectations, threats of downsizing or demotion, and accepted management styles that put pressure on employees to increase performance were perceived by many to be organizational bullying (MacIntosh, 2005).

Famously, Jack Welch, the former chief executive officer of General Electric, decided that every employee should be ranked and the bottom 10% should be eliminated (Murray, 2009). This practice become known as "rank and yank," though Welch tried to distance his rationale from such a visceral label. Still, when asked where he learned this lesson of what he called "differentiation," Welch freely admitted this was an early lesson from "out on the playground picking a team." He stated that business is really no different from picking teams in childhood where the poor performers are discarded. Many other companies employed similar ranking systems after Welch increased General Electric's profits year after year. Thus, an organization itself can foster—if not outright create—an environment where bullies may employ tactics to push others down to the bottom rung in hopes of saving their own jobs.

Leadership

In many cases, bullying in the workplace is often tacitly accepted by the organizational leadership (Vega & Comer, 2005). This creates an environment of psychological distress that directly and negatively impacts productivity, to say nothing of employee relations and job commitment. Citing other research that harassment exists in workplaces because it is allowed to do so, Einarsen and colleagues (1994) found that bullying is actually a symptom of inadequate leadership. Interestingly, this was the case even when supervisors were not the studied bullies because of the reality that misbehavior prospers when leadership is lax.

In contrast to Welch, who create an organizational company culture of bullying, some managers in leadership roles let the pendulum swing too far in the other direction. Hauge and colleagues (2007) found statistical interactions between workplace bullying and laissez-faire leadership. Indeed, Salin (2003) noted that a laissez-faire style of leadership is more conducive to bullying. There could be many reasons for this, from the personality styles of the leaders themselves, to leaders toeing the corporate line (organizational roles), to perhaps even the leaders being ill equipped to tackle the problem and instead marching ahead behind a banner of avoidance.

Conflict

Another source of prolonged bullying, according to Leymann (1996), is poor conflict management and resolution on the part of supervisors and managers. This problem becomes even more apparent when the supervisor is part of the problem, such as in group bullying. In such a situation, the supervisor will be forced to take sides and thus is not likely to side against himself or his compatriots.

Not all problematic conflict is tied to supervisors and managers. Many studies listed in this chapter cite conflict between peers as a source of bullying (Ayoko et al., 2003; Einarsen et al., 1994; Gilbert, Raffo, & Sutarso, 2013; Sheehan, Barker, & Rayner, 1999; Thomas, 2013). All reviewed sources explored levels of conflict and how subsequent emotional reactions shaped bullying behaviors. Most concluded that the longer the duration of conflict, the greater the likelihood that bullying would occur. This suggests that addressing interpersonal conflict, perhaps at a group-dynamics level, could have a fairly significant impact on bullying.

PREVALENCE OF BULLYING IN THE WORKPLACE

Determining the actual prevalence rate of workplace bullying is quite challenging and depends on methodological moderating variables (Birkeland Nielsen, Berge Matthiesen, & Einarsen, 2010). Different definitions of bullying and different instruments for measuring reactions and symptoms, cultural norms, legal terminology, and self-report bias are many factors that impede a global consensus on how much bullying occurs. Studying bullying behaviors, like any other field of study, would typically involve direct observation. With bullying in the workplace, Agervold (2007) informs us, we must rely instead on self-report of the victims. The problem with this approach is that without a clear definition of what is reportable, we are likely to get inconsistent and variable reports. Also, Rayner and Hoel (1997) noted that victim self-reports include an inherent natural bias and subjectivity. Though defining bullying is central to obtaining good data (Rayner & Hoel, 1997), it is also quite difficult, because in the adult version of bullying, there is rarely physical violence. Instead the wide range of more subtle tactics is harder to qualify and quantify. This begs the question of just how far does must bullying proceed before it is reported. What is the threshold? How much might that vary from person to person?

International Prevalence

Workplace bullying has consistently received more attention in the international community than in the United States. As noted at various points in this chapter, European countries have been on the forefront of this research, and subsequently they have gathered far more statistical data. Scandinavian research has reported prevalence rates from 3.5% to 16% (Privitera & Campbell, 2009). Their study found that 89% of respondents reported that they experienced negative behaviors either face to face or via cyberattack. Of those, 34% would meet Leymann's criteria for bullying, as defined earlier in this chapter. Of that subset, another 25% reported weekly bullying. And of all the respondents, almost 11% reported cyberbullying as a component. Privitera and Campbell (2009) applied a Chi-square analysis to their findings to determine any effects based on the size of the company, type of organization, and hierarchical status of victims of bullying. Interestingly, they found no significant relationships and concluded that there is an equal chance of being bullied regardless of those factors.

Gemzøe Mikkelsen and Einarsen (2002) reported a staggeringly high 88% of respondents in Denmark who revealed negatively aggressive interpersonal acts consistent with bullying within their past six months of employment. A separate Danish study found that 8.3% of respondents had been bullied within the past year (Ortega, Høgh, Pejtersen, & Olsen, 2009). The majority, 71%, indicated peer bullying, with 32% reporting it was a supervisor. Gender was not a factor. Ortega and colleagues believe this is consistent with the 2% to 10% rates obtained in other European countries. To be sure, their number was vastly lower than that found by Gemzøe Mikkelsen and Einarsen (2002). However, there was no readily apparent explanation for this discrepancy. A reasonable hypothesis might be that at least some of the difference may be attributable to the time period each studied. Perhaps there is greater bullying at the onset of employment to weed out coworkers—a vocational variant of "thinning of the herd."

Prevalence rates reported in other European countries have been even higher, with some countries reporting millions of impacted workers (Privitera & Campbell, 2009). A full 40% of Canadians report weekly workplace bullying (Oliver, 2013). Rayner (1997) found that there was a

53% lifetime prevalence rate in the United Kingdom, although she noted that was higher than she had anticipated and may have stemmed from how bullying is defined. Most surprising was her finding that 71% of bullies were supervisors, which was contrasted with 40% reported in Scandinavian studies. She believed this was due to their higher rates of peer and group bullying. A Spanish study (Escartín, Rodríguez-Carballeira, Zapf, Porrúa, & Martín-Peña, 2009) found a 10% prevalence rate of workplace bullying. What was interesting about this study is that participants rated the severity of various behaviors, rather than just the number of times things had happened. Emotional abuse was evaluated as the most severe type of bullying. Also notable was the fact that all workers rated their bullying as severe, regardless of the duration. It was expected that those who had suffered for longer periods of time would rate theirs as more severe, but across the board all victims provided high ratings.

Birkeland Nielsen and colleagues' (2010) more recent meta-analysis of Scandinavia, other European countries, and non-European countries established a 14.6% prevalence rate for workplace bullying, which they termed a substantial problem. Because their study included Europe and beyond, this appears to be a good global estimate of the prevalence of workplace bullying. This is clearly the antecedent to legal protections in those countries. In the United Kingdom, a trust was set up to fund a nonpolitical, nonprofit charity tasked solely with the issue of workplace bullying (Vega & Comer, 2005). Also, unions in the United Kingdom have played a large role in promoting a better understanding of workplace bullying and ways to solve this problem. Bullying was so pervasive in Austrian workplaces that a government task force was commissioned to explore and make recommendations (Vega & Comer, 2005). They identified 19 "common" behaviors that were tied to bullying. These ranged from foul language, to taunting, to overloading of work, to direct threats. That report concluded, not coincidentally, with 19 recommendations, including reminders about laws protecting workers from abuse. Thus, some countries are seriously examining the data and trying to address a clearly systemic epidemic.

U.S. Prevalence

Gilbert and colleagues (2013) have summarized why U.S. numbers are harder to determine. Because bullying is not illegal in the United States, as it is in the European countries where research is more common, it is easier to ignore it altogether. Nevertheless, we are beginning to gather large amounts of data, and much of that has greater stratification than we have seen in the European studies. Alterman, Luckhaupt, Dahlhamer, Ward, and Calvert (2013) found that 7.8% of surveyed workers in the United States reported having been threatened, harassed, or bullied in the workplace. Of that total, there were higher rates for women (9.3%) than men (6.5%). With respect to race or ethnicity, the category of "non-Hispanic other race" showed a 16.9% prevalence rate, as compared to 7% to 8% ranges for white, black, and Hispanic people. Divorced persons (11.9%) were bullied far more than married (6.7%) and never married (7.8%) individuals. Though the data are unclear as to what constituted "living with partner," that category was 10.2%. Presumably this would include lesbian, gay, bisexual, and transgender, which can be an entire class of bullying not protected by law. There was little difference based on the size of the metropolitan area, with all ranges between 7% and 8%. Likewise, the ranges were 7% to 8% for all four cardinal regions of the country.

No profession in the United States seems to be immune to bullying behaviors, according to Lewis and colleagues (2002). This phenomenon spans the gamut, from manufacturing to retail to higher education to health care. They further noted that despite the known prevalence, bullying behaviors are underreported unless there is a physical violence component. Despite almost all professions being affected, Alterman et al. (2013) found significant reporting variability based on the industry, with the lowest being 5% in construction up to a high of 16.2% in public administration. For occupations within industries, protective service workers (presumably such as police, fire department, or similar, though not defined in the article) fared the worst at 24.6%, followed by 15.7% for community and social service workers. The lowest rates were 3.9% for architecture and engineering, followed by 4.4% for computer and mathematical workers. Education level did not seem to be a factor, with less than 2% variance between those without a high school diploma (6.3%) and those with bachelor's degrees or higher (7.7%). Thus, when reviewing the occupation and industry tables, this is consistent with the variability rates seen across all entries. Thus, we should not conclude that those with greater education will necessarily land jobs where bullying is less likely to occur.

The most recent data by the WBI, whose mandate is to study workplace bullying in the United States, is more disturbing than the numbers above. According to the WBI (2014), a full 27% of Americans report experiencing abusive conduct at work. Another 21% have witnessed bullying in some capacity. This suggests that 37 million workers have been bullied, while 65 million were impacted by collateral damage. Probably most shocking is that 72% were aware of bullying occurring in their workplace whether or not it was directly observed. Stratified demographics by the WBI (2014) revealed that 69% of bullies are men and 60% of targets are women. Women bullies chose women targets 68% of the time. These two facts indicate there is a clear gender component inherent in bullying. White workers reported the lowest rates of victimization by bullying at 24%, and African Americans, Hispanics, and Asians all hovered between 32% to

33%. In terms of occupational rank, 48% reported their bullies were superiors, and 28% reported same-level bullying. Nearly 10% where bullied by
their own subordinates. All of these data further support the previously
discussed notion that a power imbalance is a central component to workplace bullying (Salin, 2013). Another interesting statistic from the WBI
(2014) is that 23% of bullying is perpetrated by more than one bully. The
WBI numbers did not differentiate cyberbullying, which would have been
an interesting statistic to review.

As has been noted, there is no federal law in the United States that
makes workplace bullying illegal. Presumably, the civil courts could take
up the matter via torte law. Having said that, the WBI's 2014 survey found
that 93% of respondents are aware of workplace bullying and support
some form of law outlawing such behaviors. A full 63% strongly support
such legislation. One cannot help but wonder if the U.S. numbers would
be more consistent with European findings if similar legal sanctions were
applied.

EFFECTS OF BULLYING IN THE WORKPLACE

The experience of workplace bullying can have a host of negative consequences. To be sure, there are detriments to the physical and emotional
well-being of victims. Also, there is collateral damage for those who witness bullying. Within the workplace, specific effects can include reduced
workplace morale, reduced job commitment, lowered job satisfaction, increased absenteeism, increased turnover, and impaired communication
with cohorts, subordinates, and supervisors (Privitera & Campbell, 2009).
The unfortunate reality is that bullying that occurs in the workplace
wreaks all manner of havoc that transcends the job site and impacts psychological functioning, which is the focus of this chapter.

Psychological Effects

In reviewing numerous studies, Vega and Comer (2005) found that the
effects of bullying can be catastrophic to the individual. They cited studies
in the United States, United Kingdom, Norway, Finland, and Sweden that
show a relation between bullying and depression, anxiety, aggression, insomnia, psychosomaticism, somatic complaints, PTSD, and even suicide
(Vega & Comer, 2005). Psychological consequences reported by Lewis and
colleagues (2002) included depression, feelings of powerlessness, self-
blame, shame, self-deprecation, insecurity, inadequacy, and lack of self-
confidence. These effects can all contribute to a self-fulfilling prophecy
such that targets who believe they are incompetent become so. Without
reviewing all of the diagnoses listed in the *Diagnostic and Statistical Manual
of Mental Disorders'* fifth edition (*DSM-5*; APA, 2013) that could correlate

with workplace bullying, we will concentrate on the diagnoses seen most in outpatient clinical treatment settings.

Affective Disorders

Affective disorders, more commonly referred to as mood disorders, are characterized primarily by a disturbance in mood as the predominant feature (APA, 2013). Respondent's in MacIntosh's (2005) research described a lack of joy, lack of hope, lack of confidence, anger, depression, disappointment, lack of self-confidence, and withdrawal from their social support network. These are all recognized symptoms of a depressive disorder. In a study to determine how bullying compares to other job stressors (role ambiguity, job demands, role conflict, and decision authority) in terms of depressed workers, Hauge, Skogstad, and Einarsen (2010) found that bullying was a far greater contributor to depression. In fact, it was the strongest predictor of depression in their study.

The *DSM-5* lists lifetime prevalence rates for various affective labels, such as 7% for major depressive disorder and up to 1.8% for bipolar mood disorders. The *DSM-5* does not specify these rates by gender for all disorders. Interestingly, these numbers are lower than prior *DSM* edition published rates. They are also lower than the 16.9% for major depressive disorder and 4.4% for bipolar mood disorders published by the National Comorbidity Survey (NCS; 2007). Prevalence of affective disorders is thought to be higher in women than men, and even more so for women who are in their childbearing years (Kuklarni, 2008). This is not, coincidentally, also during the prime working years of most women. Chima (2004) cited statistics that 20% of women will experience at least one major depressive episode in their lives. This holds special significance given the statistics that most victims of bullying are women.

Anxiety Disorders

Anxiety has many manifestations, and the *DSM-5* details 10 discrete anxiety-related diagnoses. Prevalence rates can vary, with some anxiety conditions reportedly affecting up to 9% of the population (APA, 2013). The NCS (2007) prevalence rate for anxiety disorders was 31.2%. As in the case of affective disorders, the highest prevalence rate was found during the prime working ages of 30 to 59. Hauge and colleagues (2010) reported that bullying was a potent contributor to anxiety. MacIntosh (2005) indicated that bullying was strongly associated with the feelings of fear, which are precursors to anxiety. Other studies also linked anxiety symptoms due to bullying to the development of a post-traumatic stress reaction (Berge Matthiesen & Einarsen, 2004; Leymann, 1996; Nielson & Einarsen, 2012; Tehrani, 2004). As with affective disorders, it is noteworthy that anxiety disorders are more common in women. In fact, the *DSM-5* suggests a two-to-one ratio (APA, 2013). Again, this may have special significance given the number of women who are targets of workplace bullying.

Post-traumatic Stress Disorder

According to *DSM-5*, PTSD is no longer classified as an anxiety disorder. There is now an entire classification for trauma- and stress-related disorders that is independent of anxiety and affective conditions. Per the *DSM-5*, the lifetime prevalence rate for PTSD is 8.7% (APA, 2013). The NCS (2007) was slightly lower at 6.8%, and as with other conditions, the NCS showed greater rates in the prime working ages of 30 to 59, with those rates ranging from 8% to 9%. Leymann (1996) hypothesized as far back as the 1990s that repeated bullying might be a cause of PTSD. He felt that bullied workers who literally aged within an organization found their ability to find a new job diminished, resulting in a state of powerlessness tied to rumination often seen in those with PTSD. Balducci et al. (2011) found a significant interaction between bullying and PTSD symptoms. Tehrani (2004) found that 44% of respondents who had been bullied within the past two years had clinically significant symptoms of PTSD.

When reviewing symptomatology, Berge Matthiesen and Einarsen (2004) employed various measures, including instruments specifically measuring bullying behaviors and PTSD symptoms. In their study, respondents endorsed higher rates of PTSD when they also reported bullying. Seven specific negative behaviors correlated significantly with the PTSD measures: ridiculing, hostility, ignoring, downgrading due to age, downgrading due to gender, exploiting, and negative reactions to productivity or work style. Not surprisingly, these authors found that the passage of time since bullying behaviors ended led to a reduction in reported post-traumatic stress. Their substantial meta-analysis (N = 77,721) of 66 published studies showed that bullying is most strongly related to symptoms of post-traumatic stress. They cautioned about making conclusions that post-traumatic symptoms always evolved into PTSD, as many of the research samples focused only on symptom criteria and did not address the nature of the trauma or the degree of impairment. Nevertheless, these data evidence that bullying does result in post-traumatic symptoms, which could be a precursor to the development of PTSD. Once again, women in prime working age are more likely to experience PTSD (APA, 2013; NCS, 2007).

Substance Abuse

Tracking substance abuse can be a bit trickier than some of the other mental health labels because of how few gainfully employed people are likely to disclose potentially illegal activity. And we can imagine that employees using any substance to mitigate stress might be even less likely to disclose such information. NCS (2007) data indicate lifetime prevalence rates of 13.2% for alcohol abuse or dependence and 8% for drug use or dependence. The drug of choice for the majority of those surveyed was nicotine, which accounted for 29.6%. Because smoking has many deleterious health consequences, these data are even more problematic. None of the studies reviewed for this chapter clearly listed substance abuse as a reaction to bullying in the workplace. However, given the nature of substance use as "self-medication," it is not a stretch to consider that employees may be self-medicating for some of the other psychological conditions associated with bullying.

Personality Disorders

We are hesitant to engage in a discussion of personality disorders affecting the workplace as a result of workplace bullying. Personality disorders by definition in the *DSM-5* represent "an enduring pattern of inner experience and behavior that deviates markedly from the expectations of the individual's culture" (APA, 2013, p. 646). Clearly there is going to be some bias by the majority who do not experience what we are labeling as a disorder of the minority. As has been stated before, we believe that of all the disorders in the psychiatric realm, personality disorders have the most complex interplay with many employment dynamics, to the degree that a mere portion of a book chapter alone could not adequately begin to overview this phenomenon (Parks, Lundberg-Love, Luft, Stewart, & Peddy, in press).

Having said that, in fairness to other disorders, we must include some prevalence data. The *DSM-5* (APA, 2013) details the prevalence rates for personality disorders ranging from 0.2% to 7.9% in the general outpatient population, depending on the specific disorder. The National Institutes of Health (n.d.) estimates 12-month prevalence rates for personality disorders of up to 9.1% of the U.S. population. This was noted to be based on data from the NCS, though we were unable to download the specific datasets in question and believe this falls in the restricted datasets available to current research projects. As you can see, obtaining specific data on personality disorders in the workplace is not as accessible as that for other diagnosable conditions. One study by Persson et al. (2009) observed bullied workers to have higher scores of neuroticism. They noted this was consistent with at least five prior studies. Their conclusion was that these workers had a self-image dominated by worry, mistrust, embitterment, irritability, and impulsivity. To that end, and despite lacking the desired amount of statistical data, we will work from the assumption that there are employed persons with personality disorders, but perhaps not to the same degree that we see with respect to affective or anxiety disorders.

Burnout

Burnout, though not a diagnostic category per se, is clearly problematic. Parks, Lundberg-Love, Galusha, and Deitrick (2013) reviewed the onset of employee burnout subsequent to recurrent stress in the workplace. It was noted that stress impacts mental illness, which in turn impacts stress. These authors noted that prevalence rates for burnout were hard to derive due to confounds in the current research and the potential for missed data. Still, their conclusion was that burnout had a significant psychological toll on workers and a financial toll on the economy. This is consistent with Lewis and colleagues (2002), who found that bullying behaviors can lead to burnout, which in turn can lead to exiting an established career entirely.

ECONOMIC COST OF BULLYING IN THE WORKPLACE

No look at the impact of bullying in the workplace would be complete without considering the economic realities. Leymann (1990) reported that bullying can result in long periods of sick leave, loss of productivity, increased in interaction with human resource personnel or similar consultations, increased interactions with managers that lowers their own productivity, and increased health insurance premiums for the company. Leymann estimated a cost of between $30,000 to $100,000 per year for an employee exposed to bullying in the workplace. He further remarked that this yearly cost can be staggering when one considers that victims report having been bullied for years.

Leymann (1990) did not explain how he came to his estimate, and the WBI (n.d.) freely admits it is difficult to calculate the real cost of bullying. Still, the WBI provided some numbers for consideration. To calculate turnover, they suggested multiplying an employee's yearly wage by 1.5 for recruiting and training costs. Absenteeism is more straightforward by multiplying an employee's hourly cost by the hours missed, which may actually count against the sick time benefit or paid time off. The most difficult cost estimate is that of litigation, and the WBI estimates conservatively that if a lawsuit is filed, it will cost a company upward of $60,000 in pretrial costs, plus judgments and damages if the company loses the case.

The cost to businesses can impact the bottom line in many ways (Dewa, McDaid, & Ettner, 2007; Lewis et al., 2002; MacIntosh, 2005; Nielson & Einarsen, 2012; Parks et al., 2013; Privitera & Campbell, 2009):

1. Absenteeism: Simply put, most absenteeism related to mental illness is in the form of sick days. When the absence is prolonged, it may manifest in short-term disability or even long-term disability. Absent workers simply are not productive workers, and their missed work

or revenue must be accounted for by others or lost entirely. For those workers who do not receive the benefit of sick leave, they may be more likely to leave one job for another with such a benefit.

2. Presenteeism: This is a newer term to describe working with impaired functioning in order to avoid absenteeism. One estimate for U.S. workers cited by Dewa and colleagues (2007) reported that four hours of depression-related presenteeism in a two-week period could result in a total loss of $36 billion to the U.S. economy. Presenteeism actually costs more than the estimated $8.3 billion in absenteeism.

3. Early Retirement: Workers with mental illness are more likely to exit the workforce early. This could be due to unemployment, burnout, chronic absenteeism, or basic psychology of being a "broken person." Early retirement is a drain on pension plans and government-supported programs. It also can reduce workforce readiness and leave unfilled vacancies, both of which impact a business's overall gross productivity.

4. Loss of Productivity: When employees are scared to share their ideas, lost creative potential quickly adds up. In a global economy where innovation is favored, this can be almost a death knell. On top of lost potential earnings or savings, there is genuine lost productivity and efficiency that result in an immediate loss of revenue

5. Spillover: Because we rarely work in isolation, there is bound to be some tainting of the well water. Many studies have shown that those who witness bullying have a negative and somewhat vicarious reaction. This is not limited to the identified victims alone, and as more people are impacted, it results in a change to the entire company's culture.

It is easy to focus on the economics of mental illness in relation to bullying. In fact, there is no way to approach this topic within a business model without considering economics. But we, as mental health professionals, would be remiss not to focus on the cost of mental illness in terms of human capital and psychic damage. People with mental illness are often the most disadvantaged and disenfranchised members of any community (Parks et al., 2013). Privitera and Campbell (2009) noted that the consequences of bullying impact functioning in family, social, and vocational domains. Family members and significant others may become frustrated by the suffering of their loved ones, in part because they simply cannot understand what is happening, but also because of a perceived lack of action by the victim (Lewis et al., 2002). Although we must balance the needs of the organizations we serve when consulting about the effects of bullying, we also must remember the victim's welfare and act accordingly.

Intervention

There is no one way to address workplace bullying. Also, as we have seen, there is no one way to understand the phenomenon, much less begin to solve the problem of workplace bullying. What is becoming clear is that strategies cannot be uniform for all companies. In fact, D'Cruz and Noronha (2013) posited that how we deal with bullying even depends on the type of bullying involved. Management and human resources need to be aware of the events, as well as how to address them appropriately. Still, D'Cruz and Noronha fear that victims will be reticent to use company resources to address bullying based on a belief that it will not do any good in a company culture where the bullying occurred in the first place. This is not an unreasonable concern. Additionally, victims reported underreporting because they feared they would not be taken seriously, because their manager was the bully, and because they believed it would make the situation worse rather than better (Tehrani, 2004). Hence, there is a corporate culture that must be overcome in order to address workplace bullying.

Application

Readers of most books frequently search them looking for a list of specific interventions and strategies. With that premise that in mind, we offer a list of possible interventions with the caveat that no one chapter could provide an all-inclusive, detailed, or manualized list similar to specific treatment guides. This is a brief list of suggested preventative measures based on the collective review of the research for this chapter (Ferris, 2009; Lockhart, 1997; Lutgen-Sandvik & Tracy, 2012; MacIntosh, 2006; Oliver, 2013; Piotrowski, 2012; Pomeroy, 2013; Rayner & Hoel, 1997; Sheehan, Barker, & Rayner, 1999; Spurgeon, 1997; Thomas, 2013; Woodrow & Guest, 2014).

Prevention

- Implement a clearly worded, highly visible policy on workplace bullying that includes strict zero-tolerance standards:
  - There should be a clear definition of prohibited, abusive, or bullying behaviors. Examples should be provided.
  - Standards on workplace friends and romantic relationships need to be explicit, with clear repercussions when conflicts arise.
  - The policy must confirm that cyberbullying is workplace bullying and will be treated accordingly.
  - Partner with mental health professionals to raise awareness, develop policy, provide training, assist in resolution, assist in the

investigation process, coach human resources personnel and leadership, and create reward systems to encourage respectful behaviors.

- ○ Information, including the policy itself, should be posted publically where all employees, managers, vendors, contractors, representatives, or any others conducting business can review the information.
- ○ All who review the information should sign a statement to that fact, acknowledging not only the policy but also the consequences for violating the policy.
- • Training in how to deal with bullying situations should be mandatory for managers and supervisors. The training would be required to identify patterns in behavior, given that bullying, by definition, is not a discreet incident:
  - ○ When bullying is uncovered, there should be documentation of the prohibited behavior.
  - ○ Policies should be enforced with measurable consequences.
  - ○ Assurances against retaliation for coming forward should be provided.
  - ○ Immediate corrective action should ensue if wrongdoing is confirmed. Managers should also remain vigilant to any signs of intimidation, threat, emotional outbursts, or suspicious messaging.
- • Execute a complaint procedure that requires employees experiencing or witnessing bullying to report it:
  - ○ The posted policy should be unambiguous for how complaints are handled.
  - ○ Investigations should be prompt, thorough, and impartial.
  - ○ Ensure that there will be no negative consequences for reporting bullying behaviors regarding one's superior, and delineate a plan of action if that superior is in charge of handling bullying complaints
  - ○ Encourage bystander witnesses to support victims and come forward against bullies.
- • There should be a monitoring system or feedback loop to monitor the effectiveness of the program measures.
- • Company culture should reflect a commitment to eliminating workplace bullying:
  - ○ Lead from the top down. Avoid mixed messages for managers when comparing the advice in the policy with advice provided by their own supervisors. This lack of top-down accountability can

lead to de facto subcultures within the organizational whole, which can lead to grossly inconsistent or mismanaged policies.

o Promote a positive and respectful workplace. Make this a priority and reference it often in handouts, flyers, announcements, meetings, and trainings.

o Take a proactive stance that includes supervision, support staff group facilitation, walkabouts, training programs for awareness, a liaison, career succession planning, and organizational consultation.

Acknowledging that even with the best preventative measures workplace bullying will occur, companies should be prepared to act immediately in the best interests of the victim, the alleged bully, and the company as a whole. This is a brief list of suggested intervention measures based on the collective review of the research for this chapter.

Intervention

- Immediately initiate an investigation:
  - o Listen empathetically.
  - o Take complaints seriously and follow written procedures for investigation.
  - o Care should be taken to protect both the accused and the accuser through the investigation process. Certainly this makes sense from a human resources standpoint where liability is a concern, but it also makes sense from a psychological standpoint if rehabilitation is to succeed.
  - o When documenting abuse, the narrative needs to be clear and coherent, specific, and without emotionality. There should be a clear story with relevant details about specific behaviors, witnesses, dates and times, negative effects, and reduced productivity. Not only does this better communicate the necessary information, but victims can also better make sense of this situation for themselves and understand the need to fight the good fight.
  - o Enlist human resources personal in the process from the outset. In theory, they are specially trained in handling these types of issues, including understanding the legal implications of what may occur.
  - o Seek legal guidance from in-house or retained counsel.
  - o Follow the published workplace bullying policy to the letter. Just as there should be zero tolerance for bullying among employees,

there should be zero tolerance for anybody who fails to act in accordance with the policy.

- Therapeutic Measures—Victim:
  - Provide employee assistance programs (EAPs) for initial counseling.
  - Provide or encourage individual psychotherapy. Goals of therapy can include journaling and documentation, assisting in empowerment and development of a social network, advocating for the victim, providing psychoeducation, and assisting in the decision-making process regarding job change.
  - Bibliotherapy (journaling) allows clients to safely explore what has occurred, normalize their experiences, identify coping strategies, identify intervention strategies, and regain a sense of empowerment.
- Therapeutic Measures—Alleged or Proven Perpetrator:
  - Be cognizant that bullies are people too, and there can be benefit in rehabilitation and retaining employees.
  - Provide EAPs for initial counseling.
  - Require individual therapy. Goals for therapy can include gaining insight into the nature and origin of prohibited behavior, developing a prosocial worldview, anger management, problem solving, improving interpersonal relationships, among others. The exact treatment plan would be based on the actions in question.

Any therapeutic intervention will require mental health professionals to have knowledge and awareness of bullying and workplace harassment. In fact, counselor awareness is paramount because victims many times do not have the inclination or the insight to recognize that they are even being bullied. Perhaps this should even become more of a focus within counselor training programs, so that clinicians are at least considering this possibility during intake interviews and initial counseling sessions. Although there is no *DSM* diagnosis for bullying, it is quite possible that many employed clients presenting with the aforementioned diagnoses are unaware that the workplace is the source of their distress. When you stop and think about the percentage of waking hours in a week spent working—up to 35% if you work full time and sleep eight hours per night—from a therapeutic standpoint, it would be easy to see how a client might choose to consciously or unconsciously "overlook" work as the source of distress, given the importance of employment and being good at our work, in terms of self-concept. On the flip side, it would be tragic for an uninformed counselor to inadvertently "blame" a client for his or her own distress. In fact, Lewis et al. (2002) noted that attributing the effects of bullying to a preexisting condition could intensify suffering. Imagine counseling a victim from a cognitive-behavioral orientation and focusing on distorted thinking, when in reality the thought-emotion link is rooted in genuine abuse! Whatever the approach, Lewis et al. echo what is taught in so many books on counseling theory and technique: provide a counseling experience rooted in empathic listening, where being genuine and offering hope are critical.

FUTURE RESEARCH CONSIDERATIONS

The reality is that no one book, much less one chapter, can adequately address the realities of bullying in the workplace. It would be foolhardy to believe we could reduce such a broad and troubling experience to brief snippets or cookie-cutter wisdom. What is desperately needed is far more research that focuses on current and future trends in societal bullying which ultimately are reflected in a workplace microcosm. Future researchers would do well to focus on some of these key concepts:

- For American businesses and clinicians, more U.S.-based studies are needed. This was quite clear in Nielsen and Einarsen's meta-analysis from 2012, when they noted that workplace bullying is a relatively new construct for North American researchers, despite years of prior study in the European continent. The reality is we emphasize a sociocultural perspective, yet having the bulk of the research outside the United States represents a missed opportunity for this culture. Also, it may be sending the message that American businesses and researchers simply do not care about this problem.

- We need a better understanding of why bullies bully in general. Not only might this prevent workplace bullying to begin with, but perhaps it can assist victims with a more gestalt understanding of what has occurred and why (Lutgen-Sandvik & Tracy, 2012). Including bullies in the research process may further this goal.

- Rayner and Hoel (1997) argued quite smartly that the wide diversity in academic backgrounds and research approaches skews the accuracy of any statistical models. They believe that cross-disciplinary efforts will be required to truly understand the nature and extent of bullying.

- An interesting question remains about the link between childhood and workplace bullying. Perhaps longitudinal research would provide greater insight. There may be several areas of focus to that end, such as whether or not counseling of childhood bullies impacted adult aggression and whether or not childhood victims become adult victims. Also, we might consider whether childhood victims take a paradoxical role in adulthood and themselves become bullies.

There is no doubt that as more research commences, future authors will highlight additional areas for future research. That is, in fact, the nature of scientific inquiry. The topics highlighted in this chapter represent but a few areas of potential future research directions that could provide a wealth of valuable information.

CONCLUSION

To date, research regarding workplace bullying has been derived from the work of European scholars whose countries have had more focus on this topic. Nevertheless, there is still not a good understanding of why bullying happens. Though no one disputes the fact there is a growing trend in aggressive and hostile behaviors in the workplace, in the United States there appears to be little interest in curtailing the problem via legal regulation. Without legal protection, which may actually be problematic to initiate; and given the lack of clear definitions and working models of workplace bullying, companies are left to police themselves. Mental health professionals have a unique opportunity to be part of that police action, from the development of antibullying policies to in vivo consultation as bullying is identified and investigated with the goal of treating both victims and perpetrators. We are well poised to better understand the psychosocial factors that lead to bullying behaviors, as well as understand the psychic damage to victims who have endured bullying and are trying to put their lives back together. Given that the development of workplace bullying may have multiple etiologies, and that complex personality traits and factors will always be a confounding issue for both research and treatment, the way to make any lasting inroads to curbing workplace bullying is to better define what it is and assist companies in establishing policies and procedures. From a business perspective, it is understandable why companies are now starting to look at ways to protect their talent pool, if not for actual cost benefit, then from a public relations standpoint. There is no obvious or easy solution, but growing research shows there are significant monetary and psychological costs related to bullying in the workplace, and we simply cannot afford to let these events continue.

REFERENCES

Agervold, M. (2007). Bullying at work: A discussion of definitions and prevalence, based on an empirical study. *Scandinavian Journal of Psychology, 48*, 161–172.

Alterman, T., Luckhaupt, S., Dahlhamer, J., Ward, B., & Calvert, G. (2013). Job insecurity, work-family imbalance, and hostile work environment: Prevalence data from the 2010 National Health Interview Survey. *American Journal of Industrial Medicine, 56*(6), 660–669.

American Psychiatric Association (APA). (2013). *Diagnostic and statistical manual of mental disorders* (5th ed.). Arlington, VA: Author.

Ayoko, O. B., Callan, V. J., & Härtel, C. J. (2003). Workplace conflict, bullying, and counterproductive behaviors. *International Journal of Organizational Analysis, 11*(4), 283–301.

Baillien, E., Neyens, I., De Witte, H., & De Cuyper, N. (2009). A qualitative study on the development of workplace bullying: Towards a three way model. *Journal of Community & Applied Social Psychology, 19*(1), 1–16.

Balducci, C. B., Fraccaroli, F., & Schauefil, W. B. (2011). Workplace bullying and its relation with work characteristics, personality, and post-traumatic stress symptoms: An integrated model. *Anxiety, Stress & Coping, 24*(5), 499–513.

Berge Matthiesen, S. G., & Einarsen, S. (2004). Psychiatric distressed and symptoms of PTSD among victims of bullying at work. *British Journal of Guidance & Counseling, 32*(3), 335–356.

Birkeland Nielsen, M., Berge Matthiesen, S., & Einarsen, S. (2010). The impact of methodological moderators on prevalence rates of workplace bullying. A meta-analysis. *Journal of Occupational & Organizational Psychology, 83*(4), 955–979.

Chima, F. O. (2004). Depression and the workplace: Occupational social work development and intervention. *Employee Assistance Quarterly, 19*(4), 1–20.

D'Cruz, P., & Noronha, E. (2013). Navigating the extended reach: Target experiences of cyberbullying at work. *Information and Organization, 23*, 324–343.

Dewa, C. S., McDaid, D., & Ettner, S. L. (2007). An international perspective on worker mental health problems: Who bears the burden and how are costs addressed? *Canadian Journal of Psychiatry, 52*(6), 346–356.

Einarsen, S., Raknes, B., & Matthiesen, S. (1994). Bullying and harassment at work and their relationships to work environment quality: An exploratory study. *European Work & Organizational Psychologist, 4*(4), 381.

Escartín, J., Rodríguez-Carballeira, A., Zapf, D., Porrúa, C., & Martín-Peña, J. (2009). Perceived severity of various bullying behaviours at work and the relevance of exposure to bullying. *Work & Stress, 23*(3), 191–205.

Ferris, P. A. (2009). The role of the consulting psychologist in the prevention, detection, and correction of bullying and mobbing in the workplace. *Consulting Psychology Journal: Practice and Research, 61*(3), 169–189.

Gemzøe Mikkelsen, E. E., & Einarsen, S. S. (2002). Relationships between exposure to bullying at work and psychological and psychosomatic health complaints: The role of state negative affectivity and generalized self-efficacy. *Scandinavian Journal of Psychology, 43*(5), 397–405.

Gilbert, J. A., Raffo, D. M., & Sutarso, T. (2013). Gender, conflict, and workplace bullying: Is civility policy the silver bullet? *Journal of Managerial Issues, 25*(1), 79–98.

Grusec, J. E. (1992). Social learning theory and developmental psychology: The legacies of Robert Sears and Albert Bandura. *Developmental Psychology, 28*(5), 776–786.

Hall, R., & Lewis, S. (2014). Managing workplace bullying and social media policy: Implications for employee engagement. *Academy of Business Research Journal, 1*, 128–138.

Hauge, L., Skogstad, A., & Einarsen, S. (2007). Relationships between stressful work environments and bullying: Results of a large representative study. *Work & Stress, 21*(3), 220–242

Hauge, L. J., Skogstad, A., & Einarsen, S. (2010). The relative impact of workplace bullying as a social stressor at work. *Scandinavian Journal of Psychology, 51*, 426–433.

Hoel, H., & Cooper, C. L. (2000). Destructive conflict and bullying at work. Paper. Manchester School of Management, University of Manchester Institute of Science and Technology.

Hoel, H., Cooper, C., & Faragher, B. (2001). The experience of bullying in Great Britain: The impact of organizational status. *European Journal of Work & Organizational Psychology, 10*, 443–465.

Kuklarni, J. (2008). Women's mental health. *Australian and New Zealand Journal of Psychiatry, 42*, 1–2.

Langos, C. (2012). Cyberbullying: The challenge to define. *Cyberpsychology, Behavior, and Social Networking, 15*(6), 285–289.

Lewis, J., Coursol, D., & Wahl, K. (2002). Addressing issues of workplace harassment: Counseling the targets. *Journal of Employment Counseling, 39*(3), 109.

Leymann, H. (1990). Mobbing and psychological terror at workplaces. *Violence and Victims, 5*(2), 119–126.

Leymann, H. (1996). The content and development of mobbing at work. *European Journal of Work and Organizational Psychology, 5*(2), 165–184.

Lockhart, K. (1997). Experience from a staff support service. *Journal of Community & Applied Social Psychology, 7*(3), 193–198.

Lutgen-Sandvik, P., & Tracy, S. J. (2012). Answering five key questions about workplace bullying: How communication scholarship provides thought leadership for transforming abuse at work. *Management Communication Quarterly, 26*(1), 3–47.

MacIntosh, J. (2005). Experiences of workplace bullying in a rural area. *Issues in Mental Health Nursing, 26*, 893–910.

MacIntosh, J. (2006). Tacking work place bullying. *Issues in Mental Health Nursing, 27*(6), 665–679

Murray, A. (2009, April 7). Should I rank my employees? *Wall Street Journal.* Retrieved from http://guides.wsj.com/management/recruiting-hiring-and-firing/should-i-rank-my-employees/.

National Comorbidity Survey. (2007). Harvard Medical School. Retrieved from http://www.hcp.med.harvard.edu/ncs/index.php.

National Institute of Mental Health. (n.d.). Statistics. Retrieved from http://www.nimh.nih.gov/statistics/index.shtml?utm_source=winter-inside-nimh&utm_medium=email&utm_campaign=staff

Nielson, M. B., & Einarsen, S. (2012). Outcomes of exposure to workplace bullying: A meta-analytic review. *Work & Stress, 26*(4), 309–322.

Oliver, S. (2013). Not just in the schoolyard. *CA Magazine, 146*(5), 46–47.

Olmstead, J. (2013). The cure for workplace bullying. *Nursing Management, 44*(11), 53–55.

Ortega, A., Høgh, A., Pejtersen, J., & Olsen, O. (2009). Prevalence of workplace bullying and risk groups: A representative population study. *International Archives of Occupational & Environmental Health, 82*(3), 417–426.

Parks, W. S., Lundberg-Love, P. K, Galusha, J. M., & Deitrick, S. (2013). Understanding the mechanism for employee burnout subsequent to recurrent stress in the workplace. In M. A. Paludi (Ed.), *Psychology for business success* (Vol. 1, pp. 171–192). Santa Barbara, CA: Praeger/ABC-CLIO.

Parks, W. S, Lundberg-Love, P. K., Luft, C., Steward, A., & Peddy, H. (in press). Understanding mental disorders in women in the workplace to mitigate deleterious effects. In M. L. Connerley (Ed.), *Handbook of the well-being of working women*. New York, NY: Springer.

Persson, R., Hogh, A., Hansen, Å., Nordander, C., Ohlsson, K., Balogh, I., & . . . Ørbæk, P. (2009). Personality trait scores among occupationally active bullied persons and witnesses to bullying. *Motivation & Emotion, 33*(4), 387–399.

Piotrowsi, C. (2012). From workplace bullying to cyberbullying: The enigma of e-harassment in modern organizations. *Organization Development Journal, 30*(4), 44–53.

Pomeroy, E. (2013). The bully at work: What social workers can do. *Social Work, 58*(1), 5–8.

Privitera, C., & Campbell, M. A. (2009). Cyberbullying: The new face of workplace bullying? *CyberPsychology & Behavior, 12*(4), 395–400.

Rayner, C. (1997). The incidence of workplace bullying. *Journal of Community & Applied Social Psychology, 7*, 199–208.

Rayner, C., & Hoel, H. (1997). A summary review of literature relating to workplace bulling. *Journal of Community & Applied Social Psychology, 7*, 181–191.

Salin, D. (2003). Ways of explaining workplace bullying: A review of enabling, motivating and precipitating structures and processes in the work environment. *Human Relations, 56*(10), 1213–1232.

Samnani, A., & Singh, P. (2014). Performance-enhancing compensation practices and employee productivity: The role of workplace bullying. *Human Resource Management Review, 24*(1), 5–16.

Saunders, P., Huynh, A., & Goodman-Delahunty, J. (2007). Defining workplace bullying behavior professional lay definitions of workplace bullying. *International Journal of Law and Psychiatry, 30*, 340–354.

Sheehan, M., Barker, M., & Rayner, C. (1999). Applying strategies for dealing with workplace bullying. *International Journal of Manpower, 20*(1–2), 50.

Spurgeon, A. (1997). Commentary I. *Journal of Community & Applied Social Psychology, 7*, 241–244.

Tehrani, N. (2004). Bullying: A source of chronic post traumatic stress? *British Journal of Guidance & Counseling, 32*(3), 357–366.

Thomas, J. P. (2013). Get ahead of legislation: 8 steps to a strong anti-bullying policy. *HR Specialist: Employment Law, 43*(6), 7.

Vega, G., & Comer, D. R. (2005). Sticks and stones may break your bones, but words can break your spirit: Bullying in the workplace. *Journal of Business Ethics, 58,* 101–109.

Woodrow, C., & Guest, D. E. (2014). When good HR gets bad results: Exploring the challenge of HR implementation in the case of workplace bullying. *Human Resource Management Journal, 24*(1), 38–56.

Workplace Bullying Institute. (WBI). (n.d.). Estimating the costs of bullying. Retrieved from http://www.workplacebullying.org/individuals/solutions /costs/.

Workplace Bullying Institute. (WBI). (2012). *The WBI website 2012 instant poll A— why bullying happens.* Bellingham, WA: Gary Namie, Ph.D.

Workplace Bullying Institute. (WBI). (2014). *2014 WBI U.S. workplace bullying.* Bellingham, WA: Gary Namie, Ph.D.

Chapter 4

The Role of the Victim and the Perpetrator-Victim Relationship in Understanding Workplace Aggression

Jennifer Bozeman and M. Sandy Hershcovis

Workplace aggression is a serious problem faced by organizations and their members. Schat, Frone, and Kelloway (2006) found that more than 41% of working Americans were subjected to some form of workplace aggression in a 12-month period, while Tepper, Duffy, Henle, and Lambert (2006) estimated aggression from supervisors alone costs organizations $23.8 billion annually in employee withdrawal, reduced productivity, and health care expense. Further, several meta-analytic studies (Bowling & Beehr, 2006; Hershcovis, 2011; Hershcovis & Barling, 2010) have shown that there are serious negative consequences for victims of workplace aggression.

There is a growing body of literature that investigates the intentions and characteristics of perpetrators of workplace aggression (Aquino, 2000) and what organizations can do to defend employees against these

Portions of this chapter appeared in M. Paludi (Ed.). (2012). *Managing diversity in today's workplace*, Volume 3: *Workplace politics* (pp. 49–75). Santa Barbara, CA: Praeger.

aggressors (Baron & Neuman, 1996). Fewer studies have looked at how victim characteristics may play a role in victimization (Aquino, 2000). In studying victimology, criminologists and psychologists have found that individuals sometimes put themselves in situations in which they can be victimized easily, even repeatedly (Sparks, Genn, & Dodd, 1977). It is often uncomfortable and unpopular to talk about the victim as having a hand in his or her own victimization because it appears as though the victim is to blame. However, evidence suggests that victims—at least some of the time—contribute to their own victimization. It is therefore crucial to consider which victim behaviors and personal characteristics might put people at higher risk.

A study on the prevalence of workplace aggression by Schat et al. (2006) found that 31.4% of workers who reported experiencing psychological aggression at work reported experiencing it on a weekly basis, while 21.6% of individuals who reported experiencing physical aggression at work reported experiencing it on a weekly basis. In addition, although less common, there seems to be a minority of individuals who are repeatedly victimized, whereas the majority of individuals never experience targeted aggression (Sparks et al., 1977). This chapter looks at the extent to which victims' characteristics and behaviors help precipitate victims' mistreatment. We consider three types of victim precipitation: (a) active precipitation (i.e., provoking someone), (b) behavioral precipitation, and (c) trait-based precipitation.

This chapter first defines our relevant constructs and reviews the literature on perpetrator and situational characteristics that have been found to relate to workplace aggression. Second, it provides an overview of the victim precipitation literature in criminology and psychology. Third, it considers the ways in which the victim may contribute, either actively or passively, to his or her own victimization at work. Fourth, it suggests how victim, perpetrator, and situational characteristics may interact to increase the likelihood of victimization. Finally, it concludes with a brief discussion of future directions.

DEFINITIONS AND CONSTRUCTS

Victimization

Aquino, Grover, Bradfield, and Allen (1999) defined victimization as a person's belief that he or she has been exposed to mistreatment by another or others on one or more occasions. This definition considers the victim's perception of being exposed to aggression, not the intention of the person perceived to be behaving aggressively. Therefore, it is possible that some individuals may perceive themselves as victims when others do not perceive them as victims. At the same time, it is possible for someone to be aggressed upon without perceiving that he or she is a victim.

Aggression

Aggression, as defined by Baron (1977), is any action intended to injure (harm) another individual who wishes to avoid such behavior. Workplace aggression, then, is any aggressive act directed toward an organization or its members by a current or past employee (Baron & Neuman, 1998). We distinguish workplace aggression from victimization in that workplace aggression is *enacted by a perpetrator*, whereas victimization is *experienced by a victim*.

This chapter focuses on workplace aggression targeted toward individuals and individual perceptions of victimization at work. Workplace aggression has also been referred to as workplace incivility (Andersson & Pearson, 1999), social undermining (Duffy, Ganster, & Pagon, 2002), emotional abuse (Keashly, 1998), abusive supervision (Tepper, 2000), mobbing (Leymann, 1990), workplace bullying (Adams & Crawford, 1992), workplace harassment (Bjorkqvist, Osterman, & Hjelt-Back, 1994), verbal abuse (Cox, 1991), and psychological abuse (Sheehan, Sheehan, White, Leibowitz, & Baldwin, 1990). Consistent with Hershcovis (2011), who argued that, despite different labels, these constructs are operationalized in a similar manner and are related in the same way to the same outcomes, we treat them interchangeably in this chapter.

VICTIMIZATION AT WORK: PERPETRATOR AND SITUATIONAL PREDICTORS

Before considering how the victim may contribute to his or her own victimization, we provide a brief overview of how perpetrator characteristics and the work environment factor into workplace aggression. Following this, we will draw on prior research to consider characteristics of the victim that—when combined with what is known about situational and perpetrator characteristics—provide a more informed picture of the predictors of workplace victimization.

Most research to date has considered the characteristics of the perpetrator and the situation as key predictors of workplace victimization. Characteristics of the perpetrator primarily refer to trait-based characteristics such as personality, whereas situational characteristics refer to perceptions of the organizational environment and of the job itself. Below we briefly summarize the research on perpetrator and situational characteristics.

Perpetrator Characteristics

In terms of perpetrator characteristics, Berry, Ones, and Sackett (2007) examined meta-analytically a range of trait-based correlates of workplace aggression. They reported that three of the five "Big Five" predictors—emotional stability, conscientiousness, and agreeableness—were negatively related to interpersonal workplace aggression (i.e., deviance). Although they also examined gender and found that men were more likely to behave aggressively than women, this finding was weak. In another meta-analysis, Hershcovis et al. (2007) similarly found a weak but significant relation between gender and aggression, with men more likely to behave aggressively than women. Further, these authors found that trait anger was the strongest predictor of interpersonal aggression and predicted both organizational and interpersonal aggression.

In addition to these meta-analytic findings, researchers have also investigated a range of other perpetrator characteristics. Douglas and Martinko (2001) theorized and found that individual differences account for a considerable amount of variation in workplace aggression. Specifically they found that those with revenge attitudes, a hostile attribution style (vs. nonhostile), a past history of exposure to an aggressive culture, and trait anger (perpetual feelings of anger that can lead to aggressive behavior; Berkowitz, 1993; Spielberger, Jacobs, Russell, & Crane, 1983) reported engaging in greater instances of workplace aggression.

In thinking about perpetrator characteristics, Aquino and Lamertz (2004) developed a model that placed perpetrators in two broad categories: domineering or reactive. Domineering perpetrators prefer situations in which they control others and demonstrate their power and authority over their subordinates or coworkers. This type of perpetrator prefers to closely supervise others, be overly punitive, and highlight hierarchical and social status differences between themselves and lower-status others (Ashforth, 1997). Alternatively, reactive perpetrators aggress against others because of a perceived personal threat or an infringement on a recognized social norm and are motivated through perceiving themselves to be victims.

Situational Antecedents

A significant body of research has also investigated situational antecedents of workplace aggression. In their meta-analytic study, Hershcovis et al. (2007) found that situational factors such as interpersonal conflict, job dissatisfaction, and situational constraints were the strongest predictors of aggression targeted toward the organization, while interpersonal injustice and interpersonal conflict were the strongest situational predictors of interpersonal aggression. They further found that inadequate leadership and interpersonal injustice were significantly stronger predictors of aggression targeted toward supervisors than toward coworkers.

In another meta-analysis, Bowling and Beehr (2006) found that environmental factors such as role conflict, role overload, role ambiguity, and work constraints were related to higher levels of harassment in the workplace. Work that has little meaning, is ambiguous (Agervold & Mikkelsen,

2004), uninteresting (Einarsen, Raknes, & Matthiesen, 1994), or takes place in a competitive, stressful environment has also been found to be related to higher levels of victimization.

This section summarized the individual (perpetrator-based) and situational antecedents of workplace aggression. We now turn to victimization and consider the research that has examined the victim's role in workplace aggression. We begin by summarizing the victimization literature in criminology and psychology. We then consider the research on victim precipitation in the workplace aggression literature.

VICTIMIZATION IN CRIMINOLOGY AND PSYCHOLOGY

Before turning to the workplace aggression and victimization literature, we briefly review an early work on victim precipitation that emerged from criminology and psychology literatures. Sparks et al. (1977) argued that criminologists have neglected the role that a victim might play in his or her own victimization as the overarching assumption has been that the victim is a passive element. These authors suggested that most previous research considered offenders to be the main element in the offense, while victims were randomly chosen from society. According to these authors, there are three ways in which a victim may aid in his or her victimization. First, an individual may behave in a manner that precipitates the perpetrator to victimize him or her. For example, if an individual insults or physically attacks another, he or she would likely have an increased likelihood of becoming a victim of a crime due to his or her initial provocation. In an organizational setting, precipitation of mistreatment could include acts such as gossiping about others, acting rudely toward coworkers or supervisors, displaying annoying or disagreeable behaviors, or not doing one's share of the work.

Second, victims may unintentionally put themselves in harm's way, creating an opportunity for a perpetrator. For example, if an individual is known for not speaking up for him- or herself, a coworker may take credit for the other's work product or ideas. Lastly, Sparks et al. (1977) suggested that an individual's appearance, conduct, or social position may make him or her more or less likely to be victimized than others.

In a study that looked at child victims of bullying, Olweus (1978) found that most of the victims could be labeled as provocative or active or submissive or passive. Provocative or active victims are often seen as aggressive and may threaten or provoke others into acting out against them. On the other hand, submissive or passive children were even more likely than provocative children to be victimized by others, and they commonly held negative attitudes about themselves and their circumstances. In other words, those who feel negatively about themselves may be more prone to viewing themselves as victims.

Smith, Singer, Hoel, and Cooper (2003) theorized that many of the traits exhibited by schoolyard victims, such as low self-esteem and shyness, are compounded through victimization and can potentially contribute to depression and anxiety in adulthood, which may in turn increase the likelihood that these individuals are victimized in the workplace. In their study on victimization in school and the workplace, Smith et al. surveyed 5,288 adults from various organizations and industries about their experiences with bullying and victimization both as adolescents in the schoolyard and as adults in the workplace. In comparing schoolyard victims of bullying with those who reported no bullying, individuals victimized in the schoolyard reported significantly more workplace victimization within both the six-month and five-year periods preceding the survey.

Smith et al. (2003) also found that individuals who reported both bullying and being bullied at school reported more victimization in the workplace in the 6-month and 5-year periods prior to the survey than those who were only victims or were neither victims nor bullies. These data support the finding of Sparks et al. (1977) for a correlation between reports of being violent and reports of being victimized. These researchers found that regardless of gender or race, those who reported acting in a violent manner more often also reported violent victimization. Accordingly, those who treat others aggressively may be reciprocally treated and victimized. The norm of reciprocity (Goulder, 1960) suggests that the recipient of a kind or wrongful act will perceive an obligation or strong desire to return the behavior of others. If certain individuals have a tendency to treat others aggressively, then those individuals may also experience more victimization than those who treat others kindly.

Reiss (1980) found that the number of multiple victimizations evident in the U.S. national crime survey data showed victimization to be a nonrandom event. Similarly, Farrell (1992), in a review of nine studies on repeat victimization, found that "two or three percent of respondents to victim surveys who are the most victimized report between a quarter and a third of all incidents" (p. 98) and also concluded that this pattern could not be a chance happening. This argument supports the notion that perpetrator characteristics are only one factor in predicting victimization, and victim characteristics might also help explain why some individuals are targeted with aggression and some are not. This argument is not meant to put the blame on the victim, but rather to suggest that there are individuals who either actively or passively put themselves in situations in which they are likely to be targeted.

VICTIM PRECIPITATION

The previous section discussed how situational and perpetrator characteristics relate to victimization in the workplace. The following sections will discuss how victim characteristics can factor into the likelihood that individuals will be victimized at work. First, we consider victim provocation, followed by situations created by victims that can contribute to their victimization, and finally, individual traits that can increase an individual's chances of being the victim of workplace aggression.

Active Precipitation

There is evidence that many individuals are both victims and perpetrators (Aquino & Lamertz, 2004), suggesting that victims may provoke their own victimization through their aggressive actions. Olweus (1978) posited that provocative or active victims are often seen as aggressive and may threaten or provoke others into acting out against them. Aquino and Bradfield (2000) investigated the role of victim characteristics in workplace victimization among government employees and found that the group who perceive they were victimized the most was also the most aggressive of the survey respondents. Other researchers found that those who experience chronic anger (anger directed at coworkers) were less likely to perceive themselves as recipients of respectful treatment from a supervisor (Gibson & Barsade, 1999) and more likely to perceive themselves as victims.

In addition, the literature on revenge and retaliation suggests that these behaviors are reactions to perceived mistreatment aimed at injuring or punishing the wrongdoer (Aquino, Tripp, & Bies, 2001; Bies & Tripp, 1996). Treating a coworker in an aggressive manner can result in reciprocal victimization or revenge (Aquino et al., 2001). Researchers have found that workplace aggression motivates negative behaviors such as revenge (Folger & Skarlicki, 1998), antisocial behaviors (Robinson & O'Leary-Kelly, 1998), theft (Greenberg, 1990), and violence (Folger & Baron, 1996).

The idea that certain behaviors (precipitators) can lead to revenge in the workplace (Bies & Tripp, 1996; Bies, Tripp, & Kramer, 1997) is consistent with research suggesting that aggression can result in a tit-for-tat spiral (Andersson & Pearson, 1999). By mistreating others at work, individuals can foster a sense of injustice from their coworkers who may retaliate and target revenge toward those they believe mistreated them (Skarlicki & Folger, 1997). This back-and-forth behavior can result in an escalating spiral (Andersson & Pearson, 1999).

Behavioral Precipitation

An individual's behavior or lack of a behavior can also factor into his or her victimization. In the following section, we consider three behaviors that are empirically linked to victimization. These behaviors represent (a) the manner in which victims cope with victimization, (b) the level of control they exert in social interaction, and (c) their work behaviors. Though there are other behaviors that may increase the likelihood that an individual is targeted for victimization, we have chosen these to help explain why some individuals may be singled out for aggression and some are not.

Coping

Victims who choose not to speak out to report victimization may experience greater instances of victimization, as these victims may appear to be weak or unable to protect themselves. Viano (1989) suggested that there are several reasons victims may not report their experiences. First, individuals may fear that they will not be believed. This may be particularly likely if their aggressor has higher status within the organization, for example, a supervisor. Second, victims may be concerned about the effect that reporting their victimization may have on their relationship with their aggressor. This may be of particular concern in a work situation in which the relationship is ongoing and the victim must interact with their aggressor daily (Hershcovis & Barling, 2007).

Third, there are social and psychological factors that may prevent victims from coming forward and reporting their victimization. Viano (1989) suggested that how society views victims, even innocent ones, can dissuade individuals from reporting the behavior of their aggressor, with victims often considered "losers" by society. Victimized individuals may fear that reporting their victimization could change the perceptions that others at work hold of them. Additionally, being considered a "loser" by management and coworkers could also negatively affect the victim's career plans and opportunity for upward mobility within the organization. Finally, he suggested that reporting victimization may increase the likelihood that either the original aggressor or new aggressors may target this individual as he or she may appear to be an easy target because of the social stigma related to reporting victimization. Bowling and Beehr (2006) argued that those who are victimized often perceive themselves to lack power and be of lower status, which these victims may attempt to hide from their coworkers and organizations through their decision not to report their aggressors and the victimization.

Although failing to report victimization may enable the aggression to continue, there are also downfalls to reporting victimization. In particular, Cortina and Magley (2003) found that victims who reported their mistreatment to others were more likely to be targeted with even more severe social retaliation in response to the reporting than those who remained silent about their victimization. Additionally, those who confronted their aggressors directly were more likely to experience increased work-related aggression in response to the confrontation. Both those who confronted or reported aggression from a higher-status other experienced greater aggression in response to their actions than those who reported or confronted aggression from a perpetrator who was not of higher organizational status. According to this research, options for victims of workplace aggression seem bleak. If they keep silent, they may be considered weak and easy targets for aggression; if they speak up, they may be considered aggressive and provoke further mistreatment from their aggressors.

Control

Aquino et al. (1999) posited that self-determination (a component of empowerment, relating to how much control individuals assert over their environments, including choosing with whom they interact) could be another factor that affects the likelihood that an individual experiences aggression from others at work. In particular, those who exhibit low self-determination (i.e., who appear weak and have little control) would be more likely to be victimized at work than those high in self-determination (i.e., those who have more control). Those who are high in self-determination should be better able to choose with whom they interact, which should enable these individuals to avoid situations that lead to victimization. Aquino et al. (1999) suggested that individuals low in self-determination may be comparable to Olweus's (1978) submissive or passive victims.

Aquino and Byron (2002) posited that the use of control needs to be balanced. That is, individuals very high in dominating behaviors (socially forceful and provocative) and those very low in dominating behaviors (unassertive and weak) are more likely to experience aggression and report victimization than those who exert more moderate levels of control over their social situation. These two ends of control are consistent with Olweus's (1978) findings that provocative and submissive children were most likely to be victims of bullying. Drawing from literature on chivalry bias, Aquino and Byron (2002) suggested that women are often treated with more leniency than men, as leniency bias assumes they have more of a need to be protected (Moulds, 1980). They hypothesized that the relation between extremely high and low dominating behavior and victimization will be attenuated for women as both men and women will act more leniently toward them (Glick & Fiske, 1996). The results were consistent with their hypotheses, suggesting that victim characteristics contribute to the likelihood that someone is singled out for victimization.

Consistent with the above findings, research has found that victims of bullying who reported shyness and a lack of conflict management and coping skills (i.e., unassertive) were at increased risk of being bullied (Einarsen et al., 1994). Similarly, Coyne, Seigne, and Randall (2000) found that victims were less competitive, assertive, and outspoken than their nonvictimized counterparts. Victims in their study had an inclination to avoid conflict and failed to confront their aggressor or report the mistreatment—in other words, they may have been "easy targets." Furthermore, consistent with the findings in the previous section, these victims may create an opportunity for their own victimization.

Work Behavior

In addition to their coping styles and the way in which victims interact with their social environment, a victim's behavior may also contribute to his or her own victimization. In the work environment, employee performance is of key significance, particularly to supervisors. Therefore, it is likely that low-performing individuals may be at higher risk of mistreatment. Tepper, Moss, and Duffy (2011) suggested that lower performers may precipitate their mistreatment by irritating and bothering their supervisor, making them more difficult to work with and creating a situation that encourages their negative treatment. These authors examined 183 supervisor–subordinate dyads working in the health care industry and found that when supervisors perceived their subordinates as low performers, they were likely to view them as having low utility and were more likely to target them for mistreatment. Following Opotow (1990, 1995), these authors posited that every individual has a *scope of justice*, which allows one to identify which individuals deserve to be treated in a moral manner and which individuals are undeserving of fair treatment. Those who are seen as undeserving of fair treatment can then be excluded from such treatment. Exclusion can occur when individuals are viewed as different, as offering low utility, or as creating conflict between themselves and another individual (Hafer & Olson, 2003) who may then become aggressive toward them because they are morally excludable and undeserving of fair treatment.

It has also been reported that those who perceive victimization by their supervisors enact aggression against their aggressive supervisors (Mitchell & Ambrose, 2007). For example, Tepper, Duffy, and Shaw (2001) found that when supervisors treated their subordinates aggressively, their subordinates tended to use dysfunctional resistance (e.g., ignoring requests made by the supervisor) to cope with the aggression. This research suggests that behaving aggressively at work can precipitate victimization.

Similarly, Aquino and Boomer (2003) found that employees who were considered by their supervisors to display less citizenship behaviors (a type of prosocial performance; Rotundo & Sackett, 2002) than their fellow coworkers also reported more victimization. These researchers found that citizenship behavior was more negatively related to perceptions of being victimized by lower-level workers than by managers, suggesting that citizenship behavior could possibly reduce the likelihood that an individual will be victimized.

TRAIT-BASED PRECIPITATION

In addition to the behavioral characteristics described above that may put individuals at higher risk of victimization, an individual's personality and gender may also precipitate victimization. Traits that annoy (e.g., negative personality traits) or threaten (e.g., intelligence) a potential perpetrator may put individuals in a more vulnerable position. In this section, we consider some of the personality traits that are prevalent among victims and the role gender plays in victimization.

Negative Affect

There has been a considerable amount of research on the relation between negative affect and workplace victimization. Individuals who are high in negative affect are predisposed to experience negative emotions such as fear, anger, sadness, and anxiousness (Watson & Clark, 1984). That is, they focus on what is negative about themselves and the situations they find themselves in (Watson & Pennebaker, 1989). They also tend to experience emotional distress, which can interfere with their work behaviors and their social interactions with others (Watson & Pennebaker, 1989).

Aquino et al. (1999) hypothesized that those with negative affect had an increased likelihood of being targeted in the workplace. In a meta-analysis, Bowling and Beehr (2006) similarly found that negative affectivity was the dispositional characteristic that was most related to victimization. Aquino and Bradfield (2000) suggested a threefold reason that individuals high in negative affect may be more likely to be victimized. First, individuals high in negative affect may irritate or annoy others. That is, these individuals may be more likely to be pessimistic about organizational decisions or ideas and may be more likely to complain or express displeasure about work and work-related activities than those low in negative affect. Individuals who frequently display negative emotions may drain or grate on the nerves of those around them or thwart the work efforts of potential perpetrators, resulting in frustration. Consistent with this notion, research on the frustration-aggression hypothesis suggests that when something or someone gets in the way of a goal or objective, the individual whose goal is being thwarted may become aggressive (Berkowitz, 1989; Dollard, Doob, Miller, Mowrer, & Sears, 1939; Spector, 1975).

A second reason why individuals with high negative affect may be victimized is related to the discussion in the earlier section on opportunity. Aquino and Bradfield (2000) suggested that those high in negative affectivity may display distress and act passively, providing potential perpetrators with the opportunity to behave aggressively. They suggested that by behaving in a manner consistent with feelings of anxiety and distress, individuals high in negative affect may be perceived to be submissive and therefore easy targets for aggression.

A third reason for the relationship between negative affectivity and self-reported victimization is that those high in negative affect may incorrectly perceive ambiguous or neutral behavior as aggressive (Aquino & Bradfield, 2000; Bowling & Beehr, 2006). Aquino and Bradfield (2000) found that individuals high in negative affect viewed themselves more frequently as victims of indirect victimization and suggested that personality traits factor into the likelihood that an individual will perceive that he or she is being victimized. In another study, Matthiesen and Einarsen (2004) found that victims of workplace aggression reported being suspicious of the intentions of others, which may have led them to perceive some innocuous behavior as aggressive.

The Big Five

In addition to negative affect, some the Big Five personality traits have been associated with victimization, whereas others are unrelated or show mixed results. Milam, Spitzmueller, and Penney (2009) found that individuals who reported victimization were less agreeable and more neurotic than their nonvictimized coworkers by both self-report and other reports of agreeableness and neuroticism. This finding is consistent with the arguments above that those who display negative emotions (i.e., those who are disagreeable or emotionally unstable) may irritate or frustrate others, leading them to experience higher levels of victimization. However, research on extroversion is mixed. Some research indicates that victims are more introverted (Coyne, Craig, & Chong, 2004), while other research indicates that victims are more extroverted (Glaso, Matthiesen, Nielsen, & Einarsen, 2007), or that there is no difference between introverts and extroverts related to victimization (Milam et al., 2009; Vartia, 1996). Research on conscientiousness is also mixed, with some research finding no relation between this personality trait and victimization (Coyne, Chong, Seigne, & Randall, 2003), which contradicts earlier findings that those who are more conscientious experience more victimization (Coyne et al., 2000).

Cognitive Ability

Another trait that has recently been associated with victimization is an individual's cognitive ability. In a recent study, Kim and Glomb (2010) hypothesized that those with high cognitive ability would be faced with more victimization than their lower cognitive ability counterparts. They argued that those with high cognitive ability may create situations that invite victimization, as others at work make comparisons between themselves and those who are top performers, which has been linked to cognitive ability

(Schmidt & Hunter, 1998). They found a positive relationship between cognitive ability and victimization and also found that those with high cognitive ability, who were also high in agency (i.e., individualism, personal growth, and dominance; Bakkan, 1966), experienced significantly more victimization than those low in agency. They suggested that those who were more self-focused and had high cognitive ability provoked more victimization than those who were more group focused and possessed high cognitive ability. Their findings suggested that when the brightest stars are targeted for mistreatment, organizational performance may be affected through decreased motivation, satisfaction, and individual performance on behalf of the victim (Glomb, 2002).

Gender

Though a lay assumption tends to be that men are more aggressive and women are more frequently victims, research does not support this assumption. For example, some researchers have found that men report victimization less than women (Aquino & Bradfield, 2000; Cortina, Magley, Williams, & Langhout, 2001), while others found women report less victimization than men (Jennifer, Cowie, & Ananiadou, 2003), and some found no difference (Vartia, 1996). In a meta-analytic review, Bowling and Beehr (2006) found that the gender of the victim did not differ in a practically significant way. That is, it appears that women are no more likely than men to be victimized. Similarly, in a review of victim characteristics, Aquino and Thau (2009) suggested that demographic variables, such as gender, are not strong predictors of victimization.

VICTIM AND PERPETRATOR INTERACTION

Based on our reviews in the previous section, victim characteristics and personality may precipitate aggression from perpetrators. However, as noted earlier, Douglas and Waksler (1982) argued that "perpetrator and victim commonly appear to be involved in a social encounter where the acts of each affect those of the other" (p. 249). Therefore, while certain behaviors and traits may put individuals at higher risk of victimization, it is important to consider the role of the perpetrator in the aggressive interaction. To date, most aggression research has been conducted from the perspective of victims, without acknowledging that aggressive behavior is, in fact, an interaction between two people. That is, aggression occurs in the context of a social relationship, and the nature of the relationship will dictate its enactment and the outcomes and coping methods of victims (Hershcovis & Barling, 2007, 2010). Consistent with Folger and Skarlicki's (1998) popcorn model of revenge, which argues that situational and individual characteristics combine to create a recipe for someone to "pop" (i.e., enact revenge), we argue that aggression or victimization is likely to arise out of a "chemical reaction" between perpetrators and targets. Specifically, a mismatch between perpetrators' and targets' characteristics and behaviors may mix to create an aggressive explosion. Below we discuss two potential relational factors—diversity and performance or competition—that might lead to a recipe for aggression.

Diversity

Diversity has been defined as "a mixture of people with different group identities within the same social system" (Nkomo & Cox, 1996, p. 339). According to Harrison, Price, and Bell (1998), workgroup diversity can be divided into two categories: surface-level and deep-level diversity. Surface-level diversity as described by Milliken and Martins (1996) consists of overt demographically and visible differences such as sex, race, age, and ethnicity. These types of overt group-level differences make "social classification" by others and oneself relatively simple (Harrison, Price, Gavin, & Florey, 2002). Deep-level diversity includes individual differences that are not visibly or readily noticeable such as attitudes, values, and personality (Harrison et al., 1998). Deep-level differences are often overlooked early in a relationship and are more likely to be noticed and create conflict over time through repeated interactions (Harrison et al., 2002).

Deep-level diversity between coworkers or supervisors and their subordinates can create a situation where victimization is more likely. For example, Tepper et al. (2011) posited that when supervisors view their subordinates as holding differing views and attitudes than they do, they may act aggressively toward them. These dissimilarities can also lead to conflict through opposing opinions in the workplace (Harrison & Klein, 2007). The research of Tepper et al. (2011) indicated that perceived deep-level dissimilarity between the supervisor and the subordinate (e.g., attitudinal) predicted relationship conflict and aggression from one's supervision, which also negatively predicted subordinate performance.

Related to these findings, Vartia (1996) found that approximately 20% of those who reported victimization attributed it to being different from those with whom they worked. Social identity theory suggests that individuals may show prejudice toward those outside their social ("in-") group to cast light on the positive attributes of their group or social identity through negative comparison with another (Hogg & Abrams, 1988). Rubin and Hewstow (1998) suggested that social self-esteem is the collective attitude of the group's members about their group's surface-level attributes, often in relation to another group. Group members may attempt to increase their social self-esteem by discriminating against or otherwise mistreating members of other social groups. In such instances, it may be the differences between the aggressor's and the victim's groups that lead to the victimization.

Diversity may also help explain the inconsistent findings in the research examining the Big Five traits described earlier. That is, some studies found that introverts were more likely to be victimized, while others found that extroverts were more likely to be victimized. A diversity perspective suggests that who is victimized may depend on a combination of the traits of aggressor and the victim. It is therefore possible that more introverted aggressors may aggress against more extroverted or provocative victims, while extroverted aggressors may aggress against more introverted or submissive victims. Tett and Burnett (2003) suggested that in work environments, some personality traits become salient due to task, social, and organizational cues. These cues can activate specific traits, which can affect saliency of similar or opposing traits in others. It is possible that when traits are salient to a particular work task, diversity may be a relevant factor in victimization. That is, when a particular trait such as extroversion is needed to effectively perform an interactive task, and when a member of the interaction does not exhibit the necessary trait, the interaction partner who does exhibit the needed trait may become aggressive toward the interaction partner.

PERFORMANCE AND COMPETITION

In addition to issues of diversity, aggression may occur as a result of an incompatibility in goals or behavioral orientation between perpetrator and targets. As a result, some behaviors or traits might pose a threat to some perpetrators but not others. For instance, the findings mentioned earlier that low performers are more likely to be victimized than high performers are inconsistent with the findings that those with high cognitive ability are more likely to be victimized than those with low cognitive ability. This inconsistency suggests that aggressive action may depend not only on the traits and behaviors of the target, but also on those of the perpetrator. An insecure perpetrator may perceive cognitive ability as a personal threat to his or her power and position, whereas a secure individual may perceive someone with high cognitive ability as an organizational asset worth learning from and cultivating. In contrast, a secure employee may behave aggressively toward a poor performer or social loafer because this individual may increase his or her workload, whereas an insecure individual may perceive the same individual as a nonthreat to his or her position and therefore behave civilly toward the poor performer.

Similarly, some researchers have found that victims tend to be less competitive than nonvictims (Coyne et al., 2000). Other researchers have found that a key factor leading to aggression in the workplace is competition for promotion or a supervisor's attention (Vartia, 1996). Taken together, these studies suggest that a more competitive individual may be more likely to victimize another competitive individual, possibly to diminish his or her ability to garner the positive attention of his or her supervisor or gain a promotion. On the other hand, it is less likely that the noncompetitive individual would see as much benefit in aggressing against his or her colleague as diminishing his or her colleague's reputation to gain some organizational end and will yield less of a perceived benefit to the less competitive individual.

It may also be true that an organization can create a culture or environment of competition that may invite more aggression or victimization into the workplace. Organizations with a competitive environment generally recruit and select competitive individuals as employees. Competitive personalities may be more inclined to behave aggressively when faced with competitive others. This clash between two or more competitive individuals is likely to turn multiple parties into both aggressors and victims. In such a situation, aggression is likely to spiral or escalate (Andersson & Pearson, 1999).

Smith et al. (2003) found that the most victimized group was the group of individuals who reported being both the bully and the victim. Regardless of an aggressor's reason for mistreating a victim, acting aggressively invites others to mistreat the perpetrator. That is, regardless of the original aggressor trait–victim trait combination, those who act aggressively invite aggression. These aggressors invite aggression not only from those they victimize, but likely also from others who witness the aggressive behavior and retaliate on behalf of the victim, especially if the victim is perceived as being unable to defend him- or herself (O'Reilly & Aquino, 2011). This is a particularly troublesome scenario for organizations, as the actions of one aggressor not only create a victim, but also precipitate third parties to participate and victimize the original aggressor.

CONCLUSION

It is important for organizational researchers to gain a better understanding of why some individuals are victimized in the workplace and others are not. This chapter reviewed the literature that suggests victims may put themselves in a vulnerable position to experience mistreatment (Aquino & Bradfield, 2000), either by providing perpetrators with the opportunity or by virtue of precipitating behaviors or traits. Research has shown that regardless of the intentions of the victim, victims have participated in some form or another to their own victimization (Gottfredson, 1981), whether knowingly or unknowingly provoking or entering situations that place them at a higher risk for victimization (Sparks et al., 1977).

Gobert (1977), a criminologist, also suggested that individuals may either intentionally or unintentionally precipitate their own victimization, and that when a crime is precipitated by the victim, the offender may have been provoked. He argued that because some individuals would not have acted aggressively unless precipitated, controlling precipitative behavior could reduce the incidence of crime. For this reason, he suggested that penalties for precipitated crimes should be lighter than for those that were not. Though this may be too strong a position to take in the workplace aggression literature—aggression in the workplace should not be condoned whatever the reason—we argue that at a minimum, researchers need to consider the factors that may put victims at higher risk. Perhaps more importantly, researchers should stop examining workplace aggression outside its social context. Aggression is a result of the interaction between two people, the perpetrator and the victim, and the behaviors and traits of both parties factor into the interaction. Therefore, an understanding of the social relationship is crucial to a complete understanding of the resulting aggressive interaction. It is only recently that researchers have begun to examine the role of victims in this interaction. This research has demonstrated that sometimes responsibility for a negative act may not lie solely with the perpetrator. Therefore, more research examining victim precipitation would help complete the currently one-sided take on this two-sided interaction.

REFERENCES

Adams, A., & Crawford, N. (1992). *Bullying at work: How to confront and overcome it*. London: Virago Press.

Agervold, M., & Mikkelsen, E. G. (2004). Relationships between bullying, psychosocial work environment and individual stress reactions. *Work and Stress, 18*, 336–351.

Andersson, L. M., & Pearson, C. M. (1999). Tit for tat? The spiralling effect of incivility in the workplace. *Academy of Management Review, 24*, 452–471.

Aquino, K. (2000). Structure and individual determinants of workplace victimization: The effects of hierarchical status and conflict management style. *Journal of Management, 26*, 171–193.

Aquino, K., & Bommer, W. H. (2003). Preferential mistreatment: How victim status moderates the relationship between organizational citizenship behavior and workplace victimization. *Organizational Science, 14*, 374–385.

Aquino, K., & Bradfield, M. (2000). Perceived victimization in the workplace: The role of situational factors and victim characteristics. *Organization Science, 11*, 525–537.

Aquino, K., & Byron, K. (2002). Dominating interpersonal behavior and perceived victimization in groups: Evidence for a curvilinear relationship. *Journal of Management, 28*, 69–87.

Aquino, K., Grover, S., Bradfield, N., & Allen, D. G. (1999). The effects of negative affectivity, hierarchical and self-determination on workplace victimization. *Academy of Management Journal, 42*, 260–272.

Aquino, K., & Lamertz, K. (2004). A relational model of workplace victimization: Social roles and patterns of victimization in dyadic relationships. *Journal of Applied Psychology, 89*, 1023–1034.

Aquino, K., & Thau, S. (2009). Workplace victimization: Aggression from the target's perspective. *Annual Review of Psychology, 60*, 717–741.

Aquino, K., Tripp, T. M., & Bies, R. J. (2001). How employees respond to personal offense: The effects of blame attribution, victim status, and offender status on revenge and reconciliation in the workplace. *Journal of Applied Psychology, 86*, 52–59.

Ashforth, B. (1997). Petty tyranny in organizations: A preliminary examination of antecedents and consequences. *Canadian Journal of Administrative Sciences, 14*, 126–140.

Bakkan, D. (1966). *The duality of human existence*. Reading, PA: Addison-Wesley.

Baron, R. A. (1977). *Human aggression*. New York, NY: Plenum.

Baron R. A., & Neuman, J. H. (1996). Workplace violence and workplace aggression: Evidence on their relative frequency and potential causes. *Aggressive Behavior, 22*, 161–173.

Baron, R. A., & Neuman, J. H. (1998). Workplace violence and workplace aggression: Evidence concerning specific forms, potential causes, and preferred targets. *Journal of Management, 24*, 391–419.

Berkowitz, L. (1989). Frustration-aggression hypothesis: Examination and reformulation. *Psychological Bulletin, 106*, 59–73.

Berkowitz, L. (1993). *Aggression: It's causes, consequences, and control*. Philadelphia, PA: Temple University Press.

Berry, C. M., Ones, D. S., & Sackett, P. R. (2007). Interpersonal deviance, organizational deviance, and their common correlates: A review and meta-analysis, *92*, 410–424.

Bies, R. J., & Tripp, T. M. (1996). Beyond distrust: "Getting even" and the need for revenge. In R. M. Kramer & T. R. Tyler (Eds.), *Trust in organizations: Frontiers of theory and research* (pp. 246–260). Thousand Oaks, CA: Sage.

Bies, R. J., Tripp, T. M., & Kramer, R. M. (1997). At the breaking point: Cognitive and social dynamics of revenge in organizations. In R. A. Giacalone & J. Greenberg (Eds.), *Antisocial behavior in organizations* (pp. 18–36). Thousand Oaks, CA: Sage.

Bjorkqvist, K., Osterman, K., & Hjelt-Back, M. (1994). Aggression among university employees. *Aggressive Behavior, 20*, 173–184.

Bowling, N. A., & Beehr, T. A. (2006). Workplace harassment from the victim's perspective: A theoretical model and meta-analysis. *Journal of Applied Psychology, 91*, 998–1012.

Cortina, L. M., & Magley, V. J. (2003). Raising voice, risking retaliation: Events following interpersonal mistreatment in the workplace. *Journal of Occupational Psychology, 8*, 247–265.

Cortina, L. M., Magley, V. J., Williams, J H., & Langhout, R. D. (2001). Incivility in the workplace: Incidence and impact. *Journal of Occupational Health Psychology, 6*, 64–80.

Cox, H. C. (1991). Verbal abuse nationwide part 1: Oppressed group behavior. *Nursing Management, 22*, 32–35.

Coyne, I., Chong, P. S-L., Seigne, E., & Randall, P. (2003). Self and peer nominations of bullying: An analysis of incident rates, individual differences, and perceptions of the working environment. *European Journal Work and Organizational Psychology, 12,* 208–228.

Coyne, I., Craig, J., & Chong, P. S-L. (2004). Workplace bullying in a group context. *British journal of Guidance and Counseling, 32,* 301–317.

Coyne, I., Seigne, E., & Randall, P. (2000). Predicting workplace victim status from personality. *European Journal of Work and Organizational Psychology, 9,* 335–349.

Dollard, J., Doob, L., Miller, N., Mowrer, O., & Sears, R. (1939). *Frustration and aggression.* New Haven, CT: Yale University Press.

Douglas, J. D., & Waksler, F. C. (1982). *The sociology of deviance.* Boston, MA: Little Brown.

Douglas, S. C., & Martinko, M. J. (2001). Exploring the role of individual differences in the prediction of workplace aggression. *Journal of Applied Psychology, 86,* 547–559.

Duffy, M. K., Ganster, D. C., & Pagon, M. (2002). Social undermining in the workplace. *Academy of Management Journal, 45,* 331–351.

Einarsen, S., Raknes, B. I., & Matthiesen, S. B. (1994). Bullying and harassment at work and its relationship with work environment quality: An exploratory study. *European Work and Organizaitonal Psychologist, 4,* 381–401.

Farrell, G. (1992). Multiple victimisation: Its extent and significance. *International Review of Victimology, 2,* 85–102.

Folger, R., & Baron, R. A. (1996). Violence and hostility at work: A model of reactions to perceived injustice. In E. Q. Bulatao & G. R. VandenBos (Eds.), *Violence on the job: Identifying risks and developing solutions* (pp. 51–85). Washington, DC: American Psychological Association.

Folger, R., & Skarlicki, D. P. (1998). A popcorn metaphor for employee aggression. In R. W. Griffin, A. O'Leary-Kelly, & J. Collins (Eds.), *Monographs in organizational behavior and industrial relations.* Vol. 23. *Dysfunctional behavior in organizational: Part A. Violent and deviant behavior* (pp. 43–81). Greenwich, CT: JAI Press.

Gibson, D. E., & Barsade, S. G. (1999, August). T*he experience of anger at work: Lessons from the chronically angry.* Paper presented at the annual meeting of the Academy of Management, Chicago, IL.

Glaso, L., Matthiesen, S. B., Neilsen, M. B., & Einarsen, S. (2007). Do targets of workplace bullying portray a general victim personality profile? *Scandinavian Journal of Psychology, 48,* 313–319.

Glick, P., & Fiske, S. T. (1996). The ambivalent sexism inventory: Differentiating hostile and benevolent sexism. *Journal of Personality and Social Psychology, 70,* 491–512.

Glomb, T. M. (2002). Workplace anger and aggression: Informing conceptual models with data from specific encounters. *Journal of Occupational Health Psychology, 7,* 20–36.

Gobert, J. J. (1977). Victim precipitation. *Columbia Law Review, 77,* 511–553.

Gottfredson, M. R. (1981). On the etiology of criminal victimization. *Journal of Criminal Law & Criminology, 72*, 714–726.

Goulder, A. W. (1960). The norm of reciprocity: A preliminary statement. *American Sociological Review, 25*, 161–178.

Greenberg, J. (1990). Employee theft as a reaction to underpayment inequity: The hidden costs of pay cuts. *Journal of Applied Psychology, 75*, 561–568.

Hafer, C. L., & Olson, J. M. (2003). An analysis of empirical research on the scope of justice. *Personality and Social Psychology Review, 7*, 311–323.

Harrison, D. A., & Klein, K. J. (2007). What's the difference? Diversity constructs as separation, variety, or disparity in organizations. *Academy of Management Review, 32*, 1199–1228.

Harrison, D. A., Price, K. H., & Bell, M. P. (1998). Beyond surface relational demography: Time and the effects of surface- and deep-level diversity on work group cohesion. *Academy of Management Journal, 41*, 96–107.

Harrison, D. A., Price, K. H., Gavin, J. H., & Florey, A. T. (2002). Time, teams, and task performance: Changing effects of surface- and deep-level diversity on group functioning. *Academy of Management Journal, 45*, 1029–1045.

Hershcovis, M. S. (2011). "Incivility, social undermining, bullying . . . oh my!": A call to reconcile constructs within workplace aggression research. *Journal of Organizational Behavior, 32*, 499–519.

Hershcovis, M. S., & Barling, J. (2007). Towards A relational model of workplace aggression. In J. Langan-Fox, C. L. Cooper, & R. Klimoski (Eds.), *Dysfunctional workplace: Management challenges and symptoms* (pp. 268–284). Cheltenham, UK: Edward Elgar.

Hershcovis, M. S., & Barling, J. (2010). Towards a multi-foci approach to workplace aggression: A meta-analytic review of outcomes from different perpetrators. *Journal of Organizational Behavior, 31*, 24–44.

Hershcovis, S. M., Turner, N., Barling, J., Arnold, A. A., Dupré, K.E., Inness, M., . . . Sivanathan, N. (2007). Predicting workplace aggression: A meta-analysis. *Journal of Applied Psychology, 91, 6*, 1–11.

Hogg, M. A., & Abrams, D. (1988). *Social identifications: A social psychology of intergroup relations and group processes*. London: Routledge.

Jennifer, D., Cowie, H., & Ananiadou, K. (2003). Perceptions and experiences of workplace bullying in five different working populations. *Aggressive Behavior, 29*, 489–496.

Keashly, L. (1998). Emotional abuse in the workplace: Conceptual and empirical issues. *Journal of Emotional Abuse, 1*, 85–117.

Kim, E., & Glomb, T. M. (2010). Get smarty pants: Cognitive ability, personality, and victimization. *Journal of Applied Psychology, 95*, 889–901.

Leymann, H. (1990). Mobbing and psychological terror at workplaces. *Violence and Victims, 5*, 119–126.

Matthiesen, S. B., & Einarsen, S. (2004). Psychiatric distress and symptoms of PTSD among victims of bullying at work. *British Journal of Guidance and Counselling, 32*, 335–356.

Milam, A. C., Spitzmueller, C., & Penney, L. M. (2009). Investigating individual differences among targets of workplace incivility. *Journal of Occupational Health Psychology, 14,* 58–69.

Milliken, F. J., & Martins, L. L. (1996). Searching for common threads: Understanding the multiple effects of diversity in organizational groups. *Academy of Management Journal, 21,* 402–433.

Mitchell, M. S., & Ambrose, M. L. (2007). Abusive supervision and workplace deviance and the moderating effects of negative reciprocity beliefs. *Journal of Applied Psychology, 92,* 1159–1168.

Moulds, E. F. (1980). Chivalry and paternalism: Disparities of treatment in the criminal justice system. In S. K. Datesman & F. R. Scarpitti (Eds.), *Women, crime and justice* (pp. 277–299). New York, NY: Oxford University Press.

Nkomo, S. M., & Cox, T. (1996). Diverse identities in organizations. In S. R. Clegg, C. Hardy, & W. R. Nord (Eds.), *Handbook of organization studies* (pp. 338–356). London: Sage.

Olweus, D. (1978). *Aggression in schools: Bullies and whipping boys.* Washington, DC: Hemisphere.

Opotow, S. (1990). Moral exclusion and injustice: An introduction. *Journal of Social Issues, 46,* 1–20.

Opotow, S. (1995). Drawing the line: Social categorization, moral exclusion, and the scope of justice. In *Conflict, cooperation, and justice: Essays inspired by the work of Morton Deutsch* (pp. 347–369). San Francisco, CA: Jossey-Bass.

O'Reilly, J., & Aquino, K. (2011). A model of third parties' morally-motivated responses to mistreatment in organizations. *Academy of Management Review, 36,* 526–543.

Reiss, A. J. (1980). Victim proneness in repeat victimisation by type of crime. In S. E. Fienberg & A. J. Riess (Eds.), *Indicators of crime and criminal justice: Quantitative studies* (pp. 41–53). Washington, DC: U.S. Department Bureau of Statistics.

Robinson, S. L., & O'Leary-Kelly, A. M. (1998). Monkey see, monkey do: The influence of work groups on the antisocial behavior of employees. *Academy of Management Journal, 41,* 658–672.

Rotundo, M., & Sackett, P. R. (2002). The relative importance of task, citizenship, and counterproductive performance to global ratings of job performance: A policy-capturing approach. *Journal of Applied Psychology, 87,* 66–80.

Rubin, M., & Hewstone, M. (1998). Social identity theory's self esteem hypothesis: A review and some suggestions for clarification. *Personality and Social Psychology Review, 2,* 40–62.

Schat, A. C. H., Frone, M. R., & Kelloway, K. E. (2006). Prevalence of workplace aggression in the U.S. workforce. In K. E. Kelloway, J. Barling, & J. J. Hurrell Jr. (Eds.), *Handbook of workplace violence* (pp. 47–90). Thousand Oaks, CA: Sage.

Schmidt, F. L., & Hunter, J. E. (1998). The validity and utility of selection methods in personnel psychology: Practical and theoretical implications of 85 years of research findings. *Psychological Bulletin, 124,* 262–274.

Sheehan, K. H., Sheehan, D. V., White, K., Leibowitz, A., & Baldwin, D. C. (1990). A pilot study of medical student abuse. *Journal of the American Medical Association, 263*, 533–537.

Skarlicki, D. P., & Folger, R. (1997). Retaliation in the workplace: The roles of distributive, procedural, and interactional justice. *Journal of Applied Psychology, 82*, 434–443.

Smith, P. K., Singer, M., Hoel, H., & Cooper, C. L. (2003). Victimization in the school and the workplace: Are there any links? *British Journal of Psychology, 94*, 175–188.

Sparks, R., Glenn, H., & Dodd, D. (1977). *Surveying victims*. London: Wiley.

Spector, P. E. (1975). Relationships of organizational frustration with reported behavioural reactions of employees. *Journal of Applied Psychology, 60*, 635–637.

Spielberger, C. D., Jacobs, G. A., Russell, S. F., & Crane, R. S. (1983). Assessment of anger: The State-Trait Anger Scale. In J. N. Butcher & C. D. Spielberger (Eds.), *Advances in personality assessment* (Vol. 2, pp. 161–189). Hillsdale, NJ: Erlbaum.

Tepper, B. J. (2000) Consequences of abusive supervision. *Academy of Management Journal, 43*, 178–190.

Tepper, B. J., Duffy, M. K., Henle, C. A., & Lambert, L. S. (2006). Procedural injustice, victim precipitation, and abusive supervision. *Personnel Psychology, 59*, 101–123.

Tepper, B. J., Duffy, M. K., & Shaw, J. D. (2001). Personality moderators of the relationship between abusive supervision and subordinates' resistance. *Journal of Applied Psychology, 86*, 974–983.

Tepper, B. J., Moss, & Duffy, M. K. (2011). Predictors of abusive supervision: Supervisor perceptions of deep-level dissimilarity, relationship conflict, and subordinate performance. *Academy of Management Journal, 54*, 279–294.

Tett, R. P., & Burnett, D. D. (2003). A personality trait-based interactionist model of job performance. *Journal of Applied Psychology, 88*, 500–517.

Vartia, M. (1996). The sources of bullying-psychological work environment and organizational climate. *European Journal of Work and Organizational Psychology, 5*, 203–215.

Viano, E. C. (1989). Victimology today: Major issues in research and public policy. In E. C. Viano (Ed.), *Crime and its victims: International research and public policy issues* (pp. 3–14). New York, NY: Hemisphere.

Watson, D., & Clark, L. A. (1984). Negative affectivity: The disposition to experience aversive emotional states. *Psychological Bulletin, 3*, 465–490.

Watson, D., & Pennebaker, J. W. (1989). Health complaints, stress, and distress: Exploring the central role of negative affectivity. *Psychological Review, 96*, 234–254.

Part II

Bullying across Occupations and Organizations

Chapter 5

Prime Targets: Identity Markers as the Secret Rationale for the Preponderance of Bullying in Academe

Jennifer L. Martin, Martina L. Sharp-Grier, and
Kathleen Piker-King

> Not everything that is faced can be changed. But nothing can
> be changed until it is faced.
>
> —James Baldwin

In one of the author's experiences, she has found that standing up to bullies can be an effective measure of self-protection. She learned this lesson in seventh grade, when entering a new school with unfamiliar students. A group of older girls surrounded her and began to taunt her. Instinctively, she held her head up and broke through the circle, stalking away with measured strength and feigned nonchalance. They never bothered her again. Fast-forward 30 years. This author is in her first year of her first tenure track job. She gets into a discussion that turns into a debate with a tenured full professor over issues of educational equity. It ends on a friendly note, or so she thinks. The weekend passes; but unbeknownst to her, her colleague's anger grows.

The explosion came when they passed in the hallway: she was loaded down with books, having to set her things on the floor to unlock her office door—he had a simple paper cup of coffee in his hand. Another colleague, ignorant to the debate that had occurred days before and unsure if they knew each other, introduced them. The man with the coffee cup barked, "Yes, she embarrassed me in front of a table full of colleagues last week." Now, when they parted ways, he had offered his hand for her to shake and conceded the argument. They had agreed to disagree. However, all was not well in his mind. She replied, "I thought we parted on good terms, but now you want to publicly shame me in front of a colleague? Okay." And she walked into her office, shaking with her heart racing. But that would not be the end of it. He stood at her office door, the paper coffee cup shaking in his hand. He stated, "You know, I think we may have more in common than not, I see the posters on your wall, and I can relate to them. May I come in and sit down? Can we talk?"

After an hour of contentious debate, she never backing down and they again parted on somewhat good terms. But he never challenged her again. In fact, from then on, he only ever approached her with respect. The seventh-grade lesson she learned about standing up to bullies was again realized in a current workplace situation, as far as she knew. Although, at the time of this writing, two years later, she had not experienced any overt forms of aggression from this particular colleague, she had no way of knowing if he had engaged in any covert forms of aggression or character assassination against her.

According to Farrington (2010), "Like in the schoolyard, office bullies go after the weak, the marginalized and the least likely to fight back. But only by standing up to bullies can schools eliminate their negative effect on individual careers and the campus workplace" (p. 9). Standing up to bullies may or may not be effective on an individual level; for some this may work, for others not. However, the problem is not just an individual one. It is an institutional problem that must be addressed on a grander scale.

Crawford conceptualizes workplace bullying under the broader umbrella of violence (as cited in Simpson & Cohen, 2004). To wit, workplace bullying is often seen as an abuse of power where actual physical violence does not always come into play. Harassment, sexual harassment being one form, is typically defined in the literature as victims being targeted because of their marginalized or protected statuses (Martin, Kearl, & Murphy, 2013; Meyer, 2009). One of the questions we raise in this chapter is whether or not workplace bullying, specifically bullying in academe in this context, targets victims in more vulnerable classes. Or to put it more succinctly, do bullies within the higher education context disproportionately target those who possess nondominant identity characteristics not made explicit in the types of bullying experienced? For example, are women and people of color more vulnerable to bullying in academe, although the content of bullying may mask the reasons why they are targeted? In the above example, was the author targeted because she is a woman? Would a man who argued with this male colleague have faced similar repercussions? Somehow, we doubt this. Was it more "embarrassing" for this colleague because a woman was disagreeing with his opinion?

The examples shared above do not suggest that dealing with or standing up to bullies can be that easy. In fact, some do not feel comfortable confronting a bully or addressing the situation directly. This chapter will identify those who might be the most vulnerable targets of workplace bullying and present strategies to deal with and end the bullying that occurs in colleges and universities. To operationalize our viewpoint, we define bullying in academe as pervasive, interpersonal, aggressive acts, which may involve single incidents or behavior exhibited over time, including verbal slights, threats or intimidation, rumor spreading, overly negative and sustained criticism, inequitable division of labor, and marginalization (Lester, 2013), with the overall impact of derailing careers. According to Fox and Stallworth (2005), these behaviors may include subtle and even unconscious manifestations of raced, sexed, and gendered inequitable treatment (microaggressions). Bullying in academe is both structural and interpersonal and includes mobbing, which Zapf (1999) describes as extreme psychological stress inflicted by a group of perpetrators, rather than an individual bully, racist bullying, and homophobic bullying (Misawa, 2010). All of these forms of bullying target individuals because of their nonmajority status.

The authors of this chapter identify as female professors, two of whom work at four-year institutions and one at a two-year institution. One of the authors is a white education professor in her third year in higher education. Another of the contributors is a queer African American assistant professor of sociology, in her ninth year of higher education instruction. The other author is a white tenured full professor, having spent her career at the same institution of higher education in the department of sociology.

This chapter is informed by a multifaceted theoretical framework. First, we approach this topic through a critical race feminist lens. Critical race feminism includes the recognition of race and racism in society, a critique of the traditional Western values of objectivity and neutrality, a reliance on the knowledge and experience of people of color in the definition of its tenants, an interdisciplinary focus, with the goal of the elimination of all forms of oppression, and, we would argue, critical race feminism necessitates the advocacy of antiracist/pro-feminist whites.

Critical race feminism seeks to determine how oppression is perpetuated, for the purpose of undermining it. Dismantling bullying is part and parcel of this proposition. As a logical extension of critical race feminism, sociologically, we have chosen to analyze the phenomenon of bullying in academe utilizing a conflict theoretical approach, one that critically evaluates the use of mechanisms of power and control by those who hold preferred status to ensure both their hegemonic stronghold and their access to resources. This perspective, as Collins (1971) suggests, aptly reflects how group membership status within organizational structure is wielded by those in control, in order to "manipulate others to carry out their wishes" (p. 1010) and maintain their prestige. We argue that bullying in academe reinforces structural stratification and serves to ensure limited access to privilege and status within organizations.

IDENTITY MARKERS AS HIDDEN BULLYING

Bullying in academe is an age-old problem that has only recently begun to be examined (Simpson & Cohen, 2004). According to Simpson and Cohen (2004), workplace bullying involves organizational power, is based on individual characteristics, and may involve unfair criticism, work overload, and excessive micromanaging, whereas harassment is based on group characteristics. Lester (2013) argues that bullying in the workplace involves interpersonal aggression and is "frequent, intense, and occurs over a specific time period" (p. ix). The effects include loss of confidence and self-esteem and anxiety (Simpson & Cohen, 2004). The terms "bullying" and "harassment" are often used interchangeably, which can be problematic.

Many have argued that bullying can mask harassment based on protected categories (Martin et al., 2013; Meyer, 2009), especially if the bullying behaviors do not directly highlight the individuals' identities. There is a limited amount of research on identity-based bullying (harassment) in higher education; more research exists on generic bullying, or, in other words, on the topic of bullying in general (Misawa, 2010). This semantic quandary is a cause for concern: schools have a vested interest in maintaining the generic conception of bullying because it can free them from liability if targets do not understand that their civil rights have been violated because bullying is generally not illegal. If those possessing hegemonic power have defined bullying, those with marginalized identities have had no opportunity to be part of the discourse. This semantic quandary becomes even more problematic if targets of bullying and harassment are unaware of civil rights protections that are in place. That the onus is on the victim and this is problematic in and of itself; this problem is exacerbated when institutions mask civil rights violations through minimization: by framing and relabeling them as bullying as opposed to harassment (Brown, Chesney-Lind, & Stein, 2007; Thornton, 2004). In these instances, the bully is protected in an overall attempt to preserve the reputation of the institution.

According to Sallee and Diaz (2013), individuals in more vulnerable identity classes, while protected by civil rights laws, are more susceptible to bullying in academe (e.g., those possessing nonhegemonic identities, such as racial and ethnic minorities, sexual minorities, and women). Women are more likely to report being bullied—and more likely victims of bullying that takes on the form of sexual harassment (Sallee & Diaz, 2013). Bullies tend to target only those who are the most vulnerable for a variety of reasons (Kohut, 2008), such as identity characteristics. Also relevant to this discussion is the degree of the bully's personal feelings of inadequacy, often in relation to the target, who is often high performing. Those faculty members who possess multiple minority statuses, because of their multiple marginalized identities, experience what we suggest is intersectional bullying. For these individuals, the experience of bullying cannot be understood in the context of only one of their identities; rather, as suggested by Misawa (2010), the intersection of multiple stigmatized identities results in stacked experiences of bullying that serve to further marginalize the targets and sanction their differences. Those individuals who possess minority or multiple minority statuses understand that they have to work harder to be taken seriously (Steele & Aronson, 1995). Moreover, these individuals often have to be very high performing as a measure of self-protection because the institution does not often reward nondominant statuses, particularly if those individuals seek to dismantle the status quo (Martin, in press). The latter situation may be particularly threatening to the bully who has been well served by the status quo. The relative positions of power of the target and the bully and the bully's ability to harm the target without facing consequences are pertinent to this conversation (Kohut, 2008). In sum, there are clear differences between bullying and harassment, particularly pertaining to protected classes; in fact, bullying may constitute implicit harassment—by the very nature of the identities of the targets.

According to Misawa (2009), institutions of higher learning understand the value of including diverse populations and multiculturalism in their practice; however, institutions must examine the treatment of social justice scholars who may bear the brunt of bullying and harassment for bringing issues to light. In order for this to occur, more research is necessary to understand how identities such as race, gender, and sexual orientation intersect with the targets of bullying. We have an understanding of how sociocultural positions influence people's interactions; however, more research is necessary to gain a clearer understanding of how the identities of targets influence the behavior of the bully.

Gender differences, upon which a fair amount of research exists, for example, can cause myriad issues within the phenomenon of bullying and harassment. Differences in sex role socialization, differential expectations for the "opposite" sex, privilege or lack thereof, and (dis)/identification with victims can influence the dynamic greatly. Simpson and Cohen (2004) argued that there are differences in reporting levels of bullying between women and men. We would argue that this is not because of an essentialist division between women and men, but because of the lived experiences of those possessing relative privilege. Women tend to be the more likely victims of violence in the workplace and likewise are more often the victims of bullying, "male aggression towards women in the workplace is often motivated by a desire to disempower and control them, then overruling an individual's decisions is a public and potentially powerful strategy—more powerful, perhaps, than unfair criticism or intimidation" (Simpson & Cohen, 2004, p. 179). Simpson and Cohen (2004) also found differences in perceptions of bullying between women and men; for example, women are more likely to perceive certain behaviors as threatening. Because of these differences, conflict can arise when women report bullying behaviors to male supervisors who may not deem the reported behaviors as threatening.

Men may define the conduct in question as something other than bullying because their lived experiences do not mesh with female victims' definitions or the resultant effects of the behaviors. Male supervisors may define said behaviors as something other than bullying and thus fail to act; the "no action taken" may result in victims' experiences of further bullying and retaliation and thus further negative emotional consequences. However, failure to act can result in an escalation of bullying. In sum, as Simpson and Cohen (2004) stated, "While sexual harassment is 'overtly' gendered, bullying also needs to be seen as a gendered activity—although at a different, and perhaps more deep-seated, level. Bullying therefore needs to be put in a gendered context in order to further our understanding of this behavior" (p. 183). According to Jaschik (2014), the University of Colorado at Boulder is revising its policy specifically pertaining to the department of philosophy and requiring mandatory training of faculty in an attempt to change a culture that is hostile to women and thus rife with complaints of sexual harassment and bullying. Women faculty members and graduate students bear the brunt of such treatment. The report also stated that many faculty members appear unaware of federal and state laws relative to sex bias and harassment. The University of Colorado at Boulder example is relevant because the report indicates that bullying and harassment, particularly of women, is a pervasive problem in higher education, which has historically been "written off."

PERSONAL STORY: POWER, STATUS, AND MOBILITY

The level to which bullying behavior reflects the changing organizational structure of the university and the desire to enforce institutional norms exacerbates the pervasive nature of bullying within academe. Thornton (2004), in her analysis of the then emerging phenomenon of the corporatization of academe, suggests that the business-oriented model of administration, previously nonexistent in higher education, is fast transforming

academe into a location rife with organizational inequities and mechanisms to ensure acquiescence to administrative control by faculty and
staff. Lutgen-Sandvik (2006) echoed Thornton's premise, indicating that
"increased oppression and excessive control" (p. 408) represent mechanisms used by management to ensure their power.

Finally, Keashley and Newman (2010) categorized academe as a venue
within which conditions are ripe for hostile interpersonal behaviors and
structure because of the power status between the actors—both within
and between similarly "powered" groups. This within-group power differential exists despite evidence (Lutgen-Sandvik, 2006) that suggests
that much of workplace bullying occurs as a function of supervisor–
subordinate relationships and includes behaviors such as being given
tasks with unreasonable deadlines, experiencing abrupt changes to work
assignments, and being ordered to work on less prestigious assignments
and tasks than indicated in job descriptions or expectations.

Peer-to-peer bullying, or mobbing (Zapf, 1999), is often experienced as
threats to professional reputation or status, isolation, and the "blocking"
of mobility within the organizational structure. Einarson (1999) identified
envy and competition for status, job duties, and advancement as the most
salient rationales for bullying behavior among organizational peers.
Interestingly, the tools used in "faculty-on-faculty" bullying are likely to
be provided by the organization itself, as in the case of performance evaluations and oftentimes ambiguous and subjective procedures for obtaining
tenure or academic rank (Keashly & Newman, 2010). The experience of
one of the current authors in navigating such a process provides empirical
backing to the findings of the aforementioned researchers.

At the midpoint of her academic career, one of the current authors, having met the seniority, pedagogical, and organizational involvement benchmarks identified as the minimum criteria for movement to the next
academic rank, compiled a portfolio (complete with student and peer recommendations for promotion) and submitted it for review by the interdi-
visional committee charged with promotions and rank. Early on in the
process, she became aware that an administrator with whom she had previously had a very public disagreement had been appointed to the committee. This appointment served to be catastrophic for the author, who
was denied academic movement without being provided a clear and substantive rationale, despite the overwhelming support of her students and
colleagues. Further, upon appeal of the committee's decision, the selection
process and outcome were upheld, despite upper managerial acknowledgment of inconsistencies associated with the decision. The author was
advised to resubmit portfolio materials during the next advancement cycle, as a new committee would be convened, and, as such, a different outcome was expected. In short, the subjectivity of the process made it
vulnerable to compromise, which allowed the motives or opinions of

individuals to render the process idiosyncratic. Although this process was acknowledged as inherently flawed, and despite recommendations for change having been articulated, the procedural methodology remains opaque; while there are public criteria outlined for consideration for academic mobility, the process itself remains secretive and subjective—which leaves the possibility for this phenomenon to reoccur. According to Keashley and Neuman (2010), the lack of transparency of processes, such as the one outlined, has resulted in junior faculty experiencing stress-related job insecurity and incivility when these processes are used as instruments of retaliation or mobbing. Despite its onetime occurrence, Randall (1997) suggests that such behavior rises to the level of bullying because of its aggressive and disruptive nature.

Although the aforementioned incident appears to represent only general bullying within the academy, which, according to Misawa (2010), may be experienced by any individual in the workplace and is unrelated to marginalized identities, its latent manifestations are reflective of racist bullying, which is defined as the intersection of racism and bullying (Misawa, 2010). The latent function of the denial of rank constitutes a stereotype threat, which has been found to result in significant emotional distress (Sharp-Grier, in press; Steele & Aronson, 1995). Steele and Aronson (1995) define stereotype threat as being at risk of corroborating, through one's own actions, a negative stereotype or label about a group or category to which one is associated. This threat, in tandem with the denial of academic movement, served to render what would have been an instance of general bullying in the workplace setting to an instance of racist bullying. As an African American woman, the aforementioned author was stigmatized not only as a jilted faculty member, but as a jilted black faculty member who was confronted with the reality that she now bore the brunt of a negative label associated with African American identity. This stigmatized identity brought about increased stress, emotional distress, and a heightened sense of racial awareness.

Critical race theory provides support for viewing this situation through a lens that allows for the interrogation of social, educational, and political issues by prioritizing marginalized voices (Chapman, 2007). Critical race theory possesses an activist component, the end goal of which is social justice (DeCuir & Dixson, 2004). In other words, it is crucial that the identities of targets are taken into consideration when examining issues of bullying, such as the one discussed above. Such experiences also have different and multifaceted implications for the targets that can impact them both personally and professionally. In the above author's experience, she was one of the few African American professors at her institution, which can lead to larger perceptions that she is representative of her racial identity group. Such is not the case for whites. According to Chaisson (2004), the identity of whiteness is neither "problematized nor particularized" in racial discourses because a sense of normalcy is presumed. That is, "the racial identities of minority group members are centered in the discourses on race, but whiteness remains largely unexamined as a racial identity. This non-particularity or normalcy of whiteness makes it 'transparent.' It circumvents the questioning of whiteness, in effect legitimizing it as normal" (Chaisson, 2004, p. 347). The unmarked nature of whiteness is still present in our universities.

BULLYING IN ACADEME

The instance outlined above is reflective of a larger culture of bullying in academe. According to Hollis (2012), 62% of higher education professionals reported experiencing workplace bullying, a number significantly higher than the 35% of the general public who reported bullying on the job. A meta-analysis of studies of bullying in academe yielded results that suggested that rates vary from 32% (Keashly & Neuman, 2008, as cited in Lester, 2013) to 80% (Lester, 2013). Lester (2013) noted that the academy tends to promote uncivil cultures perhaps because of the intersection of academic freedom and the debate of ideas, which is the nature of the university. However, Keashly and Neuman (2010) surmised that the academic milieu, because of its unique structure and work features, bears an increased likelihood that hostile behaviors will manifest. The literature also suggests that competitive organizational cultures such as academe can foster negative workplaces, which foster bullying environments (Simpson & Cohen, 2004; Thornton, 2004).

Thornton (2004) suggests that the emergence of the corporate culture in higher education as one that emphasizes assessable outputs has contributed to the volatility of the academic environment. Twale and DeLuca (2008) pointed out that the corporatization of the academy is a change from what has traditionally been knowledge driven—with the faculty being the producers and the possessors of this knowledge. This model change ignores the established role of the faculty and creates an environment characterized by overwork, exploitation, individualism, and hyper-competitiveness (Cleary, Walter, Horsfall, & Jackson, 2012; Thornton, 2004). Further, Twale and DeLuca (2008) argued that the change in emphasis to "market forces, managerial accountability, budget strategies, student as consumer, and university as knowledge seller" (p. 135) has dramatically altered higher education. In short, higher education has become an environment where quantitative, performance criteria are valued and rewarded, and a setting in which there are clearly defined winners and losers. Twale and Deluca argued that this new culture results in a structure where administrators become adept at "overlooking, ignoring, or side-stepping" (p. 145) inappropriate actions, such as incivilities or bullying behaviors.

This organizational refocus has resulted in a culture wherein competition and status are highly salient to the experiences of faculty. This reality is further complicated by the nature and culture of higher education. In traditional academe, interpersonal aggression existed for a vast number of reasons and occurred across multiple levels of academe. To wit, higher education emphasizes performance, competition, and achievement (Cleary et al., 2013). Faculty members are expected to maintain professional scholarly activities while simultaneously performing service to the university and teaching graduate and undergraduate students. There is often little direct institutional reward for many of these activities, save the achievement of long-term goals, including obtaining tenure and being promoted in rank.

Despite the aforementioned, bullying in academe is a phenomenon that has, until relatively recently, not been acknowledged. One of the reasons for the academy's reticence to recognize the phenomenon as problematic is, in our estimation, the cultural legacy of academe. Thornton (2004) describes the academic culture as one traditionally imbued with the notions of collegiality and peer regulation and guidance. The premise that the academy is comprised of a group of well-educated, civil, and autonomous (Keashly & Neuman, 2010) scholars who come together to create and impart knowledge has tacitly suggested that it is insulated from the pathology of bullying and hierarchical jockeying observed in other venues. The image of the academy as collegial, civil, and free from internal strife and bias is patently incorrect. Individuals enter into the milieu with the idea that they will be regarded and interacted with on the basis of their merit, and believe that it is that merit that will shape their experience.

Despite this ideology, an undercurrent of institutional hierarchical maintenance has become salient within what has traditionally been seen as one of the only venues where meritocracy reigns. This hierarchical maintenance, as suggested by Thornton (2004), has increasingly been used to shape a culture where bullying is normalized. Purcell (2007), in his analysis of the marginalized status of nontenure-track faculty in academe, stated the following of the academy's lack of attention to the growing use of what has been identified as bullying behavior in higher education: "they have failed in their duty to scrutinize the embedded and growing oppression that flows from the institutional hierarchies that structure their professional life. . . . Institutional status remains so naturalized . . . that it is not even viewed as problematic" (p. 122). Moreover, these methods are identified as mechanisms of othering—of establishing or reinforcing the marginalized status of nonmajority faculty who must navigate a venue that continuously "reminds them" that they are different (Purcell, 2007; Sharp-Grier, in press). Ironically, however, as noted above, the reality that marginalized faculty have been able to breach the bubble of higher education, coupled with the presumed nature of academe—civility, meritocracy, autonomy—serves to render their experiences of bullying and marginalization invisible and stifles the voices of marginalized faculty when they speak out. It also serves to discredit them when they are heard, by labeling them as troublemakers, malcontents, and ungrateful workers (Hoel & Cooper, 2000; Purcell, 2007; Thornton, 2004). This reality underscores why the work of critical race and social justice scholars is crucial to institutions of higher education, and why analyses such as those included in this chapter are necessary.

Individuals who have experienced bullying in higher education, identity-based, intersectional, or general, suggest that it is a painful and devastating experience, which leaves long-term scars, including post-traumatic stress disorder (Farrington, 2010), depression, difficulty concentrating, and lowered self-esteem (Lutgen-Sandvik, 2006). In addition to the psychological and emotional effects experienced by the victims of bullying within academe, individual behavioral outcomes of the phenomenon include alcohol abuse, increased use of sick or vacation leave, reduced productivity, high turnover, and negative interactions with students (Hoel & Cooper, 2000; Keashly & Numan, 2010; Lutgen-Sandvik, 2006). As suggested, bullying behaviors in academe range from general to raced, from subtle to overt, and from nonverbal to verbal actions and can include microaggressions and microinequities that are singular or cumulative. Sue (2010) identified microaggressions as seemingly benign digs, jabs, and attacks aimed at minorities. These microaggressions serve to devalue and undermine nonmajority faculty and perpetuate the culture of othering, especially when wielded in tandem with other bullying behaviors. Microaggressions invoking stereotype threat (Steele & Aronson, 1995) call into question marginalized faculty's ability and efficacy (Sharp-Grier, in press) and are often wielded to validate marginalized faculty's subordinate status.

Although experts can identify what encompasses interpersonal aggression in the workplace, and specifically what it is in higher education, existing law does not label these behaviors as illegal in the United States. Unless there is a physical assault or a violation of civil rights, no illegal behavior has occurred (Weeks & Gilkes, 2013). It is precisely this limited definition of bullying that allows for the powerful to define the transgression, to usurp the voice of the victim, and redefine and characterize the experience of the marginalized. Although bullying in the workplace often results in deep emotional and psychological trauma and, as noted above, is lodged at individuals not only as a response to their hierarchical status within the institution but also because of their marginalized status, the institution's response to and definition of bullying can serve to reframe reality and redirect resources (and remedies) away from the victim. This redefining is a function of institutional power and serves to insulate stakeholders from potential criminal investigation. The removal of bullying from the definition of what could be considered a violation of federal Equal Employment Opportunity Commission (EEOC) rules and into general institutional behavior also serves as a warning and deterrent to potential whistleblowers; this serves to steer victims away from reporting bullying by illuminating the institutionally manufactured futility of bringing forth a complaint.

As iterated above, according to the tenets of academic culture, individuals are hired into the academy based on merit—their expertise. Moreover, academe has primarily been a location of peer review (Thornton, 2004). Reflected in the concept of peer review, there is an expectation that faculty members will critique each other in peer-oriented processes such as tenure and promotion consideration. Peer review is also common in the process of reviewing manuscripts for publication. As illustrated by the author's experience listed above, peer-review processes are often venues where microaggressions and tacit bullying occur. These venues, because of their institutionalized and collective makeup, generally serve to mask targeted bullying and provide legitimacy to the outcome. Targeted faculty are often unsure as to whether or how to lodge complaints. As a result, many faculty members will remain quiet about the bullying situation rather than make the situation public (Fogg, 2008).

As noted, the personal and institutional consequences of bullying are multifaceted. At the institutional level, Weekes and Gilkes (2013) pointed out that workplace bullying is associated with employee turnover (Weekes & Gilkes, 2013), low employee morale, escalation of violence in the workplace, inability to attract new hires (Fogg, 2008), and adverse financial outcomes. The authors submit that bullied employees are more likely to terminate their employment, report lower levels of reported well-being (McKay, Arnold, Fratzl, & Thomas, 2008), and report lower levels of satisfaction with their bosses. The toxic work environment also may encourage other (bullied and nonbullied) workers to terminate their employment, which results in an institutional cost associated with continual turnover of faculty. Moreover, departments and universities develop institutional reputations based on continual research in particular areas of study. A constant flux of personnel may quell departmental academic momentum and persistence of goal attainment, which may hinder the organization's academic reputation. This diminished status may result in grants, publications, and talented graduate students being lost. In light of these findings, it is clear that junior faculty are more likely to be targets of bullying (McKay et al., 2008). It also should be noted that departments and universities are negatively influencing their collective future by the high turnover of untenured colleagues.

PERSONAL STORY: THE SOCIAL JUSTICE SCHOLAR

In the current political climate, everyone is at risk for bullying, particularly those without tenure and those possessing nondominant status, but are some scholars even more at risk? According to Patton, Shahjahan, and

Osei-Kofi (2010), "to critically engage with social justice scholarship and practice is not at the top of the list when it comes to advice for new faculty members on how to be successful in higher education today" (p. 265). One of our questions is: Do scholars doing social justice work face higher levels of bullying and microaggressions? Below, one of the authors tells of her personal experience with contra-power sexual harassment and bullying at a diverse institution.

I was teaching an introductory course in women and gender studies. I was a few weeks into the course, and all was going well—until I spoke about Title IX. I had a few male athletes in the class, and one in particular was not quiet about his hostility to the affirmative law. He was in a "less popular" male sport, and he argued with me about the three-prong test. He argued that under Title IX, all schools must comply with all three prongs of the test, thus disadvantaging men and men's sports in general. I asked him where he had learned this. He informed me that he had learned this from his coach. I attempted not only to suggest that schools must only comply with one prong of the test, but also that schools decide where their funding goes and that no school has ever had their funding pulled for lack of compliance with Title IX (although it is the case that "less popular" male sports have been cut depending upon choices made by institutions). But he would have none of it. From that day forward, he was quiet, sullen, and aggressive whenever he made a comment in class. One incident in particular was so aggressive that I eventually contacted campus security, but only after I put considerable thought into it and my friends and colleagues implored me to do so. This class was a night class and I was absolutely the last professor in the building. After I spoke to students after class, I was literally alone walking to my car across an empty parking lot. I suffered over this for about a week. I shared it with friends and they were incredulous that I, an expert in sexual harassment and a professor of women and gender studies, would question myself. Such is the nature of the beast that is bullying and harassment.

Lesson number one for me was that despite the fact that we have the knowledge, when we experience it firsthand, that knowledge flies out the window. We can teach it, but when it happens to us, we may also exhibit classic victimization characteristics: denial, minimization, and so forth. We need our sympathetic colleagues, friends, and mentors to remind us of ourselves. I was reminded, and I first contacted my direct supervisor, the director of women and gender studies; she was very supportive. She suggested that I contact campus security, explain the situation, and request an escort. A simple, innocuous request, so I thought. I e-mailed the head of security; they talked to me extensively and were very sympathetic. They asked if I thought he was making misogynistic comments. I conceded this and they were more than willing to provide me with an escort to my car each evening after class (which met once per week).

Unbeknownst to me, as a part-time faculty member, when such a request is made, the situation is relayed to the dean of students. The dean called me personally a few days later; I told her the entire scenario and how I felt unsafe walking alone to my car each evening. The beginning of this exchange was very supportive. I told her the facts, and she sympathized. She informed me that she was going to call the student into her office. I asked her to please not do this—I thought that this would make the situation worse—her perspective was then revealed: "He is an athlete—he does charity—he is a good person." My perspective was: "I want to protect myself, but not make him any angrier than he already was by the content of the course." She would not take no for an answer. She called the student in, and then called me after. She informed me that he had no idea that any problem had occurred. He denied any problems or anger and indicated shock that I had experienced any problems with him. She indicated that if I was truly afraid that I would allow her to remove him from the course: if I wanted him to stay in the course I was thus not afraid and subsequently did not need an escort. I stated that I felt removing this student from the class would exacerbate the problem, and his anger. My goal was for him to learn, despite the emotional toll this took on me.

I informed the dean that I thought this student would benefit from the course, and although I feared him, I felt that removing him from the course would do more harm than good. I was willing to sacrifice my personal psychological safety for his learning. She attempted to make this an either/or situation. She attempted to get me to admit that if I wanted him to remain in the course that I had no cause for fear. I would not do that; upon this "noncompliance," she threatened to contact the provost to report my disrespect to her. I felt bullied, and I informed her of this, but I would not back down. I indicated that I wished both for the student to remain in my class and for an escort for the remainder of the semester. That is exactly what ended up happening.

Fast-forward to the next semester. I was preparing for class, greeting my new students as they entered the classroom. I saw a tall and imposing man enter the class wearing a sports jersey from the same sport as the student from the previous semester. Was this a coincidence? I questioned myself at the time, although this incident "rang my bells." I knew something was not right. After getting to know the students on that first night, I learned that this student was an international student from Central Europe. Although he was new to the United States, he signed up for the article on Title IX for his oral presentation. Was this a coincidence or was I being bullied long distance, by that former student and, by proxy, his coach? This student attempted to make the same arguments; but he was open to learning the facts about Title IX. The semester ended well and without incident.

The above incident illustrates a multifaceted bullying experience. The author experienced contra-power bullying at the hands of her students, then also experienced hierarchical bullying by the dean of students who tried to make the professor dismiss her experience, her fear, and her concern for her own well-being. As we have previously stated, administrators, working on behalf of the institution, have a vested interest in making claims of bullying and harassment "go away" in order to avoid liability. Moreover, we argue that the content of this professor's courses, women and gender studies, made her more vulnerable to microaggressions at the hands of her students, which is, in fact, a form of bullying. The question that remains here is this: Should administrators, who have a vested interest in protecting the university at the expense of faculty safety, be the sole deciders in cases of bullying and harassment?

UBUNTU: RECOMMENDATIONS AND FRAMEWORK TO PREVENT BULLYING

According to Hollis (2012), it is leadership that drives organizational culture, and bad behavior is costly. According to Cipriano (2011), "Mean-spirited and uncivil people cause much damage to those they belittle, to the bystanders (students, staff, and department peers) who suffer the ripple effects, to the overall department performance, and to themselves. Faculty members who previously were stalwarts in the department simply disengage so that they are no longer targets to the malicious onslaught of nastiness perpetuated by this venomous person" (p. 7). Unfortunately, there is not a "one-size-fits-all" approach to stopping a workplace bully. Despite this reality, the Association of College and University Housing Officers International argued that identifying unhealthy behaviors and learning techniques to manage bullies are critical for employees and managers in higher education (as cited in Cherwin, 2013). The following techniques were recommended: ignore, confront, prove yourself, document, report, stay positive, and find a support network. This advice, although helpful on an individual level, is somewhat troubling if it is viewed in a vacuum and not within the larger social context. In order to truly address the root of bullying behaviors and put an end to them, the institution must change; the focus must be taken off the victim.

Based on our interdisciplinary study, we have framed policy prescriptions that may assist in the dismantling of bullying in higher education. First, every institution must have "watchdogs," or what we refer to as policy advocates (as described by Misawa, 2010). These are individuals who can make nonbiased recommendations that are inclusive and adhere to civil rights laws. For example, policy advocates should ensure that the university mission and vision include commitments to diversity and inclusion. They should also ensure that all antidiscrimination policies are enumerated, indicating all protected classes. Additionally, these watchdogs should ensure that bullying and harassment claims are dealt with expediently using a restorative and procedural justice model.

Latimer, Dowden, and Muise (2005) define restorative justice as "a process whereby all the parties with a stake in a particular offence come together to resolve collectively how to deal with the aftermath of the offence and its implications for the future" (p. 128). According to this definition, the restorative justice model is a collaborative process that seeks not only to hold the offender accountable for her or his actions, but also one that seeks to remedy the effects of the offense. The premise of the restorative justice model is *ubuntu* (Brathwaite, 2002), an indigenous South African ideal that reminds us that our humanity is linked with the humanity of those with whom we live. By extension, *ubuntu* suggests that offending is a violation of people and relationships—personal and social—and these relationships are important in the construction of a remedy (Latimer et al., 2005; Tylor, 2006). Reflective of the idea that relationships, not laws, are damaged by the commission of offenses, the restorative justice model holds as one of its major tenets the "voicing of victims" through victim mediation, which both encourages the offending party to take responsibility for their actions and allows the victim to confront their offender to fully articulate their experience of being victimized and work toward closure. The process of restorative justice, according to Brathwaite (2002) was "the dominant model of criminal justice throughout human history for perhaps all of the world's people" (p. 5). By definition, it is indigenous and is a standpoint, which most recently was adopted from Canadian First Nation and Native American intervention strategies.

The concept of procedural justice (Tyler, 2006) posits that it is the responsibility of the social and institutional power structure to promote a culture of legitimacy, where social norms and values are acknowledged and where the power structure itself is seen as legitimate, fair, just, and committed to promoting the best interests of individuals within the community. In other words, in order to reduce negative behavior, individuals must feel socially integrated and ideologically connected both to one another and to the institution, and it is the responsibility of the institutional structure to promote those values. It is the intersection of these two standpoints—restorative and procedural justice—that we believe represents the best framework for intervention in instances of intersectional and general workplace bullying.

According to McKay et al. (2008), a toxic organizational culture is characterized as one within which formal ethical values are promoted but are not reflected in organizational actions. Instead, unstated organizational values, which are the main and operational values, govern organizational behavior. These toxic and illegitimate (Tyler, 2006) cultures can exist within the institutional milieu and influence everyday actions. It is these values that create the culture of the institution. According to McKay et al. (2008), "To focus on prevention of bullying within academe requires a systematic proactive approach that evaluates the norms and values entrenched in the organizational culture and subculture" (p. 96). Solutions must be multidimensional at the university, department, and individual levels. Reflective of this position, we posit an intervention strategy that both changes the culture of the organization to one that discourages the acceptance of the traditional structure (enabling bullying behaviors) as legitimate, encourages social integration, and also allows for those victimized by members of the institutional milieu a voice and strategies to be made whole.

A PRESCRIPTION FOR CHANGE

We propose a structured and comprehensive framework to address the issue of workplace bullying. Our system acknowledges the organizational and interpersonal causes (and results) of the phenomenon and lays accountability at the feet of the culture, processes, and personal behaviors that serve to victimize faculty within academe. As an illustration of the framework, we have provided an outline of the prescriptions, which includes a binocular intervention strategy (Pepler, 2006) that advocates *social architecture*, a change in social structure of the institution and *scaffolding*, and dynamic support for victims and bullies (Pepler, 2006). We believe that the following strategies for intervention in general and intersectional workplace bullying provide an effective starting point for the promotion of an organizational structure that promotes a culture of valuing faculty in general and diverse faculty in particular.

I. Procedural Justice (Legitimizing Organizational Culture and Authority)

The traits of social architecture (Pepler, 2006) should include the following:

1. Management acknowledges bullying and provides a statement of awareness of the bullying culture. In so doing, it:
   a. Critically examines organizational practices that contribute to bullying.
   b. Publicly commits to and reinforces a commitment to a fair and bully-free workplace.
   c. Evaluates organizational compliance with EEOC policies and ensures adherence in practice and policy.
2. Management establishes a culture free of bullying (Hoel & Cooper, 2000):
   a. Initiates zero tolerance and bullying prevention policies.
   b. Creates comprehensive training on conflict management and resolution for faculty and administration.

      c. Provides support and training for stress management and coping skills development (Hoel & Cooper, 2000; Newman-Carlson & Horne, 2004).

      d. Initiates staff development and training on causes and consequences of bullying in the workplace (Newman-Carlson & Horne, 2004), to include identification of bullying practices (Keashley & Neuman, 2010).

  3. Management confronts and challenges abusive and bullying management styles (Hoel & Cooper, 2000):

      a. Implements a fair and accessible management structure (Tyler, 2006).

      b. Creates clear organizational and chain of command structures.

  4. Management establishes and supports fair and effective policies and interventions for bullying behavior (Hoel & Cooper, 2000; Newman-Carlson & Horne, 2004):

      a. Implements fair institutional hearing procedures.

      b. Constructs a safe reporting structure.

      c. Provides the victim protection from retribution.

      d. Develops interventions for repeated breaches of bullying policy.

      e. Initiates restorative justice victim mediation.

II. Restorative Justice (Moral/Integrative Approach: Giving Voice to the Marginalized)

In order for the most vulnerable populations to be protected by the institution, the organization must create and maintain a scaffolding approach (Pepler, 2006) to changing the culture. This involves a cumulative approach to training, continual reinforcement of goals, and periodic assessment of changes and retooling when necessary. Organizational goals should include, but are not limited to, the following:

  1. Management recognition of potential victims (Newman-Carlson & Horne, 2004) and their marginalized status:

      a. Implementation of cultural diversity training.

      b. Adoption of safe space/lesbian, gay, bisexual, transgender, and queer/questioning (LGBTQ) training and practices.

      c. Implementation of sexual harassment training.

  2. Management support of victim agency/advocacy (Keashley & Neuman, 2010):

      a. Structuring of a systemic, directive, and institutionalized support of victims' experience (Pepler, 2006).

      b. Promotion of active conflict management skills training to promote victim self-agency.

3. Management provision of support for the offender (Newman-Carlson & Horne, 2004):
   a. Provision of training for bullies to develop skills to recognize their behaviors as pathological.
   b. Implementation of active conflict management skills and training (behavioral modification).
   c. Encouragement of the utilization of chain of command to resolve issues.
4. Management allowance of the victim to have a voice—the establishment of a restorative justice mediation team:
   a. Institutionalization of an approach to allow a victim to address the bully in a safe and nonthreatening environment (mediation).
   b. Encouragement of active listening and acknowledgment of responsibility in situation.
   c. Fostering an environment of mutual problem solving and development of strategies to discourage further bullying.

The restorative justice team should include individuals representing various identities, including those who do not have a vested interest in maintaining the status quo of the university. Pertaining to this policy prescription, we ask the question: Is it not a conflict of interest for only those in positions of administration, who have a vested interest in protecting the financial interests of the university, be the only arbiters of justice?

Finally, in the interest of justice, protections must be put in place for those in the most vulnerable positions: those individuals possessing minority statuses and multiple minority statuses. If this is not done, then institutions are only paying lip service to valuing diversity. In this respect, universities must actively engage with those individuals doing social justice work on campus, for those individuals explicitly expose themselves to resistance, bullying, and harassment, simply by the nature of their courses, which involve questioning the status quo.

CONCLUSIONS

In general, academe has embraced the notion of diversity. Most institutions require at least one course in diversity. But this has come at a cost, for most institutions do not provide the necessary institutional and administrative support for professors delivering this curriculum (Ludlow, Rodgers, & Wrighton, 2005); to wit, "People at the frontlines in the war against inequality need someone at their back" (Ludlow, Rodgers, & Wrighton, 2005, p. 12). In order to put an end to bullying in academe, institutions must protect their most vulnerable faculty members. This includes new faculty, women, people of color, indigenous faculty, international faculty members, LGBTQ faculty, disabled faculty, and faculty possessing multiple minority status. Perhaps the first step in this process is to include antibullying and harassment statements in faculty handbooks along with detailed and specific instructions on how to report, including an antiretaliation statement. Institutions should publicize these changes so that both new and senior faculty are aware of them. Establishing support systems and mentoring programs is crucial for new faculty, but particularly for those possessing marginalized identities. Restorative justice models should be provided as an option for targets or victims, but only utilized if the target or victim desires to do so.

We realize that we have only just scratched the surface on what changes are essential in dismantling bullying in higher education, but we hope that we have made some salient suggestions to initiate change. In order for change to occur, advocacy is required. Critical race feminism necessitates an activist component, and it will be those activists who are the catalysts for change, because they cannot abide the unequal treatment that they face, through their work and because of who they are. Change is difficult, as is advocacy, but, as James Baldwin suggests, "nothing can be changed until it is faced."

REFERENCES

Braithwaite, J. (2002). *Restorative justice and responsive regulation.* Oxford, UK: Oxford University Press.

Brown, L. M., Chesney-Lind, M., & Stein, N. (2007). Patriarchy matters: Toward a gendered theory of teen violence and victimization. *Violence against Women, 13*(12), 1249–1273

Chaisson, R. L. (2004, October). A crack in the door: Critical race theory in practice at a predominantly white institution. *Teaching Sociology, 32,* 345–357.

Chapman, T. K. (2007). Interrogating classroom relationships and events: Using portraiture and critical race theory in education research. *Educational Researcher, 36*(3), 156–162.

Cherwin, K. A. (2013). Workplace bullying at colleges and universities. HigherEdJobs. Retrieved from http://www.higheredjobs.com/Articles /articleDisplay.cfm?ID=443.

Cipriano, R. E. (2011). *Facilitating a collegial department in higher education: Strategies for success.* San Francisco, CA: Jossey-Bass.

Cleary, M., Walter, G., Horsfall, J., & Jackson, D. (2012). Promoting integrity in the workplace: A priority for all academic health professionals. *Contemporary Nursing, 45*(2), 264–268.

Collins, R. (1971). Functional and conflict theories of educational stratification. *American Sociological Review, 36,* 1002–1019.

DeCuir, J. T., & Dixson, A. D. (2004, June–July). "So when it comes out, they aren't surprises that it is there": Using critical race theory as a tool of analysis of race and racism in education. *Educational Researcher, 33,* 26–31.

Einarsen, S. (1999). The nature and causes of bullying at work. *International Journal of Manpower, 20*(1–2), 16–27.

Farrington, E. L. (2010). Bullying on campus: How to identify, prevent, resolve it. *Women in Higher Education, 19*(3), 8–9.

Fogg, P. (2008). Academic bullies. *Chronicle of Higher Education, 55*(3), 10–13.

Fox, S., & Stallworth, L. E. (2005). Racial/ethnic bullying: Exploring links between bullying and racism in the US workplace. *Journal of Vocational Behavior, 66*(3), 438–456.

Hoel, H., & Cooper, C. L. (2000). *Destructive conflict and bullying at work.* Manchester, UK: Manchester School of Management.

Hollis, L. P. (2012). *Bully in the ivory tower: How aggression and incivility erode American higher education.* Wilmington, DE: Patricia Berkly Books.

Jaschik, S. (2014, February 3). Philosophy of sexism? *Inside Higher Ed.* Retrieved from http://www.insidehighered.com/news/2014/02/03/u-colorado-plans -change-culture-philosophy-department-found-be-sexist#ixzz2sgPvVUuO.

Keashly, L. & Neuman, J. H. (2010). Faculty experiences with bullying in higher education: Causes, consequences, and management. *Administrative Theory & Praxis, 32*(1), 48–70.

Kohut, M. R. (2008). *The complete guide to understanding, controlling, and stopping bullies and bullying at work.* Ocala, FL: Atlantic Publishing.

Latimer, J., Dowden, C., & Muise, D. (2005). The effectiveness of restorative justice practices: A meta-analysis. *Prison Journal, 85*(2), 127–144.

Lester, J. (ed.). (2013). *Workplace bullying in higher education.* New York, NY: Routledge.

Ludlow, J., Rodgers, L., & Wrighten, M. (2005). *Students' perceptions of instructor's identities: Effects and interventions.* AE-Extra. Retrieved from http://www .unco.edu/AE-Extra/2005/3/Art-2.html.

Lutgen-Sandvik, P. (2006). Take this job and . . .: Quitting and other forms of resistance to workplace bullying. *Communication Monographs, 73*(4), 406–433.

Martin, J. L. (Ed.). (In press). *Racial battle fatigue: Insights from the front lines of social justice advocacy.* Westport, CT: Praeger.

Martin, J. L., Kearl, H., & Murphy, W. J. (2013). Bullying and harassment in schools: Analysis of legislation and policy. In M. A. Paludi (Ed.), *Women and management: Global issues and promising solutions.* Vol. 2: *Signs of solutions* (pp. 29–51). Santa Barbara, CA: Praeger.

McKay, R., Arnold, D. H., Fratzl, J., & Thomas, R. (2008). Workplace bullying in academia: A Canadian study. *Employee Responsibilities and Rights Journal, 20,* 77–100.

Meyer, E. (2009). *Gender, bullying, and harassment: Strategies to end sexism and ho-mophobia in schools.* New York, NY: Teachers College Press.

Misawa, M. (2009). Racist and homophobic bullying in adulthood: Narratives from gay men of color in higher education. *New Horizons in Adult Education and Human Resource Development, 24*(1), 7–23.

Misawa, M. (2010). Racist and homophobic bullying in adulthood: Narratives from gay men of color in higher education. *New Horizons in Adult Education and Human Resource Development, 24*(1), 7–23.

Newman-Carlson, D., & Horne, A. M. (2004). Bully busters: A psychoeducational intervention for reducing bullying behavior in middle school students. *Journal of Counseling & Development, 82*(3), 259–267.

Patton, L. D., Shahjahan, R. A., & Osei-Kofi, N. (2010). Introduction to the emergent approaches to diversity and social justice in higher education special issue. *Equity & Excellence in Education, 43*(3), 265–278.

Pepler, D. J. (2006). Bullying interventions: A binocular perspective. *Journal of the Canadian Academy of Child and Adolescent Psychiatry, 15*(1), 16.

Purcell, M. (2007). "Skilled, cheap, and desperate": Non-tenure-track faculty and the delusion of meritocracy. *Antipode, 39*(1), 121–143.

Randall, P. (1997). *Adult bullying: Perpetrators and victims.* New York, NY: Brunner Routledge.

Sallee, M. W., & Diaz, C. R. (2013). Sexual harassment, racist jokes, and homophobic slurs: When bullies target identity groups. In J. R. Lester (Ed.). *Workplace bullying in higher education* (pp. 41–59). New York, NY: Routledge.

Sharp-Grier, Martina. (In press). "She was more intelligent than I thought she'd be!": Intersectionalities, stigma, and microaggressions in the academy. In J. L. Martin (Ed.), *Racial battle fatigue: Insights from the front lines of social justice advocacy.* Westport, CT: Praeger.

Simpson, R., & Cohen, C. (2004). Dangerous work: The gendered nature of bullying in the context of higher education. *Gender, Work and Organization, 11*(2), 163–186.

Steele, C. M., & Aronson, J. (1995). Stereotype threat and the intellectual test performance of African Americans. *Journal of Personality and Social Psychology, 69*(5), 797.

Sue, D. W. (2010). *Microaggressions in everyday life: Race, gender, and sexual orientation.* Hoboken, NJ: John Wiley & Sons

Thornton, M. (2004). Corrosive leadership (or bullying by another name): A corollary of the corporatised academy. *Australian Journal of Labour Law, 17*(2), 161–184.

Twale, D. J., & DeLuca, B. M. (2008). *Faculty incivility: The rise of the academic bully culture and what to do about it.* San Francisco, CA: Jossey-Bass.

Tyler, T. R. (2006). Restorative justice and procedural justice: Dealing with rule breaking. *Journal of Social Issues, 62*(2), 307–326.

Weekes, K. M., & Gilkes, E. E. (2013). Higher education confronts the workplace bully. *Lex Collegii, 36*(3), 1–6.

Zapf, D. (1999). Organisational, work group related and personal causes of mobbing/bullying at work. *International Journal of Manpower, 20*(1–2), 70–85.

Chapter 6

Bullying in Health Care: A Hazard for Caregivers and Patients

Susan Strauss

> It is an unfortunate truth that disruptive [bullying] practitioner behavior is resulting in compromised patient care in hospitals throughout the country, despite federal and state laws and accrediting agency standards that require facilities to address such behavior. Numerous surveys of healthcare providers have found that a majority of respondents perceive a strong link between poor patient outcomes and disruptive behavior. (ECRI Institute, 2009a)

Workplace bullying occurs throughout the world and in any workplace, however, health care organizations have been identified as the industry that exhibits higher rates of bullying than other types of businesses (Zapf, Einarsen, Hoel, & Vartia, 2003 cited in Lin & Bernstein, 2014). Health care workers are 16 times more likely to experience bullying than workers in other industries (Elliot, 1997), and nurses are identified as the most likely target of the misconduct (Nelson, 2014; Whittington, Shuttleworth, & Hill, 1996). The occurrence of bullying in health care is particularly egregious because of the potential of adverse outcomes to patient care. Fortunately, it is a minority of health professionals who employ bullying tactics in their professional interactions; however, their actions are successful in creating a toxic health care environment for workers and patients (Maxfield, Grenny, McMillan, Paterson, & Switzler, 2005).

Scant research has been done examining bullying across the many health care disciplines. Most studies have examined physicians' and nurses' roles in bullying, and this chapter will do the same. However, bullying has been also noted to occur with pharmacists and those working in radiology and the laboratory (Rosenstein & O'Daniel, 2005).

DEFINITION, EXAMPLES, AND PREVALENCE OF BULLYING IN HEALTH CARE

Research findings regarding the rates of bullying in the workplace vary considerably depending on the definitions used by the researchers, the types of measurement instruments employed, the country in which the study occurred, the industry studied, and the timeframes in which the study participants experienced the abuse.

Definition and Examples of Bullying in Health Care

Bullying is a persistent negative and aggressive behavior directed at one or more individuals that may be physical, verbal, or psychological perpetrated by an individual or a group that occurs repeatedly over a period of time (e.g., six months) (Becher & Visovsky, 2012; Einarsen, Hoel, Zapf, & Cooper, 2011). Workplace bullying is intimidating behavior that humiliates, degrades, and displays a lack of dignity and respect for the target (Becher & Isovsky, 2012).

Numerous terms are used to study and discuss workplace misconduct, such as bullying (Johnson & Rea, 2009), incivility (Pearson, Anderson, & Porath, 2000), disruptive behavior (Joint Commission, 2008), lateral violence (Griffin, 2004), horizontal violence (Purpora, Blegen, & Stotts, 2012), abuse (Strauss, 2007), conflict, and others. The international community will sometimes refer to bullying as harassment or mobbing (Vessey, Demarco, & DiFazio, 2010). The terms' various definitions include commonalities, such as offensive, abusive, intimidating, abuse of power, as well as differences; for example, "horizontal violence," a common term used in nursing literature, refers to hostility between two or more colleagues who share equal power or status within the organization (Johnson & Rea, 2009). For the purposes of this chapter, the term "bullying" will be used.

The Joint Commission on Accreditation of Healthcare Organizations is a nonprofit agency whose mission is to continuously improve health care by using evidence-based standards to evaluate, accredit, and certify more than 20,500 health care organizations and programs in the United States to ensure the highest quality of health care (Joint Commission, n.d.). The Joint Commission's term for bullying used to be "disruptive behavior." They have since stopped using this (although many authors writing about the behavior in health care continue to do so) because of the ambiguity of the term, in addition to some viewing the term negatively. Instead, the Joint Commission's standards identify "behavior(s) that undermine a culture of safety" rather than disruptive behavior (AORN, 2011).

The Joint Commission (2008, p. 1) identifies the following overt and covert behaviors as "disruptive behavior" (bullying): verbal outbursts; physical threats; refusing to perform assigned tasks; quietly (or not) exhibiting uncooperative attitudes during routine activities; reluctance or refusal to answer questions, return phone calls, or pages; condescending language or voice intonation; and impatience with questions. Additional health professional bullying has been identified by Neff (2000):

- Profane or disrespectful language
- Name calling and other demeaning behavior
- Sexual comments or innuendo
- Racial or ethnic jokes
- Angry outbursts
- Throwing instruments, charts, or other objects at colleagues or at things (such as walls and the floor)
- Criticizing caregivers in front of patients and staff
- Comments that diminish a patient's trust in their caregiver or the hospital
- Comments that decrease a caregiver's self-confidence
- Failure to competently address safety concerns or patient care needs when informed by other caregivers
- Intimidating behavior that causes health team members to withhold input
- Deliberate failure to follow organizational policies
- Retaliation against team members who reported a violation of the code of conduct (COC) or participated in an investigation of such an incident

McNamara (2012, p. 536) pulls from a number of researchers and lists these additional bullying behaviors: yelling, cursing; using insults; making derogatory statements, spreading rumors, backstabbing, berating someone; rude; taunting in front of others; encouraging a colleague to disregard policies and procedures; badmouthing; discrediting a coworker to management; discourteous, sarcastic, intimidating, humiliating; raising eyebrows, rolling eyes, making faces, physically turning away; excluding someone; invading someone's space to intimidate; failure to support a coworker; setting someone up for failure; silence; refusing to communicate; impatient with another's inquiry; and communicating incomplete information resulting in sabotage.

Physicians have been found to employ the behaviors listed above in addition to these forms (Pfifferling, 1999): repetitive sarcasm; lack of dignity toward others; threats of violence, retribution, or litigation; foul language; snide, cynical remarks; shaming; not responding to pages in a timely manner; lack of appropriate response to patients and staff; lack of courtesy; lack of respect for patient's autonomy, confidentiality, and welfare; failure to address concerns about clinical judgments with associates; failure to arrange for coverage when not available; not completing patient records in a timely manner; failure to participate in clinical outcome reviews; failure to comply with practice and policy standards; and withholding information.

Prevalence of Bullying in Health Care

Depending on measurement variables and definitions of the term, prevalence rates of nurses experiencing bullying vary from 21% (Berry, Gillespie, Gates, & Schafer, 2012) to 90% (Smith, Andrusynsn, & Laschringer, 2010). King-Jones (2011) found 62% of nurses experienced verbal abuse and 24% stated they would resign as a result. The strongest indicator of nurse retention was whether nurses had been bullied. Griffin (2004) found that 60% of new nurses leave their jobs due to having been targeted by bullies; Townsend (2012) asserted that one in three RNs quit due to bullying. Johnson and Rea's (2009) research discovered a little over 27% of nurses were bullied in the previous six months, with most being victimized by those in management positions—managers, directors, and charge nurses.

Silence Kills, a study by the American Association of Critical-Care Nurses and VitalSmarts, found that 53% of nurses and clinical-care providers worked with colleagues who were reluctant to help, were impatient, and refused to answer questions; 88% worked with coworkers who gossiped, formed cliques to divide the team, did not do their fair share of the work, and tried to look good at another's expense (Maxfield, Grenny, McMillan, Patterson, & Switzler, 2005). Disrespect was shown to 77% of the respondents through condescending, insulting, or rude behavior, with 33% acknowledging having worked with coworkers who yelled, shouted, swore, and name called. In addition, 52% worked with people who abused their authority by pulling rank, bullying, threatening, or forcing their point of view on others. Respondents indicated that often the misconduct was frequent and long-standing, and that attempts to discuss their concerns with the perpetrator were almost out of the question.

Berry and her colleagues (2012) found that a nurse's race and ethnicity may influence how nurses respond to bullying. The authors discovered that nonwhite nurses used an adaption strategy as a way of coping with bullying that white nurses did not use. It was theorized that the nonwhite nurses developed their strategy as a tool to deal with the white, oppressive society in which they live and work.

Research of 56 nurse managers of labor and delivery units in medical centers in Washington, Oregon, and California reported bullying in 34 of the 56 six units (ECRI, 2009). Bullying behavior increased with the number of deliveries. Physicians—neonatologists, pediatricians, family practitioners, anesthesiologists, and obstetricians—were a little over twice as likely to bully, followed by nurses—registered nurses (RNs), midwives, certified registered nurse anesthetists, and nurse administrators. The bullying was reported to occur from daily to monthly.

Out of 1,600 physician executives, 95% attested to encountering physician bullying on a regular basis, with 32% observing the misconduct weekly to monthly from primarily older and experienced physicians (Weber, 2004). Weber's study showed that bullying physicians were about 2% to 3% of the total number of medical doctors; however, this is most likely an underreporting.

THE OPERATING ROOM: A TOXIC ENVIRONMENT

The operating room (OR) is a high-risk location for bullying (Bigony et al., 2009), with the attending surgeon being the most common perpetrator (Rosenstein & O'Daniel, 2006). A study of VHA health care organizations by Rosenstein and O'Daniel (2006) found that the following surgical specialties most likely to bully: general surgeons (28%), neurosurgeons (20%), cardiac surgeons (13%), orthopedic surgeons (10%), anesthesiologists (7%), and obstetricians/gynecologists (6%). These authors believed this may be due to the personality traits of surgeons in addition to the stress of performing surgery. The most common nonsurgical clinical settings where bullying was displayed were medical units (35%), intensive care units (26%), surgical units (20%), and emergency departments (7).

Rosenstein and O'Daniel (2006) found that 74% of OR nurses, 100% of anesthetists, and 80% of surgical technicians witnessed RN bullying on a daily basis (7%) or weekly (21%). Numerous reasons have been attributed to the increased likelihood of bullying in this highly specialized area of health care: stress, the demands of staff working on-call, isolation of the OR, patient acuity, nursing shortage (Bigony et al., 2009), unrealistic scheduling, lack of adequate staffing, a push for faster turnover of patients, lack of needed supplies and equipment, favoritism, and management's failure to enforce policies and procedures (Rosenstein & O'Daniel, 2006). The bullying was reported to increase workers' stress and frustration, which negatively impacted concentration and thwarted effective communication and resulted in poor team collaboration. The ultimate impact of these issues is an increased risk of medical errors, an *adverse event*, or a *sentinel event* (discussed later). An adverse event causes a patient injury as a result of a medical (or nursing, or radiology, etc.) intervention rather than the underlying medical condition (Attarian, 2008). It is an accidental injury attributable to an aspect of health care management.

Given that many of the tools of a surgeon's trade are sharp, such as scissors, forceps, and scalpels, the OR is filled with potential weapons that can make the OR suite a dangerous place to work. Many nurses told of incidents in which the surgeon threw surgical instruments and equipment—sometimes at the nurse, sometimes at a wall or the floor (Strauss, 2007). In Strauss's (2007) study examining physician abuse as gender harassment to female and male RNs in the OR, nurses shared their stories about needing to develop a hard shell to be able to work in the OR and about managers not holding surgeons accountable. And, in many hospitals, there was a need to keep a list of who worked with a bullying surgeon to ensure that the same nurse did not have to work with him or her every day (nurses rotated their turns). One nurse exclaimed, "I find in nursing we let physicians get away with terrible behavior that would be unacceptable in any other situation. Why do we do this?" Nurses told many other stories:

- "A surgeon requested that a certain new orienting nurse not be assigned to his OR room. When this happened, he would not talk to her, ignore her, and act as if she wasn't there."

- "A patient was waiting to be rolled in to the OR from the waiting area and heard his surgeon yell and curse at a nurse. The patient was outraged and said, 'I don't want you to be my doctor. I'll find a better doctor!' The case was cancelled."

- "During the first day I worked with him I observed one of his assistants enter the room and let the door close too loudly for his [surgeon] liking. He made the assistant, a 40-year-old man, exit the room and re-enter quietly five times to practice."

- "I have been an OR nurse for close to 30 years, and in the past, I have had instruments thrown, doors slammed, etc. The verbal abuse never ends. Four more years to retirement and I cannot wait!"

Female nurses wrote of many emotions as a result of having been targeted by the bully. After surgeons, in three different incidents, yelled and threw instruments in the OR or at an employee, three different nurses made the following comments: "At first I was frightened, then stunned, then mad"; "I was shocked and a little afraid but just continued to do my job. I felt a little better after he apologized"; "Horror." One nurse explained what the staff at their hospital does when a bullying physician is misbehaving: "We have an option for handling harassment situations in our OR. It's called 'Code 66.' Whenever this announcement is called overhead, any available personnel come to the room and simply watch and listen. This provides support for the staff and makes the offender aware their behavior is being scrutinized. It usually diffuses the situation promptly."

Male nurses expressed disdain for a male (primarily) surgeon's bullying, particularly when they viewed their female colleagues as the usual target (Strauss, 2007). Male RNs found that they were treated better than their female coworkers and had job advantages because they were men. Both male and female RNs saw the influx of women surgeons as a positive influence in decreasing the abusive OR culture.

CAUSES AND CONTRIBUTING FACTORS

Health Care Culture

The role of the health care culture, including its tolerance and lack of accountability in curtailing bullying, is finally gaining notoriety as a major factor in medical errors (Joint Commission, 2008; Rosenstein, 2002, 2011). According to Porto and Lauve (2006), "the healthcare industry has begun to realize that human interaction is an important but largely ignored source of error" (p. 1). Health care has gradually begun to realize that a more teamwork-oriented approach to practicing healing, where team members work collaboratively regardless of one's status, is critical to creating a safe culture for workers and patients. Health care is beginning to examine its long-standing notion of turning a blind eye to bullying physicians, for example. Unfortunately, many hospitals have been unsuccessful in changing their abusive culture.

Brodsky (1976) asserted that "Harassment has been institutionalized as a way in which persons in certain roles should relate to each other. As such, it is not an aberration of human behavior but a formula for interacting" (p. 5). Her quote represents additional influences evident in the health care culture such as informal organizational alliances, abuse of power, and tolerance and reward for the misconduct (Brodsky, 2006). Examination of the identified organizational dynamics and structures, both formal and informal, provides an essential perspective in understanding workplace aggression and has important implications for management in establishing prevention and intervention strategies. "Bullying may be more appropriately considered a form of organizational deviance rather than simply a form of interpersonal conflict" (Hutchinson, Vickers, Jackson, & Wilkes, 2010, p. E67).

The Joint Commission (2008) issued a Sentinel Event Alert to inform health care organizations that intimidating and disruptive behaviors may result in medical errors, poor patient satisfaction, preventable adverse outcomes, increased cost of care, and increased turnover of qualified health care workers to healthier environments. The Joint Commission (n.d.b.) defines a sentinel event as an unexpected occurrence involving death or serious physical or psychological injury requiring an immediate response and investigation. They also reported that the root cause of approximately 70% of the reported sentinel events can be attributed to problem communication (see ECRI Institute [2009a] for further discussion and health care communication resources). The communication problem can take many forms, including miscommunication between the patient and the physician or caregiver. However, the primary concern is the bullying occurring among caregivers.

Poor communication exceeded other cited problems such as deficient orientation, training, staffing, and patient assessment (Rosenstein, 2011). The findings of poor communication as the most common root cause of medical errors is consistent with findings from other industries such as aviation and maritime management that, likewise, discovered that failed communication and poor teamwork, rather than technical failure, were the root of the problem (Helmreich, 1997).

Most health care workers went into their chosen professions because they were committed to helping people heal. Yet, on a daily basis throughout the United States and other countries, health care professionals, aware of their colleagues' incompetence when they make mistakes and take shortcuts, remain silent. Their silence contributes to preventable medication and treatment errors (Maxfield et al., 2005). Fifty-nine percent of nurses and other clinical-care providers asserted that it is between difficult and impossible to confront the disrespectful and rude offender, and 78% said the same regarding confronting poor teamwork. Additional barriers to speaking up include time, fear of retaliation, and not feeling it was their job. Respondents indicated that if there were conversations with colleagues and managers, the intent was *not* to solve the problems but rather to figure out a way to work around the issues, to warn coworkers, or to vent. Nurses and others found that bringing the issue to management brought no relief in stopping the misconduct.

Bullying is usually unreported, resulting in it continuing unabated because it is not addressed (Joint Commission, 2008). Nurses believe that bullying is just part of the job (Strauss, 2007). This belief system serves to keep bullying enmeshed in the fabric of the environment. Nurse managers tolerate the bullying (Lindy & Schaefer, 2010), so it becomes normalized (Ceravolo, Schwartz, Folt-Ramos, & Castner, 2012) as part of the job. Bullying tends to filter from the top down and is often seen as an acceptable way to manage and get promoted (Weinard, 2010).

Health care has become less about "caring" and more about "corporate." Tight budgets, the Affordable Care Act, reduced reimbursement rates, lack of effective management and leadership skills, nursing shortages, greater liability risks, in addition to lack of teambuilding and teambuilding training contribute to the toxic health care environment (Rosenstein, 2011). Pressure for productivity, cost containment, fear, and stress from litigation are embedded in the health care environment (Joint Commission, 2008). Add to these issues the history of hierarchy and patriarchy, which is difficult to challenge effectively (Joint Commission, 2008). The health care culture of rotating shifts, continuous daily changes, and challenges for autonomy and empowerment are continuous and provocative (Gerardi, 2004; Joint Commission, 2008). Individuals who are self-centered, immature, and defensive and lacking in interpersonal skills and the ability to cope are more likely to bully (Porto & Lauve, 2006; Weber, 2004). Seasoned physicians are feeling a loss of autonomy with the team-based approach to patient care; distributing shared power to other caregivers and the patient and creating a decrease in trust among the team create a lush ground for bullying to thrive.

Alan Rosenstein (2011) touts that the organizational tolerance for physician bullying occurred due to fear that the bullying physician—say, a pediatric neurosurgeon—would take his (almost always a male doctor) business to the hospital across town, thereby decreasing incoming revenue. Therefore, the unwritten code of silence prevailed, allowing bullying physicians to continue in their sometimes long-occurring and egregious acts (Porto & Lauve, 2006; Rosenstein, 2014). Those tasked with intervening on physician bullying are uncomfortable doing so, and the health care system's policies, such as medical bylaws and credentialing, are not followed (Leape & Fromson, 2006; Weber, 2004). As a result, the bully is indulged, the misconduct becomes normalized, and other physicians imitate the bully.

Rosenstein (2014) identified numerous barriers preventing leaders from acting to prevent and intervene on the misconduct: "cultural inertia, rich history of tolerance, embedded code of silence, fear of the bullying physician's reaction, healthcare hierarchy, conflicts of interest, lack of organizational commitment, ineffective structure or policies, and inadequate intervention skills" (p. 373).

Nursing

The nursing profession is confronted with managerial and bureaucratic processes dictating nursing's (lack of) involvement in managing health care (Jackson & Borbasi, 2000). Despite nursing comprising the largest number of hospital employees, nurses are sorely missing from financial and other decision-making matters, yet are under the continual vigilant eye of the bureaucrats who judge nursing based on their terms (Speedy & Jackson, 2004). Nurses' absence at the decision-making table denies them power over their own profession. The lack of power adds to their already stressful job, culminating in anger and hostility toward nursing and their peers, exemplifying the dynamics of oppression. Bullying among nurses may be an adaptive response to gain a sense of control over feelings of powerlessness and alienation (Hutchinson, Vickers, Jackson, & Wilkes, 2006).

A qualitative study by Hutchinson, Vickers, Wilkes, and Jackson (2009) of 26 Australian bullied nurses posited a new approach to the study of bullying in health care—one of corruption. These authors discovered that bullies formed alliances in the abuse of legitimate power and organizational processes to achieve personal gain. The alliances created enhanced group bullying, causing the organization's processes to actually normalize and excuse the misconduct and leading it to "evolve and metastasize as corruption" (p. 217). There were five elements of bullying representing the corruption (p. 217): (a) silence and censorship: the organizational milieu that includes secrecy and concealment allowing corruption to thrive; (b) coalition of hostile unofficial alliances, many long lasting, who employ bullying tactics as corruption; (c) corruption of legitimate routines and processes for personal gain; (d) reward and promotion of certain individuals by alliances to gain career advancement for those within the alliances; and (e) planned concealment of misconduct conducted by the coalition of alliances to protect their members. The authors suggest that misusing organizational power coupled with improper use of the organization's resources and conveying prestige constitute corrupt engagement. Their study reported how bullying, as a mode of corruption, became enmeshed and institutionalized to the point of becoming almost invisible and allowing it to flourish without consequences.

One factor theorized to influence bullying toward nurses is oppression (Mathieson & Bobay, 2007; Purpora et al., 2012; Roberts, 1983). Horizontal violence and oppression have been reported and discussed in nursing literature for more than 20 years (Woelfle & McCaffrey, 2007). Groups or individuals are considered oppressed when they internalize the values of those who are dominant as the way "it" is supposed to be; that the dominant group's norms are the "right" norms (Freire, 1968). Nurses are said to be oppressed from two perspectives—gender and the health care system. Most nurses are women and they work in a patriarchal system controlled by primarily male physicians and administrators. Nurses' inertia in responding to incidents of bullying is associated with nursing's history of gender oppression and marginalization (of nurse managers) from the patriarchal system of medicine (Roberts, 1983, 1996, 1997).

Scarry (1999) argued that nursing education itself oppresses students and ensures that they integrate with the status quo, which is consistent with Friere (1968), which she described as a deviant health care system. According to Freire (1968), members of oppressed groups are often silent when there is cause to express their concerns. Nurses are frequently silent out of fear of retaliation, intimidation by the oppressor, and lack of support from management and human resources. Their silence is symptomatic of nurses' feelings of shame and embarrassment about their oppression.

Studies have documented the process whereby student nurses and new graduates have become socialized into the culture of bullying and begin to adopt these behaviors (Randle, 2003). New RNs who were targeted by verbal abuse from their nurse colleagues were more likely to be unmarried and work in a hospital, have low job satisfaction, be less commitment to their employers, have less autonomy, and feel they would probably leave their job (Budin, Brewer, Chao, & Kovner, 2013). A common adage among all nurses is that nurses "eat their young," a comment made because of the bullying seasoned nurses direct toward their new colleagues. Student nurses and new graduate nurses are particularly vulnerable to bullying. Nursing educators and preceptors must be knowledgeable about bullying, ensure they model professional, respectful behavior, and provide guidance and support to the new nurses (King-Jones, 2011).

A study by Randle (2003) suggested that student nurses were bullied during their clinical experience, which negatively impacted their image as a nurse as well as diminished their sense of self and their self-esteem. The students reported feeling powerless, anxious, angry, and stressed (McKenna, Smith, Poole, & Coverdale, 2003). The hostile clinical environments may increase the risk that patients will suffer the consequences by student nurses not providing pain medication in a timely manner or assisting the patient with toileting (Dunn, 2003). Nursing and allied health education students must receive education in the myriad aspects of bullying within the health care environment to prepare themselves for what they may experience as students and what may await them as new graduates (Bigony et al., 2009).

Nurse-to-nurse bullying is a major problem confronting many nurses and the nursing profession. Nurses may bully their colleagues for political reasons; for example, to decrease competition for a promotion or other important position, task assignments, or to achieve positive performance appraisal results. Katrinli, Atabay, Gunay, and Cangarli (2010) cite political motives as an ethical factor where nurses "humiliate, devalue and degrade others for their own personal self-interest" (p. 623). The political aspects of bullying should be considered in approaches to prevent the misconduct. This study also showed that the nurse bully's desire for power was repeatedly shown as the most pressing cause for bullying. Bullying among nurses appears to be self-perpetuating as bullied nurses are likely to bully their colleagues (Vessey, Demarco, Gaffney, & Budin, 2009)

Shift work played a role in influencing bullying (Dewitty, Osborne, Frisen, & Rosenkranz, 2009). The shift with the highest incidence of "conflict" was the rotating shift (71.1%). During the evening shift, 64.2% reported conflict, and during the day shift 52.1% reported conflict as very common. The length of the shift influenced the reporting of conflict as well, with those working eight-hour shifts reporting the lowest amount of conflict at 49.1%, followed by 12-hour shifts at 61.9% and 10-hour shifts at 63.1%.

Physicians

Physicians are reported to be uncooperative without regard for professional conduct, as well as displaying rigidity in cooperative problem solving (Pfifferling, 1999). Physicians are also accused of sexual and racial harassment. Other types of physician bullying found by Rosenstein, Russel, and Lauve (2002) include disrespect (80%), berating colleagues (72%), abusive language (69%), condescension (67%), yelling (60%), berating patients (52%), insults (43%), abuse anger (43%), and physical abuse (22%).

A study of physician executives found that targeted physicians did not report bullying due to fear of retaliation (Weber, 2004). Fifty percent of medical doctors (MD) thought that only those physicians who were totally out of line were ever reported for bullying, and 63% believed that some physicians were provided more lenient consequences than others. A contributing factor perceived as influencing physician bullying is that in most instances, MDs in this study were not employed by the hospital but attained medical staff privileges through a credentialing process. Weber found that organizational leaders fail to confront bullying MDs because physicians, particularly surgeons, greatly impact the hospital's bottom line. Physician leaders responding to this study disclosed that they are friends with many of the offending physicians and the board of directors, so these leaders try to protect their bullying physician friends from consequences. As well, some administrators view the physician as a customer, and *the customer is always right.*

Another cause of physician bullying touted by Pfifferling (1999) is that physicians think they do not need to adhere to rules, standards, regulations, or even dignified behavior toward others with less power or status because they are privileged. Pfifferling refers to physician bullying as an epidemic that needs to stop. Physicians are reported to be uncooperative and disregarding professional conduct, as well as displaying rigidity in cooperative problem solving.

Gender in Health Care

Nursing, defined typically as a female profession, has historically and to the present time been defined as a professional discipline of service, dedication, duty, subservience, and compliance with the patriarchal and medical hierarchy (Lewis, 2001; Timmins, 2005). This historical, and perhaps current, context of the nursing profession helps to set the stage for health care bullying. Lee (2002) asserted that the abuse of organizational power used in bullying is gendered.

Schultz (1990) posited that if a more gender-equitable workplace is to be promoted, it is the system that requires change, specifically around the gender segregation of various jobs as is prevalent in health care. Job gender segregation refers to horizontal segregation, in which coworkers are usually the same gender, and vertical segregation, in which higher-level jobs are often held by men and women comprise lower-level jobs, as is evident in health care (Kanter, 1977; Schultz, 1990). Gutek and Morasch (1982) labeled the dynamics that play into gender segregation as *sex-role spillover*, in which the gender roles females and males hold outside of work are "spilled over" into the workplace. Gender role spillover is most evident in organizations in which the gender ratio is skewed in one direction or the other, as it is in health care. Kanter (1977) and Schultz (1990) posited that women (and men) abide by stereotypical gender roles to assimilate into and survive within the organization's system. Health care reflects the gender stereotypes of society, with female nurses the compassionate, empathetic, and caring professional and physicians as the strong, independent decision maker. Stereotypes are evolving, with more women becoming physicians, however, the same flux is not seen as much of an increase in men choosing nursing as a career. The gender power differential is portrayed within health care and is a great influence in bullying.

The nurse–physician relationship is based on a subservient yet legal partnership that ties nursing to medicine. Nurses have internalized the patriarchal system in which they find their self-worth as the historical handmaidens of the omnipotent physician (Kalisch & Kalisch, 1977). The lack of empowerment in the patriarchal system is considered one of the antecedents of nurse-to-nurse hostility (Walker & Avant, 1995).

Whereas much of the workplace abuse research measures the gender of the aggressor and the gender of the target, none of the research found draws any conclusions about the potential of discrimination with the gender disparity that is apparent in some of the researchers' conclusions. Scant research is beginning to emerge to study the relation of bullying and gender dynamics, with most focusing on male-to-female or male-to-male misconduct (Lee, 2002).

Lee (2002) stated that "It is highly unlikely that abuse of organizational power would not be gendered" (p. 207). Halford and Leonard (2001) asserted that "organizational structures do not come to reproduce male power unwittingly, but are in fact designed for this purpose, or at least, actively maintained with this in mind" (p. 50). Simpson and Cohen (2004) investigated the role of gender in bullying in higher education. They argued that bullying cannot be separated from gender and that the construct of bullying requires its relation to gender. Like others who have studied gender in organizations (Lee, 2002; Halford & Leonard, 2001; Johnson, 1997), these researchers found that a masculine infrastructure, as exemplified in health care, is the framework for a culture of bullying.

A CASE STUDY

I discovered that the one male surgeon for a small rural hospital that I was consulting with was a known bully. Within three years, five female nurse managers and numerous other female OR nurses and surgical technicians had resigned. Politically, the hospital administrator did not want to take a strong stand against the surgeon because the surgeon was credited with keeping the hospital in this small rural town afloat by admitting patients for surgery. It was well known within the medical center that he was a bully, and his bullying was contagious, with others jumping on the bandwagon by also bullying coworkers in the OR.

I met with the hospital administrator to express my concern based on the feedback I was receiving from OR and other hospital nurses. He explained that hospital politics with the hospital's board of directors refused to let the surgeon go for fear of the hospital having to close its doors. When I suggested they advertise for other surgeons, he believed no other surgeon would want to move to this small rural town to practice. He also shared that the most recent nurse manager, who confronted the surgeon's bullying and complained to the administrator and the board, was fired. She claimed that those victimized by the bullying surgeon were all women and none of the men were targets. She then filed a sexual harassment lawsuit alleging the bullying and her subsequent firing after the complaint were gender based.

I met with the hospital's board of directors to express my concern about the surgeon's behavior toward the hospital's staff and patients, the cost of maintaining this surgeon, and the impending litigation, which may have been just the tip of the iceberg. What came to light is that many of the board's members were businessmen within the community, and they feared if they let the surgeon go, patient admissions would drop to the point that the hospital would have to close. No one wanted that outcome, obviously. What became evident, however, was their underlying fear. They feared that community members would be so irate at the board for denying the surgeon ongoing privileges and putting the viability of the hospital at risk that citizens would no longer give business to the businessmen on the board, and they would be forced to close their businesses' doors! This case demonstrates the ecology of bullying that allows a toxic environment to sustain itself.

BULLYING IN HEALTH CARE AS AN INTERNATIONAL PROBLEM

Bullying within the health care milieu is not unique to the United States; health care professionals throughout the world work in toxic health care environments. A large meta-analysis of 136 articles of more than 150,000 nurses taken from 160 samples globally found that roughly 33% of nurses around the globe were exposed to physical violence and bullying (Spector, Zhou, & Che, 2014). Another approximately 33% of nurses reported some injury, while 25% were targeted with sexual harassment and 66% experienced nonphysical violence. Emergency and geriatric departments and psychiatric facilities were the most frequent locations of physical violence. Anglo countries were the most frequent site for physical violence and sexual harassment most often committed by patients, whereas the Middle East was most noted for nonphysical violence and bullying perpetrated by the patient's family and friends.

Close to 66% of physical violence was perpetrated by patients, approximately 33% was committed by family or friends, while less than 10% of assaults were carried out by MDs, nurses, or other staff (Spector et al., 2014). Patients were the most frequently identified perpetrators for nonphysical and general violence, although the perpetrators were fairly balanced among all sources, with health professionals committing the majority of nonphysical violence.

The World Health Organization, the International Labour Office, the International Council of Nurses, and the Public Services International instigated a study of abuse toward health professionals in Brazil, Bulgaria, Lebanon, Portugal, South Africa, Thailand, and Australia (di Martino, 2002). The percentage of health professionals experiencing a minimum of one incident of either psychological or physical violence in the previous year ranged from a low of 37% in Portugal to a high of 76% in Bulgaria. According to the International Council of Nurses in Geneva, roughly 70% to 80% of assaults are never reported, and some hospitals probably squelch workers from reporting it (Nelson, 2014).

A study in Copenhagen, Denmark, identified three reasons why bullied health professionals left their jobs: (a) poor leadership, (b) working in an environment of hostile behavior, and (c) poor health (Hough, Hoel, & Carneiro, 2011). Poor leadership was linked to the most critical factor for leaving. Pai and Lee (2011) examined the types of abuse RNs in Taiwan experienced and its impact on mental health. The researchers found that while patients were the most likely to be physically abusive to the RNs, coworkers, supervisors, and staff were the usual perpetrators of psychological bullying.

Additional studies of bullying of health care workers including nurses, MDs, nursing assistants, and other studies have been done in Turkey

(Katrinli et al., 2010), Canada (Higgins & MacIntosh, 2010), Australia (Roche, Diers, Duffield, & Catling-Paull, 2010), Costa Rica (Gimeno, Barrientos-Gutierrez, Baru, & Felknor, 2012), the United Kingdom (Quine, 1999), Austria (Niedl, 1996), Denmark (Mikkelsen & Einarsen, 2001), Finland (Kivimaki, Elovainio, & Vahtera, 2000), Norway, Sweden, Iceland, Italy (Andersen, Aasland, Fridner, & Lovseth, 2010), Jordan (Ashmed, 2012), South Taiwan (Lin & Liu, 2005), Hong Kong (Kwok, Law, & Li, 2006), Egypt (Samir, Mohamed, Moustafa, & About Saif, 2012), and Saudi Arabia (Algwaiz & Alghanim, 2012), among others. The similarities are striking—patients are often the primary offender outside the United States, but physicians and colleagues bully as well. Most bullying is verbal, which negatively impacts the target's mental health.

In the fall of 2014, the fourth international conference on "Violence in the Health Sector" occurred in Miami. Sponsored every two years by the Netherlands' Oud Consultancy and supported by numerous U.S. and international health care and nursing organizations, health care researchers and other health care professionals from Asia, Australia, Europe, Canada, Africa, Middle East, South America, and the United States presented at the three-day conference. In addition to increasing knowledge, each conference provided an opportunity to share international developments by emphasizing various efforts, best practices, and research to effectively respond to the breadth of the problem globally.

Impact of Bullying

There are broad ramifications when bullying is tolerated, rewarded, and sustained within health care. The health care industry itself is harmed as well as those who work within the industry such as nurses, physicians, and other staff. Perhaps the greatest negative impact is to the quality of patient care—an unforgiveable consequence of the industry not policing its own.

Impact to Health Care

There are numerous negative repercussions to the health care industry and to specific health care organizations as a result of bullying. The cost of organizations employing bullying caregivers is escalating. Bullying physicians are likely to decrease productivity of whichever department or unit with which they interface (Porta & Lauve, 2006). When a physician or other caregiver bullies, it consumes management's time, and staff time is needed to debrief and compose themselves again after an incident. If instruments are thrown and require resterilization or if supplies are contaminated, new supplies are needed, thus consuming time and resources. The ability to "work around" these incidents persists and raises costs. These authors assert that the actual costs of bullying are unknown but contribute to the escalating financial challenges of the U.S. health care system.

Repeated bullying has a cumulative effect on the staff's emotion and stress levels, which equate to turnover and absenteeism costs. There are financial risks if there is a loss of the hospital's reputation. Patient satisfaction scores may be decreased, resulting in the hospital's reduction of market share as well as increased potential for liability (Bigony et al., 2009). The Medicare Hospital Consumer Assessment of Healthcare Providers and Systems Survey compiled patient satisfaction responses and is available on their Internet site. Depending on the geography and an RN's practice specialty, the cost of replacing one RN ranges from $22,000 to $145,000, and nursing turnover costs the organization up to two times her (or his) salary (Jones & Gates, 2007).

There is a double standard in health care—physicians are often ignored or indulged when they act out; they may be offered counseling or anger management classes. Often hospitals have policies and procedures that are implemented only with the most severe types of misconduct by MDs (Porto & Lauve, 2006). This response attests to the power physicians hold within the organization. In contrast, when employees bully, there are consequences in place (although often ignored), with little if any support or coaching offered. This contrast is an obvious example of an unfair workplace and results in a "normalization of deviance" (p. 6) by physicians while creating the demise of morale. A major deterrent to reporting bullying was fear of retaliation but also the belief that it does no good because the bullying continues (Rosenstein, 2002; Strauss, 2007).

THREE LAWSUITS EXEMPLIFYING HEALTH CARE'S TOXIC ENVIRONMENT

Case One

Over a period of three years, an MD's bullying had been contemplated by the medical executive staff committee (*Eden v. Desert Regional Medical Center*, cited in ECRI Institute, 2009b). The hospital finally decided to terminate Dr. Eden's hospital privileges because of his extensive bullying. Behaviors included throwing contaminated needles onto trays held by nurses, pounding his fists on the desk of an employee in close proximity to her arm that had just recently be operated on, and writing nasty comments about an obstetrician on the patients' charts. Nurses left their employment, an obstetrician quit practicing at that hospital, and some physicians refused to admit patients as a result of the bullying MD creating a toxic and stressful health care environment. After the MD's privileges were terminated, he sued the hospital, indicating the hospital had conspired against him. However, a California court affirmed the hospital's decision to terminate Dr. Eden's privileges due to bullying.

Case Two

Dr. Dan Raess, a cardiac surgeon at St. Francis Hospital in Indiana, was outraged when there was a conflict with perfusionists' (heart-lung machine operator during surgery) scheduling, which meant he was not able to conduct emergency heart surgery immediately (*Raess v. Doeschler*, 2006). He yelled at two of the perfusionists who were present but unavailable for the surgery. The following day, Joseph Doescher, the chief perfusionist, resigned his position in protest to the doctor's bullying behavior to his colleagues the previous day. Doescher, however, continued to work as a staff perfusionist. Several days following Dr. Raess's outburst to Doescher's two colleagues, Raess approached Doescher to discuss "coverage issues." The two men engaged in an argument and Raess became so angry, his body stiffened, his face became red, and his jugular vein extended. Raess walked toward Doescher, leading Doescher to believe that Raess was going to hit him. The doctor's fists were balled, his demeanor and walk were purposeful, and he yelled at Doescher that "You're over. You're history. You're finished." Due to Raess's demeanor, the look in his eye, and his body language, Doescher believed he was going to be assaulted so he raised his hands to defend himself as he backed up against the wall. The doctor walked past Doescher without assaulting him. Doescher's victimization resulted in him becoming depressed and anxious, anorexic, suffered sleep disturbances, loss of confidence, and he did not return to work.

Doescher sued Raess for assault and battery and intentional infliction of emotional distress. For the first time, a court allowed an expert on workplace bullying to testify. The expert's testimony supported that Doescher's victimization was an "episode of workplace bullying" and that Raess is "a workplace abuser, a person who subjected Doescher to an abusive work environment" (Transcript 409: 413–414). Workplace bullying is not a recognized cause of action and therefore not a cause to bring a lawsuit, thus the complaint was for assault and battery and intentional infliction of emotional distress. The judge allowed the assault and battery complaint to go to trial but ruled against the intentional infliction of emotional distress to proceed. As a result of testimony by witnesses, the jury found for Doeschler on the assault claim (only) and awarded him $325,000.

Case Three

The largest verdict for sexual harassment ever awarded to a single plaintiff in an employment case was awarded to Ani Chopourian, a physician's assistant, for $168 million (*Chopourian v. Catholic Healthcare West et al.*, 2011). Chopourian filed as many as 18 complaints of sexual harassment and other inappropriate conduct by surgeons over a two-year period to managers at Sacramento's Mercy General Hospital (which recently changed its name to Dignity Health). Chopourian complained that one surgeon referred to her as a "stupid chick" and that she did surgery "like a girl." She was stabbed with a needle by the same surgeon who, in a rage, broke the ribs of an anesthetized patient about to undergo heart surgery. Another surgeon would greet her each morning with the phrase, "I'm horny" and slap her on the buttocks. After two years of complaints, she was fired several days following her final complaint regarding patient care and the doctors' bullying. Ms. Chopourian claims her termination of employment was retaliation.

Interestingly, all three of these precedent-setting cases involved surgeons in the operating room.

POTENTIAL IMPACT OF BULLYING ON PATIENT CARE

According to surgeon Marty Makary (2012a), medical errors kill enough patients weekly to fill four jumbo jets! Researcher James (2013) posits that the "number of premature deaths associated with preventable harm to patients was estimated at more than 4,400 per year" (p. 122). The Joint Commission (2008) acknowledged that bullying (intimidating and disruptive behaviors) in health care organizations may result in medical errors, poor patient satisfaction, preventable adverse outcomes, increased cost of care, and increased turnover of qualified health care works to healthier environments.

Appallingly, 53% of nurse managers acknowledged that bullying was a factor in near-miss incidents, while 42% of the obstetric/gynecology clinics indicated adverse outcomes were the result of bullying (Veltman, 2007). The research and this chapter do not purport to blame all medical errors and adverse patient outcomes on health care bullying. However, there is enough empirical evidence to suggest that the bullying that occurs among caregivers is negatively affecting the quality of patient care and absolutely must be addressed by the health care industry with more vehemence than it currently is.

A 2008 study of approximately 4,500 health care workers found that 67% believed there was a connection between bullying and adverse events, 71% believed there was a link between bullying and medication errors, and 27% saw a nexus between bullying and patient deaths (Rosenstein & O'Daniel, 2008). A full 18% were cognizant of an adverse event related to bullying.

It was estimated that 6.3 million measurable medical injuries occurred in 2008, of which 1.5 million were a result of medical error; indirect costs of approximately $1.4 billion were related to mortality rates (2,500 excess deaths) as a result of these errors (Shrev et al., 2010). In addition, 10 million days of work were missed due to disability

The ISMP's (2014) survey respondents indicated a widespread impact of negative workplace behaviors on medication errors. Nearly half of the nurses and a little less than 60% of pharmacists admitted that intimidating behaviors impacted the way they question or clarify medication orders. Equally concerning is that 7% of nurses and 10% of pharmacists indicated they had been involved in a medication error due to circumstances surrounding bullying.

IMPACT OF BULLYING ON PHYSICIANS AND NURSES

Physicians

Pfifferling (1999, p. 3) listed a number of ramifications to staff as a result of a bullying physician: withholding information due to fear of being belittled or criticized, not asking for help, withholding suggestions for fear of being viewed as arrogant, reduction in self-esteem due to being criticized and lack of receiving positive feedback, increased turnover, blaming others, and dysfunctional teamwork. In addition, the organization's reputation will suffer when staff are the targets of physician bullying.

Physicians who interact with bullying physicians may experience a multitude of consequences: chronic fatigue, physical illness and emotional distress, absenteeism, poor communication, poor teamwork, "dumping" on staff and patients, turnover, poor problem solving, increased likelihood of litigation from partner liability, time spent dealing with problem colleagues, fear of lawsuits, stress dealing with threats from bullying physician, withholding information from bullying physicians due to stress and fear about the bully physician's outbursts, remedying the bullying leading to loss of income-producing time, and sabotage (Pfifferling, 1999).

Physician executives and hospital administrators spend time and money in the assessment, confrontation, and monitoring process of the bullying MD (Pfifferling, 1999). In addition these executives are rightfully concerned about lawsuits; time counseling disgruntled staff, peers, patients, and family; protecting staff from the bullying MD; administrator turnover; time spent "putting out fires" and dealing with public relations; recruitment of MDs to replace bullying MD; expensive adversarial processes; conflict management; expenses to satisfy the unrealistic demands of the bullying MD; and time, energy, and expenses in rehabilitation of the MD.

Nurses

Sanford (2011) found several reasons why nurses leave their employment: workload and staff (91%), wish for a more desirable culture in which to work (79%), poor peer and management relationships (81%), poor nurse management (51%), and undesirable relationships with physicians (29%). Is it any wonder that nurses leave when considering the impact of bullying on their personal and work lives?

Nurses who are targeted by bullies report experiencing vulnerability, stress, loss of self-esteem, sleeplessness, depression, feelings of demoralization, fear, and pain (Hutchinson et al., 2006). Retention and recruitment of nurses has been blamed on bullying (Jackson, Clare, & Mannix, 2002). Bigony and colleagues (2009, pp. 689–690) list weight loss or gain, hypertension, cardiac palpitations, gastrointestinal disorders, headache, insomnia, and chronic fatigue as consequences of bullying. In addition, nurses experience a sense of powerlessness, anger, and suicidal behaviors (Vessey et al., 2010).

Merely witnessing bullying can cause lowered job satisfaction and commitment, decreased productivity (Matthiesen, Einarsen, & Mykletun, 2008), stress, depression, anxiety, and less support from their supervisor (Hansen et al., 2006; Niedhammer, David, Degioanni, Drummond, & Phillip, 2009). In addition, witnesses report less commitment to working with teammates and sharing ideas, thereby reducing creativity and teamwork (Lutgen-Sandvik, 2006).

PREVENTION AND INTERVENTION STRATEGIES

In 2009, the Joint Commission created a leadership standard specifically to address bullying ("behaviors that undermine a culture of safety") in ambulatory care, critical access hospitals, laboratories, long-term care, Medicare-Medicaid certification long-term care, and office-based surgery programs. The standard requires that leaders of these organizations (a) create a COC that defines specific behaviors that undermine a culture of safety and (b) create and implement a process for managing the identified behaviors. Additionally, the Joint Commission recommends that interpersonal skills and professionalism be included as part of the six core competencies recommended for the credentialing process of all physicians.

Because of the role that the workplace milieu plays in bullying, organization-wide efforts are crucial in the prevention and abatement of workplace bullying (Einarsen et al., 2011). Hutchinson, Vickers et al. (2010) developed a multidimensional model of workplace bullying identifying four organizational factors that have "synergistic relationships with each other" (p. 31): (a) tolerance or reward for the misconduct, (b) informal alliance networks, (c) misuse of authority, processes, and procedures; and (d) normalization of workplace bullying. Too often hospitals will not approach bullying from an organization-wide preventative perspective, thereby failing to recognize that bullying will not be prevented merely by developing policies and procedures and delivering training.

Johnson (2011) posited that addressing the problem of bullying requires an ecological approach, illustrating that bullying is a result of individual (microsystem), departmental (mesosystem), organizational (exosystem), and societal (macrosystem) interrelated factors. This author's holistic model should be considered as more than a theoretical framework but used as a practical guide in designing and developing effective bullying prevention and intervention strategies. Consider the following possibilities in designing an ecological model:

- Macrosystem: In 1999, the Bureau of Labor Statistics (Occupational Safety and Health Administration, n.d.) estimated that there were 8.3 nonfatal assaults on health care workers compared to two per 10,000 in the private sector, making health care one of the most perilous industries in which to work. One goal is to pass national or state legislation against bullying, particularly bullying and violence in health care. Thirty states have recognized that violence to health care professionals is a major issue and have passed laws making it a felony to assault health care workers. (The most likely locations for violence is the emergency department, psychiatric units, and in geriatrics.) Europe and the United Kingdom have long been ahead of the United States in addressing bullying in the workplace. Antibullying laws already exist there, recognizing that even one act of physical bullying is enough to ignite their antibullying laws, and psychological bullying must be persistent to be a violation of the law (Nelson, 2014).

- Exosystem: A greater understanding is needed on how organizational strata work in sync, as a system, to allow and sustain the toxic environment. As well, examining how the toxic environment impacts both patient and staff safety and injury rates should be a goal of the organization. Further examination of the organizational hierarchy and its role in spurring and maintaining the toxicity is required.

- Mesosystem: This level of the ecological approach probes the role of management and bystanders in both the sustainability and the prevention of bullying. In my experience in consulting with health care organizations, managers and human resources professionals often lack the knowledge to recognize bullying and are unfamiliar with the skills to intervene.

- Microsystem: Answering the following questions is a valid catalyst to explore the microsystem: What characteristics prompt an individual to bully? How does the bully select her or his target? Are there specific characteristics of a target? How do power and the types of power, both formal and informal, for example, as well as the misuse and abuse of power lay the foundation for bullying?

Holloway and Kusy (2011) developed an intervention model, the "Toxic Organization Change System." The model was built on the following principles:

- Successful interventions combine organizational, team, and individual tactics.
- If there is difficulty implementing the three interventions simultaneously, begin with organizational change followed by the team and then the individual.
- An individual with power and organizational sway should be the one who confronts the bully with necessary consequences for the misconduct.

Tactics for the Medical Staff

Physicians should share in the authorship of the organization's COC, and it must be incorporated into the medical staff standards of conduct and bylaws. The organization's administrator, in tandem with medical department chairs and the medical chief of staff, is responsible for physician behavior and accountability to the medical staff standards and bylaws. MDs should be referred to peer-review hospital committees or outside resources such as employee assistance programs, coaching, or for anger management training. If the physician's bullying resulted in compromising patient safety that resulted in an adverse event or a "near miss," the medical board should be notified (Sanchez, 2014). Rosenstein (2008, 2011) offers the following suggestions:

- Medical staff bylaws should contain a description of bullying behaviors and how they will be handled.
- Enforce medical staff bylaws.
- Identify physician champions to undertake physician accountability.
- Incorporate physician bullying into the peer review process.
- Limit or suspend privileges if required.
- Assess the offending physician with a comprehensive multidisciplinary evaluation followed with whatever corrective action is required (Pfifferling, 1999). The offending physician should be monitored following the correction.
- Medical bylaws must include the hospital's code of conduct and it must be integrated with the physician peer review responsibilities (Pfifferling, 1999).

- Respect, dignity, cooperation, collaboration, and communication need to be incorporated into formal performance reviews and physician credentialing.

- Physicians must sign a form acknowledging that they have read, understand, and commit to abide by the COC.

Tactics for Nursing

Nurses should implement nursing self-governance models and multidisciplinary task forces, including bullying as an issue in orientation programs and ensuring safe staffing and on-call requirements (Bigony et al., 2009). Additionally, the American Nurses Association (2010) stated that the art of nursing is based on caring and respect for human dignity. The standards of professional performance include collaboration, collegiality, ethics, and quality of practice, research, resource utilization, professional practice evaluation, education, leadership, and environmental health. The American Nurses Association's standards of performance should be included as a foundation for continuing education and the orientation process.

Another critical element in continuing education, staff meetings, and orientation is the nurses' code of ethics, which includes three provisions specifically addressing how nurses treat their colleagues (ANA, 2001). Provision one states that the nurse shall have a relationship with colleagues and others that forbids harassment or threatening behavior or disregard for how a nurse's actions impact others. Provision five promotes the preservation of integrity, including avoidance of verbal abuse from colleagues. The sixth provision acknowledges the nurse's responsibility for the health care environment, including a responsibility to a moral environment of respectful interactions with colleagues and support of peers. The nursing code of ethics should be posted in nursing stations and be actively discussed by nursing management throughout the organization. It should be a living document.

The nurses at Bozeman Deaconess Hospital found a successful solution to their bullying health care environment—their union filed a complaint with the National Labor Relations Board claiming the hospital's approach to conflict was one of intimidation and was ineffective and illegal (Hausen, 2013a). The union president claimed that bullying had become "crazy huge" and that nurses were so beat down they felt they did not have any other options. The union's vice president said that the nurses are "like battered women" (Hausen, 2013c, p. 1). While on strike, nurses wore red T-shirts that read "no bullying." After 28 hours of collective bargaining over two days, the union and the hospital came to a tentative agreement in which both sides agreed that the hospital would delete polices preventing nurses from speaking about investigations, and would allow nurses to have a union representative with them when they are disciplined, among other conditions (Hausen, 2013b).

Organizational Strategies

The organization's strategies must include both physicians' and nurses' tactics into their overall strategy and approach the strategy from an organization development change management initiative:

- Create a multidisciplinary change management task force to establish an antibullying mission, goals, and measurable objectives and monitor the change management initiative.
- Determine the location of a central repository where all complaints of bullying will be held.
- Yearly review all complaints to identify patterns, trends, most common perpetrators, locations, or departments where most of the misconduct occurs, the manager's response, any remedies for the target, consequences for the bully; if the bully is a physician—was the misconduct reported for peer review or the state's medical board and any impact on patient care; use the results as a teachable moment for necessary changes.
- Incorporate collaboration and communication requirements into the COC.
- Conduct an internal assessment of the organization's culture using focus groups, interviews, and a survey. The assessment should be repeated every 18 months to analyze whether the organization's antibullying change initiative is effective; the results of the assessment should be used to make additional changes using subsequent interventions. The ongoing assessments should function as an environmental monitoring of the culture. Maxwell (2005) recommended four areas for focus group discussion: how much support is there from management, teamwork, disrespectful behaviors, and micromanagement. Purposely assess the quality of communication in the organization that is negatively impacting the quality of patient care.
- Respect, dignity, cooperation, collaboration, and communication need to be incorporated into formal performance reviews of all employees, including those in administration, and used in the credentialing of physicians.
- Benchmark with best practices from the literature and from other health care organizations.

- Train the board of directors, administration, human resources, and all managers in the area of bullying.

In several qualitative studies, nurses who have experienced bullying reported that managers either did not respond to complaints of bullying or their responses were ineffective (Dzurec & Bromley, 2012; Gaffney, DeMstco, Hofmeyer, Vessey, & Budin, 2012; Strauss, 2007). In my experience in consulting with health care organizations, nurse leaders and human resources professionals do not recognize bullying, particularly the subtle nuanced forms of the misconduct that can be so enmeshed in the fabric of the organization as to be invisible. Once recognized, these leaders must learn the skills on how to intervene effectively, to monitor the behavior, and to provide consequences.

Comprehensive training for managers on the construct of bullying should include the following elements: a definition of bullying, including examples of both overt and covert behaviors; the impact to the target; the impact to patient care; review of pertinent policies and procedures including the COC, electronic communication, violence, and harassment; the manager's role in the prevention and intervention; causes and contributing factors, including the abuse of power and the hierarchical history of health care; and, finally, how to use specific communication tools in confronting a manager's direct report of someone who is engaging in bullying. Additional training is needed on teamwork, teambuilding, and communication techniques. The training needs to be face to face, not online, and enough time should be devoted to training to encompass the suggested topics, using experiential learning and recognizing adult learning principles:

- Train all employees on bullying with the same learning objectives suggested above for managers minus the manager's role.
- Develop and establish a COC as mandated by the Joint Commission that clearly defines bullying and spells out the behaviors that are and are not acceptable; the COC should include a list of behaviors for all administrators, staff, physicians and other providers, patients, families, guests, vendors, and consultants and the procedures and pertinent regulatory requirements. The COC requires wide dissemination yearly and more often if needed. It must be an active document that is viable, not a passive document stored on the organization's intranet or in an employee's drawer and not made viable. Create an expectations document that outlines the expectations of patient, family, and guest behavior, clearly indicating that harassment and bullying are not allowed, and then give the document to each patient upon admission.
- The COC must be assessed, reviewed, and revised yearly.

- Design and implement an effective quality communication plan.
- Investigations must be conducted by someone who is fair and impartial who has been trained in how to conduct investigations and is competent in doing so.
- Bullying by anyone who threatened quality patient care should conclude an immediate suspension pending the outcome of an investigation.
- Integrate all steps with quality improvement and risk management.
- Retaliation must be outlawed.

Numerous authors call for a "zero-tolerance" policy for bullying within health care (McNamara, 2012; Rosenstein, 2010, 2011) yet fail to engage in any discourse to spell out what zero tolerance translates to regarding actual behavior. Although zero tolerance makes sense at face value, what does it really mean? What behaviors require a zero tolerance? Name calling and any name or just those selected and by whom? Swearing? Ignoring? Blaming? Throwing instruments? Silence? Is a zero-tolerance policy going to be equally applied to all physicians and employees so that if a surgeon refers to a nurse in a derogatory term and a maintenance worker does the same, the consequences be consistent? Will both be removed from the institution? Or does zero tolerance mean it depends on the severity of the misconduct as to whether there is zero tolerance? If it depends on the severity of the behavior, who decides "severity"? Can there be a zero-tolerance policy yet people get second chances because this is their first offense? To be effective, the policy must be equally applied to everyone in the health care setting, whether that is the chief executive officer or the maintenance engineer. Any zero-tolerance policy requires an actual policy, not just a statement indicating that the organization has a zero-tolerance policy. The policy needs to clearly spell out the details of this expectation.

In my work as an expert witness for harassment lawsuits, I frequently observe human resources professionals and managers asked by opposing counsel during depositions what zero tolerance means at their organization. I have yet to see anyone be able to answer the question. Their policies indicated zero tolerance, but there was no definition as to what that meant.

Although all of the steps mentioned above are necessary, they are not enough to curtail the toxic health care culture of bullying, a culture that has existed and been sustained for decades. An intentional and purposeful culture change effort will be required in most health care organizations if the bullying culture is to dissipate. Culture change is messy; it is complicated and painstaking; it takes time, passion, commitment, energy, and resources. The goal is to change a bullying culture to a healthy and healing culture and then to sustain the new culture. What is absolutely essential for this effort is strong leadership and committed stakeholders who invest the necessary passion and resources to the initiative. Stakeholders need to be identified by the organization and should include employees, management, administration, the board of directors, and all providers and physicians. Consideration should be given to the community, former patients, and their families as stakeholders as well. Ulrich (1997) asserted they need to come together to ask pivotal questions about the change initiative:

- Do we have a shared mentality and if so, is it the "right" one?
- To what extent does the organization have the required knowledge, skills, and abilities to create a respectful, bullying-free workplace for staff and a healing environment for our patients?
- What needs to be designed, developed, and implemented to ensure that there are the right processes, incentives, rewards, and measurements of our outcomes to demonstrate success?
- Do we have the necessary expertise to do this, and if not, what is needed? Does the commitment exist within the organization (financial, human resources, time, etc.) to reach the desired and measureable goal?
- Who else needs to be involved in this change strategy? Would we benefit from an outside consultant to facilitate the process?
- What is required to accomplish our goal?
- How will we measure our success?
- How will our success be maintained?
- What needs to occur to ensure that the change is approached as an integrated, comprehensive effort rather than as fragmented "programs" or "training"?
- Does the organization have the leadership required to diminish bullying and create a healthy and healing culture? Will hospital leaders both "own" the process and champion it as well? Are administrators, management, staff, physicians, and other providers willing to invest what is required to reach the goal of enhancing the hospital's culture to one of respect, equality, integrity, and safety?

When the initial discussions of a change initiative begin, the answers to the above questions are often answered in the affirmative. Stakeholders are energized, excited, and express their commitment, and then—there it sits. People get busy with their own personal and professional lives, lacking the time, resources, and knowledge of how to begin or complete the process, which results in a weak or absent follow-through.

As an organization development and bullying consultant to health care (and other) organizations, one of my recent clients was a suburban medical center. They asked for my assistance to help them understand bullying and to plan an initiative to decrease the misconduct. We set up an initial full day to begin the process. I conducted training in the morning to ensure their understanding of the construct, and the afternoon was set aside to begin the planning process for successful change. The group comprised primarily the hospital's nursing management, including the chief nursing officer (CNO) who had brought me in as the consultant.

The group was actively engaged in the morning training session and worked hard in the afternoon identifying stakeholders, determining driving and restraining forces for success (force-field analysis), discussing the steps to assess the current culture and the desired culture, as well as other early planning steps. Because an afternoon timeframe only begins the planning process, there was a need to identify the next steps, which the group energetically listed. Then I asked for a show of hands of approximately five nurses who would be willing to meet to make sure that the "next steps" were not lost and the planning process could continue. Not one nurse raised her hand. It was quiet in the room. I looked at each nurse, including the CNO, waiting for someone to volunteer so that none of the energy and work done that afternoon would go by the wayside. Finally, one nurse exclaimed that no one was raising their hands because they were all too busy. Everyone agreed. Still, no one raised their hand to continue the work. Eventually the CNO raised her hand, the emergency room director raised his hand, and one other nurse manager raised her hand. Those three agreed to meet to determine how they would move forward using the "next steps."

I was fairly pessimistic that this medical center would continue on the path they had begun because there was not enough of a commitment demonstrated. I called the hospital a month later to speak to the CNO to inquire how their planning meeting went and what their "next steps" were. She told me they just had not gotten around to having that meeting. I have found similar responses in other hospitals. Often I hear that the hospital is busy with implementing some other major effort, for example, electronic medical records, and once they are done with that initiative, they would work on the bullying. When I follow through, however, the bullying issue has not been addressed.

Despite the fact that the Joint Commission (2012) has a patient safety standard that addresses bullying (*disruptive behavior*) and that they have a leadership mandate requiring a COC specifically addressing bullying, hospitals that I have consulted with were unaware of either of these standards. Each hospital employs a director-level person who is responsible for quality improvement utilizing the Joint Commission's standards to ensure his or her institution maintains its accreditation. Sometimes that person is also tasked with risk management or there is a different management position for risk management. Both of those individuals should be attending any training and planning on bullying, yet, with one exception, I have found they are not informed of the training and planning sessions. This lack of recognition of the role quality improvement plays in bullying and the bullying culture is inexcusable when one considers the risk to patients. The one hospital that did send their director of quality improvement to the training and planning session was unaware of the Joint Commission's patient safety standard related to bullying and the requirement to design a COC to address the behavior. This lack of knowledge and follow-through with regulatory requirements is just one rationale as to why, after decades and decades of ongoing bullying in health care, it still continues boundlessly.

There are several ways to address the change management process, an action research framework, one adapted from Beckhard and Harris (1987) and Ulrich (1997) that includes these steps:

Step 1: Define the current hospital culture based on an assessment of the environment, as discussed earlier in the chapter.

Step 2: Define the desired hospital culture—based on what you desire the environment to be.

Step 3: Identify the specific gaps between the current culture and the desired culture.

Step 4: Identify the driving forces (pushing for success, such as improved morale, legal concerns, respectful environment, quality patient care) and restraining forces that create barriers (such as leadership resistance and financial resources) that will impact a successful outcome.

Step 5: Design and develop an action plan with measureable goals and objectives to address the gaps between the hospital's current and desired cultures, including how to increase the driving forces and diminish the restraining forces.

Step 6: Implement the plan.

Step 7: Monitor the plan's effectiveness and make necessary changes along the way.

Step 8: Evaluate and measure the plan's effectiveness.

Metrics are a key element in intervening in the toxic health care environment. We measure what is important (Maxfield et al., 2005). Metrics need to be determined in the very beginning of the planning process and incorporated into the goals and objectives.

There may be some immediate efforts that can be planned and implemented to begin the process, such as communication training, hospital-wide bullying training, engaging physicians in the planning process, and identifying potential champions. These initial steps will be an enticement for commitment from employees to get involved in the initiative.

Even with strong leadership and commitment from stakeholders, change initiatives may fail for any number of reasons (Ulrich, 1997). By examining obstacles to change, the hospital can minimize or prevent the impact of the predictable and unpredictable reasons for failure. Many reasons exist as to why changes do not produce change:

1. The change is not tied to a strategy.
2. It is more of a quick fix or a program rather than a long-term strategy.
3. No long-term perspective is considered.
4. The politics of the organization are not planned for and will undermine the change.
5. Portentous expectations sabotage simple successes.
6. Rigid change designs create roadblocks.
7. Lack of leadership knowledge and skill around change.
8. Lack of measurable, substantial results.
9. Fear of the unknown.
10. Inability to rally required engagement and commitment to sustain change.

These causes of failure must be considered in the planning process to minimize their influence and potential sabotage of the change initiative.

CONCLUSION

The problem of bullying in health care is pervasive with often severe outcomes to nurses and other staff, physicians, and patients. Managers and human resources professionals have been informed of bullying among nurses, from physicians to nurses and other caregivers and from patients and visitors; and policies and procedures have been created, lawsuits filed, and research conducted—yet bullying and other forms of violence continue unabated, harming caregivers and negatively impacting patient care. Little progress has been made to correct the behavior. Hospitals and other health care organizations have allowed the misconduct to fester, nurses feel it is just part of their jobs, and physicians believe they are entitled to act in whatever way they want. There is a fundamental reluctance to confront not only the bully but also the culture that embeds the misconduct into a normal and often invisible reality of the industry. The consequences inherent in health care organizations where communication is inadequate and toxicity undermines optimal patient care has resulted in a system and environment that is the antithesis of healing for patients.

REFERENCES

Algwaiz, W. M., & Alghanim, S. A. (2012). Violence exposure among health care professionals in Saudi public hospitals: A preliminary investigation. *Saudi Medical Journal, 33*(1), 76–82.

American Nurses Association (AMA). (2001). *Ethical and legal resources that relate to lateral violence: American Nurses Association code of ethics for nurses with interpretive statements.* Retrieved from http://c.ymcdn.com/sites/www.sc-nurses.org/resource/resmgr/imported/Professional%20Behavior%20Standards%20from%20ANA%20Code%20of%20Ethics%20with%20Interpretive%20Statements%20rev%207-30-13.pdf.

American Nurses Association (AMA). (2010). *Scope and standards of practice: Nursing* (2nd ed.). Silver Spring, MD: Author.

Andersen, G. R., Aasland, O. G., Fridner, A., & Lovseth, L. T. (2010). Harassment among university hospital physicians in four European cities: Results from a cross-sectional study in Norway, Sweden, Iceland and Italy (the HOUPE study). *Work, 37,* 96–110.

Ashmed, A. S. (2012). Verbal and physical abuse against Jordanian nurses in the work environment. *Eastern Mediterranean Health Journal, 18*(4), 318–324.

Association of Operating Room Nurses (AORN). (2011, December, 7). Joint Commission drops term "disruptive behavior." *AORN, Public Policy News.* Retrieved from http://www.aorn.org/News.aspx?id=21745.

Attarian, D. E. (2008). What is a preventable adverse event? *AAOS Now.* Retrieved from http://www.aaos.org/news/aaosnow/may08/managing6.asp.

Becher, J., & Visovsky, C. (2012). Horizontal violence in nursing. *Medsurg Nursing, 21*(4), 210–213, 232.

Beckhard, R., & Harris, R. T. (1987). *Organizational transitions: Managing complex change* (2nd ed.). Reading, MA: Addison-Wesley.

Berry, P. A., Gillespie, G. L., Gates, D., & Schafer, J. (2012). Novice nurse productivity following workplace bullying. *Journal of Nursing Scholarship, 44*(1), 80–87.

Bigony, L., Lipke, T. G., Lundberg, A., McGraw, C. A., Pagnac, G. L., & Rogers, A. (2009). Lateral violence in the perioperative setting. *AORN Journal, 89*(4), 688–696.

Brodsky, C. M. (1976). *The harassed worker.* Lexington, MA: Lexington.

Budin, W. C., Brewer, C. S., Chao, Y-Y., & Kovner, C. (2013). Verbal abuse from nurse colleagues and work environment of early career registered nurses. *Journal of Nursing Scholarship, 45*(3), 308–316.

Ceravolo, D. J., Schwartz, D. G., Folt-Ramos, K. M., & Castner, J. (2012). Strengthening communication to overcome lateral violence. *Journal of Nursing Management, 20*(5), 599–606.

Chopourian v. Catholic Healthcare West et al. CIV. NO. S-09-2972 KJM KJN.

Dewitty, V. P., Osborne, J. W., Frisen, M. A., & Rosenkranz, A. (2009). Workforce conflict: What's the problem? *Nursing Management, 40*(5), 31–37.

di Martino, V. (2002). *Workplace violence in the health sector: Synthesis report.* Geneva: The World Health Organization (WHO), the International Labour Office (ILO), the International Council of Nurses (ICN), and Public Services International (PSI). Retrieved from http://who.int/violence_injury_prevention/violence/activities/workplace/WVsynthesisreport.pdf.

Dunn, H. (2003). Horizontal violence among nurses in the operating room. *AORN Journal, 78*(6), 977–988.

Dzurec, L. C., & Bromley, G. E. (2012). Speaking of workplace bullying. *Journal of Professional Nursing, 28*(4), 247–254.

ECRI Institute. (2009a, September). *Healthcare risk control: Supplement A: Communication.* ECRI Institute. (2009b, March). *Healthcare risk control supplement A: Disruptive practitioner behavior.* Retrieved from Retrieved from https://www.ecri.org/components/HRC/Pages/default.aspx.

Eden v. Desert Regional Medical Center. No. E035841 (Cal. App. Dist.4 01/24/2006)–CA.

Einarsen, S., Hoel, H., Zapf, D., & Cooper, C. L. (2011). The concept of bullying and harassment at work: The European tradition. In S. Einarsen, H. Hoel, D. Zapf, & C. L. Cooper (Eds.), *Bullying and harassment in the workplace: Developments in theory, research, and practice* (pp. 3–39). London: Taylor & Frances.

Freire, P. (1968). *Pedagogy of the oppressed.* New York, NY: Seabury Press.

Gaffney, D. A., DeMarco, R. F., Hofmeyer, A., Vessey, J. A., & Budin, W. C. (2012). Making things right: Nurses experiences with workplace bullying A grounded theory. *Nursing Research and Practice,* article 243210.

Gerardi, D. (2004). The emerging culture of healthcare: Improving end-of-life care through collaboration and conflict engagement among health care professionals. *Ohio State Journal of Dispute Resolution, 23*(1), 105–142.

Gimeno, D., Barrientos-Gutierrez, T., Burau, K., & Felknor, S. (2012). Safety climate and verbal abuse among public hospital-based workers in Costa Rica. *Work, 42,* 29–38.

Goodman, M. L., Morris, J. C., & Nosowsky, R. (n.d.). *Addressing disruptive behaviors in an academic environment.* Health Lawyers. Retrieved from http://www.healthlawyers.org/Events/Programs/Materials/Documents/AMC 10/goodman_nosowsky_morris_slides.pdf.

Griffin, M. (2004). Teaching cognitive rehearsal as a shield for lateral violence: An intervention for newly licensed nurses. *The Journal of Continuing Education in Nursing, 35*(6), 257–263.

Gutek, B. A., & Morasch, B. (1982). Sex ratios, sex-role spillover, and sexual harassment of women at work. *Journal of Social Issues, 38*(4), 55–74.

Halford, S., & Leonard, P. (2001). *Gender, power, and organizations.* Basingstoke, Hampshire: Palgrave Macmillan.

Hansen, A. M., Hough, A., Persson, R., Karlson, B., Garde, A. H., & Orback, P. (2006). Bullying at work, health outcomes, and psychological stress response. *Journal of Psychosomatic Research, 60*(1), 63–72.

Hausen, J. (2013a, February 7). Bozeman Deaconess Hospital nurses file complaints, allege unfair labor practices. *Bozeman Daily Chronicle.* Retrieved from http://www.bozemandailychronicle.com/news/health/article_eb636934-70eb-11e2-ac97-0019bb2963f4.html?mode=jqm.

Hausen, J. (2013b, March 28). Bozeman Deaconess Hospital, nurses reach labor settlement. *Bozeman Daily Chronicle.* Retrieved from http://www.bozemand

ailychronicle.com/news/health/article_34d42fc34-9762-11e2-a038
-0019bb2963f4.html.

Hausen, J. (2013c, February 20). Nurses picket Bozeman Deaconess Hospital. *Bozeman Daily Chronicle.* Retrieved from http://www.bozemandailychronic le.com/news/health/article_713e7bc8-7b11-11e2-bb35-001a4bcf887a .html?mode=jqm.

Helmreich, R. L. (1997). Managing human error in aviation. *Scientific American, 276*(5), 62–67.

Higgins, B. L., & MacIntosh, J. (2010). Operating room nurses' perceptions of the effects of physician-perpetrated abuse. *International Nursing Review, 57,* 321–327.

Holloway, E., & Kusy, M. (2011). Systems approach to address incivility and disruptive behaviors in health-care organizations. *Organization Development in Healthcare: Conversations on Research and Strategies. Advances in Health Care Management, 10,* 239–265.

Hough, A., Hoel, H., & Carneiro, I. G. (2011). Bullying and employee turnover among healthcare workers: A three-wave prospective study. *Journal of Nursing Management, 19,* 742–751.

Hutchinson, M., Vickers, M. H., Jackson, D., & Wilkes, L. (2006). Workplace bullying in nursing: Towards a more critical organizational perspective. *Nursing Inquiry, 13*(2), 118–126.

Hutchinson, M., Vickers, M. H., Jackson, D., & Wilkes, L. (2010). Bullying as circuits of power: An Australian nursing perspective. *Administrative Theory & Praxis, 32*(1), 25–47.

Hutchinson, M., Vickers, M.H., Wilkes, L., & Jackson, D. (2009). "The worse you behave, the more you seem to be rewarded": Bullying in nursing as organizational corruption. *Employee Responsibilities and Rights Journal, 21,* 213–229.

Institute for Safe Medicine (ISMP). (2014). *Results from ISMP survey on workplace intimidation.* Retrieved from https://ismp.org/Survey/surveyresults /Survey0311.asp.

Jackson, D., & Borbasi, S. A. (2000). The caring conundrum: Potential and perils for nursing. In J. Daly, S. Speedy, & D. Jackson (Eds.), *Contexts of nursing: An introduction* (pp. 65–74). Sydney, Australia: MacLennan & Petty.

Jackson, D., Clare, J., & Mannix, J. (2002). Who wants to be a nurse: Violence in the workplace—a factor in recruitment and retention. *Journal of Nursing Management, 10*(1), 13–20.

James, J. T. (2013). A new, evidence-based estimate of patient harms associated with hospital care. *Journal of Patient Safety, 9*(3), 122–128.

Johnson, A. G. (1997). *The gender knot: Unraveling our patriarchal legacy.* Philadelphia, PA: Temple University Press.

Johnson, S. (2011). An ecological model of workplace bullying: A guide for intervention and research. *Nursing Forum, 46*(2), 55–63.

Johnson, S. L., & Rea, R. E. (2009). Workplace bullying: Concerns for nurse leaders. *Journal of Nursing Administration, 39*(2), 84–90.

Joint Commission on Accreditation of Health Care Organizations. (n.d.a.). Retrieved from http://www.jointcommission.org/about_us/about_the _joint_commission_main.aspx.

Joint Commission on Accreditation of Health Care Organizations. (n.d.a.). Retrieved from http://www.jointcommission.org/sentinel_event.aspx.

Joint Commission on Accreditation of Health Care Organizations. (2008). *Sentinel event alert: Behaviors that undermine a culture of safety, 40*, 1–3. Retrieved from http://www.jointcommission.org/assets/1/18/SEA_40.pdf.

Joint Commission on Accreditation of Health Care Organizations. (2012). Leadership standard clarified to address behaviors that undermine a safety culture. *Joint Commission Perspectives, 32*(1). Retrieved from http://www .jointcommission.org/assets/1/6/Leadership_standard_behaviors.pdf.

Jones, C. B., & Gates, M. (2007). The costs and benefits of nurse turnover: A business case for nurse retention. *Online Journal of Issues in Nursing, 12*(3), 4.

Kalisch, B. J., & Kalisch, P. A. (1977). An analysis of the sources of physician-nurse conflict. *Journal of Nursing Administration, 7*(1), 51–57.

Kanter, R. M. (1977). *Men and women of the corporation*. New York, NY: Basic Books.

Katrinli, A., Atabay, G., Gunay, G., & Cangarli, B. G. (2010). Nurses' perceptions of individual and organizational political reasons for horizontal peer bullying. *Nursing Ethics, 17*(5), 614–627.

King-Jones, M. (2011). Horizontal violence and the socialization of new nurses. *Creative Nursing, 17*(2), 80–86.

Kivimaki, M., Elovainio, M., & Vahtera, J. (2000). Workplace bullying and sickness absence in hospital staff. *Occupational and Environmental Medicine, 57*(10), 656–660.

Kwok, R. P. W., Law, Y. K., & Li, K. E. (2006). Prevalence of workplace violence against nurses in Hong Kong, *Hong Kong Medical Journal, 12*(1), 6–9.

Leape, L. L., & Fromson, J. A. (2006). Problem doctors: Is there a system level solution? *Annals of Internal Medicine, 144*(2), 107–115.

Lee, D. (2002). Gendered workplace bullying in the restructured UK civil service. *Personnel Review, 31*(1–2), 205–228.

Lewis, M. (2001). Bullying in nursing. *Nursing Standard, 15*(45), 39–42.

Lin, F. A., & Bernstein, I. (2014). Civility and workplace bullying: Resonance of Nightingale's persona and current best practices. *Nursing Forum, 49*(2), 124–128.

Lin, Y., & Liu, H. (2005). The impact of workplace violence on nurses in South Taiwan. *International Journal of Nursing Studies, 42*(7), 773–778.

Lindy, C., & Schaefer, G. (2010). Negative workplace behaviors: An ethical dilemma for nurse managers, *Journal of Nursing Management, 18*, 285–292.

Lutgen-Sandvik, P. (2006). Take this job and . . .: Quitting and other forms of resistance to workplace bullying. *Communication Monographs, 73*(4), 406–433.

Makary, M. (2012a, September 21). How to stop hospitals from killing us. *Wall Street Journal*. Retrieved from http://online.wsj.com/news/articles/SB1000 08723963904446201045780082633344441352#printMode.

Mathieson, L. K., & Bobay, K. (2007). Validation of oppressed group behaviors in nursing. *Journal of Professional Nursing, 23*(4), 226–234.

Matthiesen, G. D., Einarsen, S., & Mykletun, R. (2008). The occurrences and correlates of bullying and harassment in the restaurant sector. *Scandinavian Journal of Psychology, 49*(1), 59–68.

Maxfield, D., Grenny, J., McMillan, R., Patterson, K., & Switzler, A. (2005). *Silence kills: The seven crucial conversations for healthcare.* American Association of Critical-Care Nurses. VitalSmarts. Retrieved from http://www.aacn.org/WD/practice/docs/publicpolicy/silencekills.pdf.

Maxwell, J. A. (2005). *Qualitative research design: An interactive approach* (2nd ed.). Newbury Park, CA: Sage.

McKenna, B. G., Smith, N. S., Poole, S. J., & Coverdale, J. H. (2003). Horizontal violence: Experiences of registered nurses in their first year of practice. *Journal of Advanced Nursing, 42*(1), 90–96.

McNamara, S. A. (2012). Incivility in nursing: Unsafe nurse, unsafe patients. *AORN Journal, 95*(4), 535–540.

Mikkelsen, E. G., & Einarsen, S. (2001). Bullying in Danish work-life: Prevalence and health correlates. *European Journal of Work and Organizational Psychology, 10*(4), 393–413.

Neff, K. E. (2000). Understanding and managing physicians with disruptive behavior. In S. B. Ransom, W. W. Pinsky, & J. E. Tropman (Eds.), *Enhancing physician performance: Advanced principles of medical management* (pp. 45–72). Tampa, FL: American College of Healthcare Executives.

Nelson, R. (2014, April 19). World report: Tackling violence against healthcare workers. *Lancet, 383*, 1373–1374.

Niedhammer, I., David, S., Degioanni, S., Drummond, A., & Phillip, P. (2009). Workplace bullying and sleep disturbances: Findings from a large scale cross-sectional survey in the French working population. *Sleep, 32*(9), 1211–1220.

Niedl, K. (1996). Mobbing and wellbeing: Economic and personnel development implications. *European Journal of Work and Organizational Psychology, 5*(2), 239–249.

Occupational Safety and Health Administration. (n.d.). *Healthcare wide hazards: Workplace violence.* Washington, DC: U.S. Department of Labor. Retrieved from https://www.osha.gov/SLTC/etools/hospital/hazards/workplace violence/viol.html.

Pai, H-C., & Lee, S. (2011). Risk factors for workplace violence in clinical registered nurses in Taiwan. *Journal of Clinical nursing, 20*, 1405–1412.

Pearson, C. M., Anderson, L. M., & Porath, C. L. (2000). Assessing and attacking workplace incivility. *Organizational Dynamics, 29*(2), 123–137.

Pfifferling, J. H. (1999, March–April). The disruptive physician: A quality of professional life factor. *Physician Executive, 25*(2), 56–61.

Porto, G., & Lauve, R. (2006, July/August). Disruptive clinician behavior: A persistent threat to patient safety. *Patient Safety and Quality Healthcare.*

Purpora, C., Blegen, A., & Stotts, N. A. (2012). Horizontal violence among hospital staff nurses related to oppressed self or oppressed group. *Journal of Professional Nursing, 28*(5), 306–314.

Quine, L. (1999). Workplace bullying in NHS community trust: Staff questionnaire survey. *British Medical Journal, 318*(7178), 228–232.

Raess v. Doescher. 883 N.E. 2d 790 (Ind. 2008).

Randle, J. (2003). Bullying in the nursing profession. *Journal of Advanced Nursing, 43*(4), 395–401.

Roberts, S. J. (1983). Oppressed group behavior: Implications for nursing. *Advances in Nursing Science, 5*(4), 21–30.

Roberts, S. J. (1996). Breaking the cycle of oppression: Lessons for nurse practitioners? *Journal of the American Academy of Nurse Practitioners, 8*(5), 209–214.

Roberts, S. J. (1997). Nurse executives in the 1990s: Empowered or oppressed? *Nursing Administration Quarterly, 22*(1), 64–71.

Roche, M., Diers, D., Duffield, C., & Catling-Paull, C. (2010). Violence toward nurses, the work environment, and patient outcomes, *Journal of Nursing Scholarship, 42*(1), 13–22.

Rosenstein, A. (2002). Nurse-physician relationships: Impact on nurse satisfaction and retention. *American Journal of Nursing, 102*(6), 26–34.

Rosenstein, A. (2011). Managing disruptive behaviors in the health care setting: Focus on obstetric services. *American Journal of Obstetrics & Gynecology, 204*, 187–192.

Rosenstein, A. H., & O'Daniel, M. (2005). Disruptive behavior and clinical outcomes: Perceptions of nurses and physicians: Nurses, physicians, and administrators say that clinicians' disruptive behavior has negative effects on clinical outcomes. *Nursing Management, 36*(1), 18–29.

Rosenstein, A. H., & O'Daniel, M. (2006). Impact and implications of disruptive behavior in the perioperative arena. *Journal of American College of Surgeons, 203*(1), 96–105.

Rosenstein, A. H., & O'Daniel, M. (2008). A survey of the impact of disruptive behaviors and communication defects on patient safety. *Joint Commission Journal of Quality and Patient Safety, 34*(8), 464–471.

Rosenstein, A., Russel, H., & Lauve, R. (2002, November–December). Disruptive physician behavior contributes to nursing shortage. *Physician Executive, 28*(6), 8–11.

Samir, N., Mohamed, R., Moustafa, E., & Abou Saif, H. (2012). Nurses' attitudes and reactions to workplace violence in obstetrics and gynaecology departments in Cairo hospitals. *Eastern Mediterranean Health Journal, 18*(3), 198–204.

Sanchez, l. T. (2014, August 21). Viewpoint: Disruptive behaviors among physicians. *Journal of the American Medical Association, 312*, 2209–2210.

Sanford, K. (2011). The case for nursing leadership development. *Healthcare Financial Management, 65*(3), 100–106.

Scarry, K. D. (1999). Nursing elective: Balancing caregiving in oppressive systems. *Journal of Nursing Education, 38*(9), 423–426.

Schultz, V. (1990). Telling stories about women and work: Judicial interpretations of sex segregation in the workplace in Title VII causes raising the lack of interest argument. *Harvard Law Review, 103*(8), 1749–1843.

Shreve, J., Van Den Bos, J., Gray, T., Halford, M., Rustagi, K., & Ziemkiewicz, E. (2010). *The economic measurement of medical errors.* Millimon. Retrieved from https://www.soa.org/research/research-projects/health/research-econ-measurement.aspx.

Simpson, R., & Cohen, C. (2004). Dangerous work: The gendered nature of bullying in the context of higher education. *Gender, Work and Organization, 11*(2), 163–186.

Smith, L. M., Andrusynsn, M. S., & Laschringer, H. (2010). Effects of workplace incivility and burnout: Impact on staff nurse recruitment and retention outcomes. *Journal of Nursing Management, 18*(8), 1004–1005.

Spector, P. E., Zhou, Z. E., & Che, X. X. (2014). Nurse exposure to physical and nonphysical violence, bullying, and sexual harassment: A quantitative review. *International Journal of Nursing Studies, 51*, 72–84.

Speedy, S., & Jackson, D. (2004). Power, politics and gender: Issues for nurse leaders and managers. In J. Daly, S. Speedy, & D. Jackson (Eds.), *Nursing Leadership* (pp. 55–68). Sydney, Australia: Churchill Livingstone.

Strauss, S. (2007). Quantitative and qualitative analysis of physician abuse as gender harassment to female and male registered nurses in the operating room. Retrieved from http://pqdtopen.proquest.com/doc/304765407.html?FMT=AI.

Timmins, F. (2005). How assertive are nurses in the workplace? A preliminary pilot study. *Journal of Nursing Management, 13*(1), 61–67.

Townsend, T. (2012). Break the bullying cycle. *American Nurse, 7*(1). Retrieved from http://www.americannursetoday.com/article.aspx?id=8648&fid=8612.

Ulrich, D. (1997). *Human resource champions: The next agenda for adding value and delivering results.* Boston, MA: Harvard Business School Press:

Veltman, L. L. (2007). Disruptive behavior in obstetrics: A hidden threat to patient safety. *American journal of Obstetrics and Gynecology, 196*(587), 587.e1–587.e5.

Vessey, J., Demarco, R., & DiFazio, R. (2010). Bullying, harassment, and horizontal violence in the nursing workforce: The state of the science. *Annual Review of Nursing Research, 28*, 133–157.

Vessey, J., Demarco, R., Gaffney, D., & Budin, W. (2009). Bullying of staff registered nurses in the workplace: A preliminary study for developing personal and organizational strategies for the transformation of hostile to healthy workplace environments. *Journal of Professional Nursing, 25*(5), 299–306.

Walker, L. O., & Avant, K. C. (1995). *Strategies for theory construction in nursing* (3rd ed.). Norwalk, CT: Appleton-Lange.

Weber, D. O. (2004). Poll results: Doctors' disruptive behavior disturbs physician leaders. *Physician Executive, 30*, 16–17.

Weinard, M. R. (2010). Horizontal violence in nursing: History, impact, and solution. *Journal of Chi Eta Phi Sorority, 54*(1), 23–26.

Wittington, R., Shuttleworth, S., & Hill, L. (1996). Violence to staff in a general hospital setting. *Journal of Advanced Nursing, 24*(2), 320–333.

Woelfe, C. Y., & McCaffrey, R. (2007). Nurse on nurse. *Nursing Forum, 42*(3), 123–131.

Zapf, D., Einarsen, S., Hoel, H., & Vartia, M. (2003). Empirical findings on bullying in the workplace. In S. Einarsen, H. Hoel, D. Zapf, & C. L. Cooper (Eds.), *Bulling and emotional abuse in the workplace: International perspectives in research and practice* (pp. 103–126). New York, NY: Taylor & Francis.

Chapter 7

Service with a Smile Meets Customer with a Snarl: Implications for Worker Well-Being

Lisa A. Marchiondo, Lilia M. Cortina, Harry S. Shannon, Ted Haines, Sybil Geldart, and Lauren Griffith

> The customer is always right.
>
> —Harry Gordon Selfridge (founder, Selfridges Department Store, London, 1909)

Organizations often adopt slogans such as the one in this chapter's epigraph to boost customer confidence and loyalty, yet these customer-centric attitudes may also contribute to *customer incivility* toward those who serve them (Harris & Reynolds, 2003). This disregard for employee dignity is insidious and potentially escalating, meriting greater attention from social scientists and practitioners alike.

To date, applied research has focused heavily on incivility instigated by organizational "insiders," meaning coworkers within the organization

This research is based on the master's thesis of Lisa Marchiondo, completed under the supervision of Lilia Cortina. We presented portions of this manuscript in August 2009 at the annual meeting of the Academy of Management. This research was funded by the Workplace Safety and Insurance Board (WSIB) of Ontario, Canada, Grant 04016.

(e.g., Pearson, Andersson, & Porath, 2000; Porath & Pearson, 2012) or peers and professors in school (Caza & Cortina, 2007; Porath, Overbeck, & Pearson, 2008). However, employees in many service environments interface with *customers* more than peers or superiors. How frequently do those service personnel encounter an uncivil public, and do those encounters diminish their well-being? Because customer incivility has a number of unique features that make it a "mild" stressor (i.e., low in intensity, lacking in overt malice, brief in duration, stemming from strangers), one could reasonably ask whether it has meaningful implications for employees' professional well-being. We might be even more skeptical about whether its effects reach beyond the work domain, spilling into facets of mental health that are not work related (e.g., general symptoms of anxiety and depression).

The contributions of this study are threefold. First, we *compare the prevalence* of customer incivility to rates of insider incivility in the lives of postal employees. Postal work is particularly well suited to research on customer incivility, because some postal personnel spend virtually all of their work days interacting with customers, potentially exposing them to many acts of customer rudeness. At the same time, employee–customer interactions tend to be extremely time limited in the postal sector and do not take place in the context of close relationships (in contrast to transactions in other applied social settings, such as law, education, and health care, where close relationships with clients and consumers are typical). This distinctive combination of exposure frequency—but also exposure brevity and superficiality—raises intriguing questions about whether customer incivility is in fact stressful if or when it occurs during fleeting service transactions. Findings from this research could be generalizable to any number of work contexts (e.g., retail, transportation) that have similar service characteristics.

These questions bring us to a second novel contribution of this project: we develop and test a model of pathways by which customer incivility relates to multiple domains of individual well-being. This adds to the emerging literature on customer incivility by investigating whether its effects extend *beyond professional well-being*, seeping into employees' non-work-related psychological health. Further, this model highlights the counterintuitive nature of workplace incivility: even when it is subtle, ambiguous, transitory, and stemming from strangers, it may still threaten employees' health and wellness.

Third, we assemble an *array of practical solutions* for protecting against the incidence and impact of incivility in service work. We also outline directions for future research that will be critical for advancing knowledge. The dramatic growth of the service industry has made it one of the largest employment sectors in the developed world (e.g., Biron & van Veldhoven, 2012; Lee & Wolpin, 2006). It is therefore important that we fully understand the social (and antisocial) dynamics of these settings.

CUSTOMER INCIVILITY DEFINED

In its most general sense, "incivility" encompasses everything "from breaches of etiquette to professional misconduct, from general civil unrest to moral decay" (Andersson & Pearson, 1999, p. 455). In an applied setting, incivility involves seemingly small acts of rudeness or discourtesy that violate basic moral standards of respect. The intentions or goals (if any) motivating the behavior are unclear to the instigator, target, or observers. The ambiguity of incivility invites varied interpretations and allows instigators to deny their misconduct (Caza & Cortina, 2007; Porath & Pearson, 2012). Although they overlap, "workplace incivility" and "workplace aggression" are not synonymous, with the latter term usually reserved for higher-intensity, overtly malicious behavior (Sliter, Pui, Sliter, & Jex, 2011; van Jaarsveld, Walker, & Skarlicki, 2010). Most workplace incivility research has examined *insider* incivility, which can occur between peers (laterally), from superiors to subordinates (top down), and even from subordinates to superiors (bottom up; Caza & Cortina, 2007; Porath et al., 2008; Porath & Pearson, 2012). Less is known about incivility springing from institutional *outsiders*, such as customers.

Similar to insider incivility, customer incivility entails rude behavior that is low level, ambiguous, and in violation of norms of respect (Sliter, Jex, Wolford, & McInnerney, 2010; Sliter et al., 2011; van Jaarsveld et al., 2010). For example, during service transactions, customers may use condescending remarks, impatient gestures, or demeaning terms of address. Despite similarities between customer and insider incivility, an important difference is the opportunity for targets to take action against the mistreatment. When an individual encounters uncivil conduct from peers, there are typically options for reporting, resisting, or resolving the situation. Opportunities commonly exist for service personnel to report aggressive customer behavior that is more overt in nature (e.g., disruptive conduct can be reported to security). However, when a customer is merely *impolite*, norms often dictate that personnel be courteous and patient, maintain positive demeanor, and remember that "the customer is always right" (Grandey, 2003; Rupp, McCance, Spencer, & Sonntag, 2008; Rupp & Spencer, 2006). For these reasons, customer incivility, compared to both insider incivility and customer aggression, poses unique challenges.

Additional features that distinguish customer versus insider incivility are the duration of the incivility and relationship with its perpetrator. In many service environments, standard transactions with customers are short lived. In addition, customers differ from coworkers and supervisors in that they are often strangers or, at best, acquaintances. For instance, letter carriers often have no deep relationships with residential mail recipients, and retail clerks rarely get to know the people making purchases. Moreover, customer-service transactions in many settings do not create the time-intensive and ongoing client relationships typical in professions like law, consulting, or in-home health care. One could ask whether the brevity and superficiality surrounding this kind of customer incivility make it a stressor of little consequence.

CUSTOMER INCIVILITY PREVALENCE

Insider incivility is prevalent across a range of applied settings, from clerical work to law enforcement to higher education (Porath & Pearson, 2012). Some suggest that incivility in organizations could be on the rise, due to greater complexity, technology, and pressure in the workforce; a "flattening" of organizations; and weaker organizational climates of community (Andersson & Pearson, 1999; Pearson et al., 2000). Moreover, sociologists have argued that incivility is increasing in society more generally, due to fewer meaningful public and professional engagements between people (Pearson et al., 2000).

The enactment of customer-to-employee incivility may be explained by an imbalance in power dynamics (Grandey, Dickter, & Sin, 2004; Mills & Bonoma, 1979). According to this perspective, employees feel that they control the sales and current operations of their organizations and, as such, desire due respect and authority. Yet some customers feel a sense of entitlement, expecting service personnel to cater to all their needs in a prompt and friendly manner (Fisk & Neville, 2011). These differing approaches to the service encounter can lead to a power struggle between workers and customers (Grandey et al., 2004). In organizations that privilege customer-centric attitudes, the power balance can be tipped in favor of the customer (Mills & Bonoma, 1979), fueling arrogance and rudeness toward employees.

Incivility stemming from customers may be more prevalent than insider incivility (Sliter et al., 2010). Related forms of mistreatment, such as customer "aggression," are more commonly committed by customers than by coworkers (Grandey, Kern, & Frone, 2007; LeBlanc & Kelloway, 2002). Grandey and colleagues (2007) argued that customers, compared to coworkers, are more likely to aggress against employees due to the *effect/danger ratio*. That is, people strive to maximize the effect of their deviant behavior on a target, while minimizing the personal danger of the deviant behavior to themselves. Applying this reasoning to workplace incivility, customers, compared to organizational members, should perceive less danger in behaving uncivilly, because customers (a) feel less bound by social norms due to their anonymity, (b) face few, if any, consequences for their unethical behavior, (c) understand that employees face repercussions for negative behavior, and (d) typically control the frequency and nature of future interactions. We thus began this study by hypothesizing that:

Hypothesis 1: Service employees will encounter more customer incivility than insider (coworker and supervisor) incivility.

IMPLICATIONS FOR WELL-BEING

Experiences of insider incivility link with declines in target well-being. These include lower career salience and performance and greater counterproductive work behavior, distress, ostracism, and injustice (Caza & Cortina, 2007; Cortina, Magley, Williams, & Langhout, 2001; Penny & Spector, 2005; Porath & Pearson, 2012). Not only can these outcomes erode one's dignity, but they can also take a financial toll on organizations, amplifying the costs of sick leave, lost productivity, stolen or damaged property, and replacement of employees who leave (Cortina, 2008; Harris & Reynolds, 2003).

Insider incivility clearly has consequences, but is the same true of customer misconduct? Though few in number, important studies have shown a relation between experiences of customer incivility and employees' job-related emotional exhaustion, performance decline, and work withdrawal (Kern & Grandey, 2009; Sliter et al., 2010, 2011; van Jaarsveld et al., 2010). This emerging research puts customer incivility "on the map" as an occupational stressor worthy of attention. It also begs the question as to the generalizability of customer incivility across job type, sector, and contextual factors inside and outside the workplace.

In this investigation, we extended this nascent scholarship by testing whether customer incivility relates to *other important job outcomes*, including satisfaction, commitment, and turnover intent. We also expanded the focus of inquiry by examining whether outcomes reach *beyond professional well-being*, spilling into employees' nonwork-related psychological health (e.g., anxiety, depression, hostility). Such effects might seem unlikely due to the unique features of customer incivility: low intensity, ambiguous intent, brief duration, and perpetration by strangers. However, there are good theoretical reasons to hypothesize these effects.

Theoretically, three concepts from the social or personality literature help explain the harms of customer incivility: emotional labor, control, and coping. When employees are expected to mask their true feelings and unconditionally support customers, they engage in emotionally suppressing behavior (i.e., emotional labor), which flourishes when service workers encounter difficult customers (Biron & van Veldhoven, 2012; Rupp & Spencer, 2006; Spencer & Rupp, 2009; Wang, Liao, Zhan, & Shi, 2011). Emotional labor can undermine employee professional well-being, including such job-related consequences as job dissatisfaction, stress, and burnout (Dormann & Zapf, 2004; Rupp et al., 2008). Mental health effects can also accompany emotional labor, as it fuels emotional exhaustion, depression, anger, and physical health symptoms (Erickson & Wharton, 1997; Grandey, 2003;

Schaubroeck & Jones, 2000). Emotional labor thus supports the adverse influence of customer incivility on service employees (Sliter et al., 2010).

Additional reasons to predict that customer incivility can threaten well-being relate to employee *control* and *resources for coping* with rude customers. Unlike overt aggression, everyday disrespect from customers is not routinely monitored by most organizations, and most do not have formal systems for employees to report customer discourtesy. Organizations may even discourage employee complaints about customers, with concerns about customer loyalty outweighing matters of employee dignity. In such contexts, employees cannot take direct action against customer incivility, and they may be left with a sense of powerlessness. Lack of control is known to exacerbate organizational stressor-strain processes (Grandey, Fisk, & Steiner, 2005), so (uncontrollable) customer incivility could be professionally and emotionally exhausting.

TOWARD A HOLISTIC MODEL

Extending the emerging work on customer incivility, we designed a model that integrates relationships between customer incivility and multiple indicators of occupational and psychological strain. Specifically, we predicted that customer incivility would link to detriments in service workers' psychological well-being (i.e., lowered job satisfaction, negative mental health symptoms), which in turn would relate to declines in their investment and energy exerted at work (i.e., decreased job commitment, increased job burnout). Subsequently, we expected that this decreased investment would foster greater intentions to leave the organization.

We based the structure of this model on several lines of research. Uncivil behaviors at work qualify as "daily hassles" (or "routine nuisances of everyday life," Cortina et al., 2001, p. 65; see also Cortina, 2008), and daily hassles can undermine psychological well-being, including lowered job satisfaction and greater mood disturbance (DeLongis, Folkman, & Lazarus, 1988; McGonagle & Kessler, 1990). In turn, job (dis)satisfaction is associated with turnover cognitions, as mediated by organizational commitment (Williams & Hazer, 1986). Organizational commitment is one of the strongest predictors of employee turnover, according to meta-analytic research (Griffeth, Hom, & Gaertner, 2000). Studies have further demonstrated a relation between job satisfaction and turnover intentions, both directly and via job burnout (Lee & Ashforth, 1996; Lim, Cortina, & Magley, 2008; Miner-Rubino & Cortina, 2007).

Related findings have emerged with regard to mental health and work outcomes. Studies show that negative work contexts and relationships play roles in the emergence of depressive symptoms (Hirschfeld et al., 2000). Such mental health problems can foster poorer performance, greater use of sick days, and general absenteeism (Kessler & Frank, 1997; Kessler,

Merikangas, & Wang, 2008; Simon, 2003). Ample medical studies have demonstrated the effects of mental health deficits on employee work productivity and investment, as well as on organizational exit behaviors (Simon, 2003; Stewart, Ricci, Chee, Hahn, & Morganstein, 2003).

In addition to job satisfaction and negative mental health's relation with distal endogenous variables, these constructs should also share a relation. Not only should customer incivility have a direct relation with negative mental health, but decreased job satisfaction may contribute to mental decline. Because most employees spend significant portions of their lives at work, poor experiences and dissatisfaction at work are bound to influence their general psychological well-being. In studies of coworker incivility, lower job satisfaction indeed relates to declines in mental health (Lim et al., 2008). Further, the demand-control-support model (Karasek & Theorell, 1990) supports the notion that workplace experiences influence well-being outside the work domain.

Taken together, prior research suggests that customer incivility (a daily hassle) will relate to declines in psychological well-being (both work-related dissatisfaction and general negative mental health symptoms), which in turn links to lower investment and energy at work (lower commitment, greater work-related burnout). The ultimate outcome of this process will be service workers' plans to exit this negative social environment. We present a diagram of these relationships in Figure 7.1 and summarize them formally in the following hypothesis:

Hypothesis 2: Employee experiences of customer incivility will relate to decreased job satisfaction and increased negative mental health symptoms. Lower job satisfaction will also relate to increased negative mental health symptoms. In turn, these outcomes will be associated with increased job burnout and decreased organizational commitment, which will then predict greater turnover intent.

THE CURRENT STUDY

We tested our hypotheses within the context of a large, public, government-owned organization (a "Crown corporation"): Canada Post Corporation. Certain features of this employment context raise intriguing and competing ideas about the presence and effects of customer incivility. On the one hand, customer incivility may be exacerbated by poor cultural attitudes toward public sector workers. On the other hand, the effect of such rudeness on postal workers may be mitigated by these workers' experiences of job security, fairer working conditions compared to private courier industry employees (Bickerton & Warskett, 2005), and greater tolerance of poor public opinions. Both possibilities deserve future empirical attention.

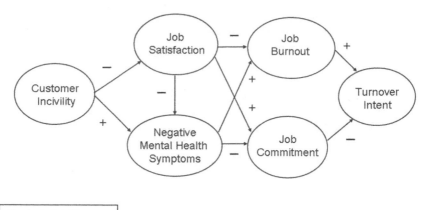

Figure 7.1 Proposed model of customer incivility's effects on work and psychological outcomes (Plus [minus] signs indicate hypothesized positive [negative] relationships.)

Method

Participants and Procedure

Following an adapted "tailored design" method (Dillman, 2000), questionnaires were mailed to 1,968 employees in 12 locations of Canada Post. After receiving survey packets by mail, 965 participants returned their completed (anonymous) questionnaires directly to the research team, yielding a 50% response rate. We excluded 15 questionnaires due to potential duplication, leaving 950 for analysis.

Because the primary focus of this study was incivility from customers, we selected only delivery and retail workers for analysis (e.g., letter carriers, counter clerks, retail personnel; $n = 544$). These were the employees who regularly encountered customers in the course of their work. Within this group of customer-interfacing employees, 64% were male and 82% worked full time. Mean job tenure was 19 years, and mean age was 47 years (age range was 20 to 69 years). Sixty-one percent of this group identified as white; however, 34% of open-ended ethnicity responses could not be coded due to vague responses (e.g., "Canadian").

Measurement

Informed by focus groups and pilot testing, this survey only included scales that have strong records of validity and reliability. For French-speaking Canadians, a French version of the questionnaire was developed, using a back-translation approach. Table 7.1 displays the summary

Table 7.1 Descriptive Statistics, Alpha Coefficients, and Intercorrelations among Study Variables

Variable	M	SD	1	2	3	4	5	6	7	8	9
1. Customer incivility[1]	1.55	0.72	.92								
2. Organizational commitment	2.89	0.84	-.22***	.89							
3. Turnover intent	2.07	1.09	.22***	-.46***	.70						
4. Job satisfaction	3.64	1.00	-.22***	.71***	-.56***	.87					
5. Job burnout	3.08	0.67	.28***	-.67***	.49***	-.72***	.85				
6. Impaired mental health	1.82	0.57	.24***	-.36***	.36***	-.48***	.62***	.94			
7. Years employed	18.98	9.82	-.08	-.24***	-.04	-.16***	.14***	.11***	n/a		
8. Supervisor incivility	1.84	0.91	.22***	-.40***	.27***	-.41***	.41***	.48***	.06	.89	
9. Coworker incivility	1.73	0.86	.29***	-.21***	.11*	-.22***	.23***	.35***	.08	.48***	.92

Note. Items were reverse-scored as appropriate. Overall index scores were developed by calculating the means of all items in each scale. Higher scores indicate higher levels of the underlying construct. Correlations are below the diagonal, and scale reliabilities (Cronbach's alphas) are italicized along the diagonal.

* $p < .05$ (2-tailed).

** $p < .01$ (2-tailed).

*** $p < .001$ (2-tailed).

[1] When computing the incivility mean based on data from *victims* of customer incivility (56% of the sample), item-level means rise to 2.43 to 2.49.

statistics, reliabilities (Cronbach's alpha), and intercorrelations for all constructs analyzed in this study.

We built features into the design of this study to minimize common method bias *ex ante*, as recommended by Podsakoff, MacKenzie, Lee, and Podsakoff (2003; see also Conway & Lance, 2010). First, to reduce evaluation apprehension and promote honest and complete responding, participants were assured that their surveys would remain anonymous, that their supervisors would never have access to their data, and that there were no right or wrong answers. Second, the surveys assessed outcomes independent of and prior to incivility measurement, creating "psychological separation" between the criterion and predictor variables. This strategy also decreased the chances that respondents' memories of customer incivility biased their answers to questions about job satisfaction, commitment, and so forth. Third, scale endpoints and formats varied across the predictor and criterion variables, which diminishes method biases stemming from anchor and endpoint effects. Fourth, we selected outcome measures from the established literature, and each measure had a strong history of construct validity. Our customer incivility items were adapted, but they asked only about recent, firsthand experiences of specific behaviors (not general impressions or hearsay). In addition to this array of procedural remedies, we conducted an *ex post* statistical analysis—the Harman single-factor test—to determine whether common method variance had unduly influenced results. We found no overarching factor, which argues against a monomethod-bias explanation of our findings.

Incivility

Participants reported incivility experiences from customers using five items from the Workplace Incivility Scale, adapted to the customer-service context (WIS-Customer; Cortina et al., 2001; see also the Appendix). Participants rated the frequency with which they had experienced each WIS-Customer behavior during the prior year, from 1 (*never*) to 5 (*many times*). Previous research supports the content and discriminant validity of the WIS (Cortina et al., 2001).

Participants rated experiences of uncivil conduct from supervisors using the same five WIS items and response options, with the stem now referring to supervisors (WIS-Supervisor). They then completed a third version of the scale, which referenced coworkers (WIS-Coworker). Together, these two subscales formed a reliable 10-item measure of "insider incivility."

Job-Related Outcomes

Job satisfaction was assessed using three items from the Michigan Organizational Assessment Questionnaire (Cammann, Fichman, Jenkins,

& Klesh, 1983). A sample item reads: "All in all, I am satisfied with my job." Participants responded to these items using a scale ranging from 1 (*strongly disagree*) to 5 (*strongly agree*).

The Oldenburg Burnout Inventory (Demerouti, Bakker, Nachreiner, & Schaufeli, 2001) measured two facets of job burnout. The disengagement subscale (six items) addressed employees' disconnections from work due to disinterest (e.g., "Lately, I tend to think less during my work and just execute it mechanically"). The exhaustion subscale (six items) addressed work burnout in relation to employees' energy on the job (e.g., "I can stand the pressure of my work well"; "When I work, I usually feel energized") (both items reverse coded). Participants responded to all items using a five-point scale (1 = *strongly disagree* to 5 = *strongly agree*).

Ten items gauged workers' commitment to the organization (adapted from Ashford, Lee, & Bobko, 1989; Cook & Wall, 1980). Items included "In my work I like to feel I am making some effort, not just for myself but for [my organization] as well" and "To know that my own work had made a contribution to the good of [the organization] would please me." Participants indicated their agreement with each statement from 1 (*strongly disagree*) to 5 (*strongly agree*).

Participants also used a 1 (*strongly disagree*) to 5 (*strongly agree*) scale to complete a two-item measure of turnover intent: "I often think about quitting this job" and "I will probably look for a new job during the next year" (Porter, Crampon, & Smith, 1976). The correlation between these two turnover items was high ($r = .70$).

Mental Health

Four facets of nonwork-related mental health were measured: symptoms of anxiety, symptoms of depression, hostile ideation, and general physical or emotional fatigue. Given the close relation among these constructs, we modeled them as indicators of an overall, nonwork-related mental health latent variable.

Items from the Brief Symptom Inventory (BSI; Derogatis & Spencer, 1983) assessed symptoms of anxiety, depression, and hostility. Sample items read: "feeling tense or keyed up" (anxiety: six items), "feeling hopeless about the future" (depression: six items), and "temper outbursts that you could not control" (hostile ideation: five items). Participants responded using a scale from 1 (*not at all*) to 5 (*extremely*). With both clinical and nonclinical populations, the BSI has proven to be reliable, valid, and correlated in appropriate ways with the Minnesota Multiphasic Personality Inventory (Boulet & Boss, 1991).

Symptoms of generic (nonwork-related) fatigue were measured using the "personal burnout" subscale of the Copenhagen Burnout Inventory (Kristensen, Borritz, Villadsen, & Christensen, 2005). These six questions (e.g., "How often do you feel tired?"; "How often do you feel weak and susceptible to illness?") assessed symptoms of physical and psychological fatigue and exhaustion, *not* specifically attributable to work or to clients. Response options ranged from 1 (*never/almost never*) to 5 (*always*).

Control Variable

Job tenure (i.e., years of employment with this organization) was controlled in all analyses to ensure that employees' reported rates of incivility and outcomes did not simply result from their seniority or lack thereof. Longer-tenured employees may experience lower rates of incivility or report fewer negative outcomes, having had more time to develop strategies for heading off or coping with the mistreatment. Controlling for job tenure also accounts for the possibility of a "survivor effect" (i.e., employees with longer tenure have remained on the job because they have experienced little incivility).

Results

Incidence of Customer Incivility

In this postal sample, 56% of service workers reported experiencing at least one instance of customer incivility within the past year. By comparison, 66% described at least one instance of incivility from coworkers, and 72% reported incivility from supervisors. Moreover, customer incivility occurred, on average, at significantly lower frequencies than either coworker incivility ($F[22, 516] = 3.90, p < .001$) or supervisor incivility ($F[25, 512] = 2.79, p < .001$). Contrary to our earlier Hypothesis 1, these results suggest that insider incivility is more pervasive than customer incivility in the context of public-sector service work.

Model of Customer Incivility

Testing the Hypothesized Model

Structural equation modeling was used to test the hypothesized theoretical model (Figure 7.1). As recommended by Anderson and Gerbing (1988), we undertook a two-stage approach to modeling. We first estimated a measurement model to ensure that the psychometric properties of the measures were adequate and loaded on the hypothesized factors. We then estimated a structural model. For all models, we evaluated overall fit using both "incremental" and "absolute" fit indices (Hu & Bentler, 1995).

In the measurement model, items were randomly allocated across three indicator "parcels" for each latent construct, except customer incivility (two indicators) and turnover intent (one indicator). In order to identify the model, we fixed the factor loading of one indicator to one for each latent construct. The measurement model represented a good fit to the data, χ^2 (85, N = 541) = 333.15, p < .01, Nonnormed Fit Index (NNFI) = .94, Comparative Fit Index (CFI) = .96, Root Mean Square Error of Approximation (RMSEA) = .07 (90% CI for RMSEA = .07 to .08). Standardized factor loadings ranged from .73 to .98 and were all statistically significant.

Next, we tested the structural model, which also fit the data well, χ^2 (94, N = 541) = 427.71, p < .01, NNFI = .97, CFI = .97, RMSEA = .08 (90% CI for RMSEA = .07 to .09). All hypothesized paths in the structural model except one were statistically significant, even after controlling for job tenure; completely standardized path coefficients are shown in Figure 7.2. In line with our earlier Hypothesis 2, customer incivility was associated with reductions in service employees' job satisfaction (β = −.28) and increases in their negative mental health symptoms (β = .11). Lower job satisfaction related to more negative mental health symptoms (B = −.50). Subsequently, lowered job satisfaction and increased symptoms both correlated with greater job burnout (βs = −.67 and .36, respectively). Lower job satisfaction but not negative mental health related to lower organizational commitment (β = .84). Ultimately, turnover intentions increased as a function of higher burnout (β = .33) and lower commitment (β = −.33). As seen in Figure 7.2, this model explained 38% of the variance in employees' turnover intent.

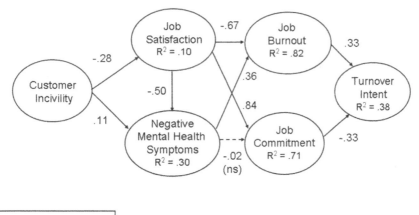

Control: Job Tenure

Figure 7.2 Completely standardized structural model results. Solid arrows represent statistically significant paths (p < .05); dotted arrows represent nonsignificance. Not shown are the paths from the control variable, job tenure, to job satisfaction (−.17, p < .05) and negative mental health symptoms (.03, ns).

Testing an Alternative Model

Even when one model fits well, other models with different substantive interpretations are virtually always possible (Bollen, 1989; MacCallum, Wegener, Uchino, & Fabrigar, 1993). In newer research domains, there is typically some degree of uncertainty about how processes operate, so methodologists advocate exploration of different modeling possibilities (MacCallum, 1995). We therefore tested two competing alternative models. The first model explicitly tested the mediating roles of job satisfaction and mental health symptoms—following procedures recommended by Holmbeck (1997). This model included all of the paths of our original hypothesized model, plus direct paths from customer incivility to job burnout and organizational commitment. With a chi-square difference test, we compared the original model against this alternative model with two additional paths, finding the alternative model to have somewhat better overall fit: $\Delta\chi^2 (2) = 8.61, p < .05$. However, the two new paths had relatively small weights (completely standardized beta coefficients of .06 and −.08, respectively), and their addition did not improve our prediction of burnout or commitment in any meaningful way. That is, the explained variance in job burnout (82%) and commitment (71%) remained unchanged from the original model. Moreover, the addition of these two paths detracted from the parsimony of our original model, which had shown good fit. Based on all of these considerations, we concluded that our original hypothesized model (with effects of customer incivility fully mediated through job satisfaction and mental health) provides a more meaningful and parsimonious explanation of these relations.

Testing Another Alternative

The frequency of supervisor and coworker incivility, as noted above, raises another plausible alternative: customer incivility may relate to employee outcomes, but not after parcing out the influences of (the more prevalent) insider incivility. Put differently, an outstanding question is whether customer incivility links to worker well-being after accounting for the effects of incivility stemming from coworkers and supervisors. To address this question, we tested a second alternative model, adding *insider incivility* as an exogenous variable with direct paths to job satisfaction and negative mental health symptoms. In other words, this model pits customer incivility and insider incivility against each other, so that they "compete" for variance in the same proximal outcomes (while still controlling for job tenure). The fit of this model was similar to that of our original hypothesized model: $\chi^2 (138, N = 541) = 554.76, p < .01$, NNFI = .96, CFI = .97, RMSEA = .08 (90% CI for RMSEA = .07 to .08). Importantly, customer incivility continued to show a significant relationship with job satisfaction ($\beta = −.20$) over and above the effects of insider incivility.

Discussion

Given the increase in the revenue and number of employees in service industries (Biron & van Veldhoven, 2012; Lee & Wolpin, 2006), it is vital that we better understand customer-service work and its consequences for health and wellness. This study examined the "dark side" of the customer–employee interface, investigating customer incivility toward service personnel and determining whether this incivility relates to multiple domains of well-being, above and beyond the effects of coworker and supervisor incivility. Here we discuss key findings and their implications for both science and practice.

Key Findings

Focusing on retail and delivery employees, we found a majority of workers describing recent encounters with uncivil conduct from customers. Customer incivility, however, took place less often than incivility from supervisors and coworkers (organizational "insiders"). This pattern runs counter to Hypothesis 1 and distinguishes incivility from more overt forms of mistreatment (e.g., aggression), which are more commonly committed by customers than coworkers (Grandey et al., 2007; LeBlanc & Kelloway, 2002).

We assume that encounters with uncivil customers were typically short lived in the postal context and did not involve intense relationships. Incivility from any individual, moreover, is subtle and ambiguous by definition (Andersson & Pearson, 1999). All of these characteristics of customer incivility (i.e., less frequent than insider incivility, transitory, no deep relationship at stake, subtle, ambiguous) trigger a critical question: even if it is common and unpleasant, is customer incivility potent enough to undermine multiple dimensions of worker well-being? Our modeling results suggest that it is.

Supporting Hypothesis 2, customer incivility linked with decrements in numerous facets of employees' occupational and mental health, even after accounting for the effects of coworker and supervisor incivility. More specifically, service workers' encounters with customer incivility were associated with lower job satisfaction—as one might expect. What is more surprising is that effects reached beyond the job context to relate to aspects of mental health (e.g., depression, anxiety, hostility) that are not specific to work. Decreased job satisfaction as a function of customer incivility was also associated with poorer mental health. In turn, these negative psychological health factors predicted greater job burnout, and job satisfaction predicted lower organizational commitment (i.e., lower investment at work). Job burnout and commitment then contributed to turnover intentions. This collection of variables accounted for well over one-third of the variation in service employees' thoughts of quitting. Because modeling analyses controlled for employee job tenure, these results cannot be attributed to workers having few (or many) years on the job. Moreover, these relations remained even after removing effects of (more prevalent) insider incivility.

Our modeling results may seem disheartening. If low-level disrespect from strangers detracts from one's well-being, then are negative outcomes inevitable for service employees? We believe not. A range of practical strategies exist, discussed below, that organizations and employees can adopt to protect against the incidence and impact of customer incivility. We also suggest a number of important directions for future research, including factors that may attenuate (or exacerbate) incivility and its outcomes.

Practical Implications

As noted earlier, the social and personality literature suggests that employees' lack of power and control might fuel relationships from customer incivility to professional and emotional outcomes. This may be particularly true when managers promote an ideology that "the customer is always right." Establishing a formal within-organization reporting system for customer incivility may reduce the effects of this mistreatment by increasing employees' perceived sense of control (Kern & Grandey, 2009). In addition, organizations could grant employees greater autonomy, more options for rotating between tasks, permission to ask uncivil customers to leave, or permission to walk away from the encounter. Some service employees have also argued for the need for local, state, and federal legislation against customer mistreatment (Harris & Reynolds, 2003).

In addition to developing new policies and reporting systems, organizations could develop methods of "armoring" service workers against customer incivility. Traditionally, service training seminars and handbooks teach employees to provide "service with a smile," regardless of their true underlying feelings (Grandey, Fisk, Mattila, Jansen, & Sideman, 2005). This promotes surface acting, which can be detrimental to employees and their interactions with customers (Grandey, Fisk, & Steiner, 2005; Rupp et al., 2008). Organizations could alternatively train personnel to build "protective shells" and to handle difficult customer interactions in a diplomatic but resolute manner. For example, some programs teach employees to adopt a feeling of detached concern, referring to a sense of balancing over- and underinvolvement during interactions with customers (Harris & Reynolds, 2003). Similarly, role separation (differentiating between one's authentic self and temporary role as a service representative) can be promoted to temper the effects of service stressors (Dollard, Dormann, Boyd, Winefield, & Winefield, 2003). Organizations can teach these skills through various mechanisms, including workshops, videos, role-playing exercises, instructions from supervisors, handbooks, and new-employee orientations (Dollard et al., 2003; Harris & Reynolds, 2003; Rupp et al., 2008). Training modules such as these can empower employees by teaching them to manage unruly customers in ways that do not undermine the quality of service they provide or their own well-being.

Organizations can also control customer incivility by managing customer expectations. For example, signs at entrances and service counters could appeal to customer courtesy and inform patrons that rude behavior will not be tolerated. Many scholars go a step further, recommending that customer expectations be framed by organizations rather than by consumers (Boulding, Kalra, Staelin, & Zeithaml, 1993; Fischer, Gainer, & Bristor, 1997). For instance, one proposal is that managers organize, stage, control, and supervise nearly all aspects of customer encounters (Harris & Reynolds, 2003). Complete oversight and control may be difficult—especially when many interactions with customers occur outside the organization (as is the case with courier work). Moreover, employees' need for respect must be balanced with their need for autonomy. The larger point, though, is that greater overall attention to employee–customer dynamics could benefit employees, organizations, and their patrons.

Outstanding Scientific Questions

With limited studies to date regarding customer incivility, a number of questions remain unanswered. For example, if employees are indeed harmed by customer incivility, the next question is how to mitigate that harm. Ideally, research should identify steps that organizations can take to enhance customer respect of service employees. One might argue, however, that customer behavior is beyond the reach of management, or that some customer incivility is inevitable in the service context. Another focus for research could therefore be organizational resources that preserve the dignity and well-being of service employees, even in the face of a hostile public. For example, could certain leadership styles or formal reporting systems act as buffers against the consequences of customer incivility? Could positive intraorganization conditions (e.g., a climate of justice and respect) reduce the detrimental effects of extraorganizational incivility? Although managing customer behavior is challenging, perhaps organizations can attenuate the impact of unpleasant customers by establishing within-organization atmospheres that boost employee morale and dignity.

The presence of exacerbating factors within organizations should also be investigated. Do some organizations have environments that foster rude customer behavior? For example, when customers wait long periods of time for service, rudeness may flourish. Negative organizational contexts may also lead to employee unhappiness, engendering employee incivility toward customers (and coworkers). In turn, these customers may reciprocate the rude behavior to the service workers, in a "tit-for-tat" fashion (Andersson & Pearson, 1999). Although not specific to incivility, related research has found that leadership behaviors affect the service climate, which in turn influences employees' organizational citizenship behavior and subsequent customer satisfaction (Schneider, Ehrhart, Mayer, Saltz, & Niles-Jolly, 2005). Similarly, employees' experiences at work have been shown to relate to the quality of service they provide to customers (Schneider, White, & Paul, 1998; Sliter et al., 2010).

Finally, factors unique to customer incivility deserve research. Although uncivil behavior (e.g., condescension, interruption, derision) may look similar regardless of who instigates it, individual responses diverge dramatically (Porath et al., 2008; Porath & Pearson, 2012). In particular, emotional sequelae could vary with the profile of the instigator (e.g., greater embarrassment following outsider incivility, but greater anger following insider incivility). In addition to consequences, the antecedents of incivility may differ depending on its source. For example, coworkers may be most likely to behave badly under conditions of poor leadership, while poor service climates may be the strongest trigger for customer incivility.

Limitations

As with any research, this study has limitations. All of the data were collected using single-source, self-report methods, which raises the possibility that correlations may be inflated due to common method bias. We did not seek data from other sources for good reason: the private nature of our constructs (e.g., internal mental health symptoms; rude conduct often lacks a witness) made the use of self-report necessary (Chan, 2009). Moreover, the sensitive nature of this study (e.g., asking employees to report supervisors' morally questionable behavior) required assurances of total anonymity; it was therefore not possible to track individual respondents and link their data to information from other sources. That said, as discussed in the "Method" section, we built four features into the study design to minimize common method bias and conducted an *ex post* statistical analysis that contests meaningful influence of common method variance.

Our cross-sectional survey data cannot support causal conclusions about customer incivility "leading to" employee outcomes. An alternative possibility is that employees' negative work-related and psychological conditions caused them to behave in ways that elicited uncivil treatment from customers (Pugh, 2001). For example, an employee with low job satisfaction and commitment may provide customers with inadequate and unfriendly service, triggering customer discourtesy, which may then aggravate the employee's dissatisfaction and distress. To minimize this concern, we rooted our model development in social and organizational theory, but different temporal and causal possibilities should be tested in future research.

The findings reported here are based on employee experiences in two segments (delivery and retail) of the service industry. The pervasiveness of customer incivility may differ between professions providing different services (e.g., optional vs. essential products). Rates might also vary across nations, cultures, or urban versus rural locations. That said, we expect that customer incivility would be common in many service environments due to the well-documented, frequent occurrence of insider incivility across disparate contexts, as well as the emerging documentation of customer incivility's prevalence in diverse organizations such as banking (Sliter et al., 2010, 2011) and call centers (van Jaarsveld et al., 2010). Moreover, we would not expect relations between incivility experiences and outcomes to vary substantially by setting.

CONCLUSION

Given the dramatic growth of the customer-service industry, customer incivility is an escalating social problem. Over half of the service employees we surveyed had been exposed to condescension, derogation, or other uncivil customer conduct in the previous year. These everyday slights and indignities may seem trivial, but we found connections between customer incivility and numerous facets of worker well-being, including nonwork-related psychological health. This last finding speaks to the counterintuitive nature of workplace incivility: even when it is subtle, ambiguous, transitory, and stemming from strangers, it still threatens employee health and happiness. In short, it behooves organizations to consider the costs of customers behaving badly and to intervene to protect worker dignity.

APPENDIX

Complete items for the Customer Incivility Measure (WIS-Customer), adapted from the Workplace Incivility Scale (WIS; Cortina et al., 2001)
During the last year while employed by [your organization], have you been in a situation where your customers did the following:

1. Put you down or were condescending to you?
2. Paid little attention to your statements or showed little interest in your opinion?
3. Made demeaning or derogatory remarks about you?
4. Addressed you in unprofessional terms, either publicly or privately?

5. Doubted your judgment on a matter over which you have responsibility?

Note. Response options for each item were 1 = *never*, 2 = *once or twice*, 3 = *sometimes*, 4 = *often*, 5 = *most of the time.*

REFERENCES

Anderson, J. C., & Gerbing, D. W. (1988). Structural equation modeling in practice: A review and recommended two-step approach. *Psychological Bulletin, 103,* 411–423.

Andersson, L. M., & Pearson, C. M. (1999). Tit for tat? The spiraling effect of incivility in the workplace. *Academy of Management Review, 24,* 452–471.

Ashford, S., Lee, C., & Bobko, P. (1989). Content, causes, and consequences of job insecurity: A theory-based measure and substantive test. *Academy of Management Journal, 32,* 803–829.

Bickerton, G., & Warskett, R. (2005). Contractors or disguised employees? A case study of couriers in Winnipeg. *Just Labour, 6–7,* 23–30.

Biron, M., & van Veldhoven, M. (2012). Emotional labour in service work: Psychological flexibility and emotion regulation. *Human Relations, 65,* 1259–1282.

Bollen, K. A. (1989). *Structural equations with latent variables.* New York, NY: Wiley.

Boulding, W., Kalra, A., Staelin, R., & Zeithaml, V. A. (1993). A dynamic process model of service quality. *Journal of Marketing Research, 30,* 7–27.

Boulet, J., & Boss, M. W. (1991). Reliability and validity of the Brief Symptom Inventory. *Psychological Assessment, 3,* 433–437.

Cammann, C., Fichman, M., Jenkins, D., & Klesh, J. R. (1983). The Michigan Organizational Assessment Questionnaire. In S. E. Seashore (Ed.), *Assessing organizational change: A guide to methods, measures, and practices* (pp. 71–138). New York, NY: Wiley.

Caza, B. B., & Cortina, L. M. (2007). From insult to injury: Explaining the impact of incivility. *Basic and Applied Social Psychology, 29*(4), 335–350.

Chan, D. (2009). So why ask me? Are self-report data really that bad? In C. E. Lance & R. J. Vandenberg (Eds.), *Statistical and methodological myths and urban legends: Doctrine, verity and fable in the organizational and social sciences* (pp. 309–336). New York, NY: Routledge/Taylor & Francis Group.

Conway, J. M., & Lance, C. E. (2010). What reviewers should expect from authors regarding common method bias in organizational research. *Journal of Business and Psychology, 25,* 325–334.

Cook, J., & Wall, T. (1980). New work attitude measures of trust, organizational commitment, and personal need non-fulfillment. *Journal of Occupational Psychology, 53,* 39–52.

Cortina, L. M. (2008). Unseen injustice: Incivility as modern discrimination in organizations. *Academy of Management Review, 33*(1), 55–75.

Cortina, L. M., Magley, V. J., Williams, J. H., & Langhout, R. D. (2001). Incivility in the workplace: Incidence and impact. *Journal of Occupational Health Psychology, 6*(1), 64–80.

DeLongis, A., Folkman, S., & Lazarus, R. S. (1988). The impact of daily stress on health and mood: Psychological and social resources as mediators. *Journal of Personality and Social Psychology, 54*(3), 486–495.

Demerouti, E., Bakker, A. B., Nachreiner, F., & Schaufeli, W. B. (2001). The job demands-resources model of burnout. *Journal of Applied Psychology, 86*(3), 499–512.

Derogatis, L. R., & Spencer, P. M. (1983). *The Brief Symptom Inventory: Administration, scoring, and procedure manual—I.* Baltimore, MD: Clinical Psychometric Research.

Dillman, D. A. (2000). *Mail and internet surveys, the tailored design method* (2nd ed.). New York, NY: Wiley.

Dollard, M. F., Dormann, C., Boyd, C. M., Winefield, A. H., & Winefield, H. R. (2003). Unique aspects of stress in human service work. *Australian Psychology, 38*, 84–91.

Dormann, C., & Zapf, D. (2004). Customer-related social stressors and burnout. *Journal of Occupational Health Psychology, 9*(1), 61–82.

Erickson, R. J., & Wharton, W. V. (1997). Inauthenticity and depression: Assessing the consequences of interactive service work. *Work and Occupations, 24*, 188–213.

Fischer, E., Gainer, B., & Bristor, J. (1997). The sex of the service provider: Does it influence perceptions of service quality? *Journal of Retailing, 73*(3), 361–381.

Fisk, G. M., & Neville, L. B. (2011). Effects of customer entitlement on service workers' physical and psychological well-being: A study of waitstaff employees. *Journal of Occupational Health Psychology, 16*(4), 391–405.

Grandey, A. A. (2003). When "the show must go on": Surface acting and deep acting as determinants of emotional exhaustion and peer-rated service delivery. *Academy of Management Journal, 46*(1), 86–96.

Grandey, A. A., Dickter, D. N., & Sin, H.-P. (2004). The customer is *not* always right: Customer aggression and emotion regulation of service employees. *Journal of Organizational Behavior, 25*, 1–22.

Grandey, A. A., Fisk, G. M., Mattila, A. S., Jansen, K. J., & Sideman, L. A. (2005). Is "service with a smile" enough? Authenticity of positive displays during service encounters. *Organizational Behavior and Human Decision Processes, 96*, 38–55.

Grandey, A. A., Fisk, G. M., & Steiner, D. D. (2005). Must "service with a smile" be stressful? The moderating role of personal control for American and French employees. *Journal of Applied Psychology, 90*(5), 893–904.

Grandey, A. A., Kern, J. H., & Frone, M. R. (2007). Verbal abuse from outsiders versus insiders: Comparing frequency, impact on emotional exhaustion, and the role of emotional labor. *Journal of Occupational Health Psychology, 12*(1), 63–79.

Griffeth, R. W., Hom, P. W., & Gaertner, S. (2000). A meta-analysis of antecedents and correlates of employee turnover: Update, moderator tests, and research implications for the next millennium. *Journal of Management, 26*, 463–488.

Harris, L. C., & Reynolds, K. L. (2003). The consequences of dysfunctional customer behavior. *Journal of Service Research, 6*(2), 144–161.

Hirschfeld, R. M. A., Montgomery, S. A., Keller, M. B., Kasper, S., Schatzberg, A. F., Möller, H. J., . . . Bourgeois, M. (2000). Social functioning in depression: A review. *Journal of Clinical Psychiatry, 61*(4), 268–275.

Holmbeck, G. N. (1997). Toward terminological, conceptual, and statistical clarity in the study of mediators and moderators: Examples from the child-clinical and pediatric psychology literatures. *Journal of Consulting and Clinical Psychology, 65,* 599–610.

Hu, L. T., & Bentler, P. M. (1995). Evaluation model fit. In R. H. Hoyle (Ed.), *Structural equation modeling: Concepts, issues, and applications* (pp. 76–99). Thousand Oaks, CA: Sage.

Karasek, R. A., & Theorell, T. (1990). *Health work: Stress, productivity and the reconstruction of the working life.* New York, NY: Basic Books.

Kern, J. H., & Grandey, A. A. (2009). Customer incivility as a social stressor: The role of race and racial identity for service employees. *Journal of Occupational Health Psychology, 14*(1), 46–57.

Kessler, R. C., & Frank, R. G. (1997). The impact of psychiatric disorders on work loss days. *Psychological Medicine, 27,* 861–873.

Kessler, R. C., Merikangas, K. R., & Wang, P. S. (2008). The prevalence and correlates of workplace depression in the National Comorbidity Survey Replication. *Journal of Occupational and Environmental Medicine, 50*(4), 381–390.

Kristensen, T. S., Borritz, M., Villadsen, E., & Christensen, K. B. (2005). The Copenhagen Burnout Inventory: A new tool for the assessment of burnout. *Work & Stress, 19*(3), 192–207.

LeBlanc, M. M., & Kelloway, E. K. (2002). Predictors and outcomes of workplace violence and aggression. *Journal of Applied Psychology, 87*(3), 444–453.

Lee, D., & Wolpin, K. I. (2006). Intersectoral labor mobility and the growth of the service sector. *Econometrica, 74,* 1–46.

Lee, R. T., & Ashforth, B. E. (1996). A meta-analytic examination of the correlates of the three dimensions of burnout. *Journal of Applied Psychology, 81,* 123–133.

Lim, S., Cortina, L. M., & Magley, V. J. (2008). Personal and workgroup incivility: Impact on work and health outcomes. *Journal of Applied Psychology, 9*(1), 95–107.

MacCallum, R. C. (1995). Model specification: Procedures, strategies, and related issues. In R. H. Hoyle (Ed.), *Structural equation modeling: Concepts, issues, and applications* (pp. 16–36). Thousand Oaks, CA: Sage.

MacCallum, R. C., Wegener, D. T., Uchino, B. N., & Fabrigar, L.R. (1993). The problem of equivalent models in applications of covariance structure analysis. *Psychological Bulletin, 114,* 185–199.

McGonagle, K. A., & Kessler, R. C. (1990). Chronic stress, acute stress, and depressive symptoms. *American Journal of Community Psychology, 18,* 681–706.

Mills, M. K., & Bonoma, T. V. (1979). Deviant consumer behavior: A different view. *Advances in Consumer Research, 6,* 347–352.

Miner-Rubino, K., & Cortina, L. M. (2007). Beyond targets: Consequences of vicarious exposure to misogyny at work. *Journal of Applied Psychology, 92*(5), 1254–1269.

Pearson, C. M., Andersson, L. M., & Porath, C. L. (2000). Assessing and attacking workplace incivility. *Organizational Dynamics, 29*(2), 123–137.

Penny, L. M., & Spector, P. E. (2005). Job stress, incivility, and counterproductive work behavior (CWB): the moderating role of negative affectivity. *Journal of Organizational Behavior, 26,* 777–796.

Podsakoff, P. M., MacKenzie, S. B., Lee, J. Y., & Podsakoff, N. P. (2003). Common method biases in behavioral research: A critical review of the literature and recommended remedies. *Journal of Applied Psychology, 88,* 879–903.

Porath, C. L., Overbeck, J. R., & Pearson, C. M. (2008). Picking up the gauntlet: How individuals respond to status challenges. *Journal of Applied Social Psychology, 38,* 1945–1980.

Porath, C. L., & Pearson, C. M (2012). Emotional and behavioral responses to workplace incivility and the impact of hierarchical status. *Journal of Applied Social Psychology, 42*(S1), E326–E357.

Porter, L. W., Crampon, W. J., & Smith, F. J. (1976). Organizational commitment and managerial turnover: A longitudinal study. *Organizational Behavior and Human Performance, 15*(1), 87–98.

Pugh, S. D. (2001). Service with a smile: Emotional contagion in the service encounter. *Academy of Management Journal, 44*(5), 1018–1027.

Rupp, D. E., McCance, A. S., Spencer, S., & Sonntag, K. (2008). Customer (in)justice and emotional labor: The role of perspective taking, anger, and emotional regulation. *Journal of Management, 34*(5), 903–924.

Rupp, D. E., & Spencer, S. (2006). When customers lash out: The effects of perceived customer interactional injustice on emotional labor and the mediating role of discrete emotions. *Journal of Applied Psychology, 91,* 971–978.

Schaubroeck, J., & Jones, J. R. (2000). Antecedents of workplace emotional labor dimensions and moderators of their effects on physical symptoms. *Journal of Organizational Behavior, 21,* 163–183.

Schneider, B., Ehrhart, M. G., Mayer, D. M., Saltz, J. L., & Niles-Jolly, K. (2005). Understanding organization-customer links in service settings. *Academy of Management Journal, 48*(6), 1017–1032.

Schneider, B., White, S. S., & Paul, M. C. (1998). Linking service climate and customer perceptions of service quality: Test of a causal model. *Journal of Applied Psychology, 83,* 150–163.

Simon, G. E. (2003). Social and economic burden of mood disorders. *Biological Psychiatry, 54,* 208–215.

Sliter, M. T., Jex, S. M., Wolford, K., & McInnerney, J. (2010). How rude! Emotional labor as a mediator between customer incivility and employee outcomes. *Journal of Occupational Health Psychology, 15*(4), 468–481.

Sliter, M. T., Pui, S-Y., Sliter, K. A., & Jex, S. M. (2011). The differential effects of interpersonal conflict from customers and coworkers: Trait anger as a moderator. *Journal of Occupational Health Psychology, 16*(4), 424–440.

Spencer, S., & Rupp, D. E. (2009). Angry, guilty, and conflicted: Injustice toward coworkers heightens emotional labor through cognitive and emotional mechanisms. *Journal of Applied Psychology, 94*(2), 429–444.

Stewart, W. F., Ricci, J. A., Chee, E., Hahn, S. R., & Morganstein, D. (2003). Cost of lost productive work time among US workers with depression. *Journal of the American Medical Association, 289*(23), 3135–3144.

van Jaarsveld, D. D., Walker, D. D., & Skarlicki, D. P. (2010). The role of job demands and emotional exhaustion in the relationship between customer and employee incivility. *Journal of Management, 36*(6), 1486–1504.

Wang, M., Liao, H., Zhan, Y., & Shi, J. (2011). Daily customer mistreatment and employee sabotage against customers: Examining emotion and resource perspectives. *Academy of Management Journal, 54*(2), 312–334.

Williams, L. J., & Hazer, J. T. (1986). Antecedents and consequences of satisfaction and commitment in turnover models: A reanalysis using latent variable structural equation modeling. *Journal of Applied Psychology, 71*, 219–231.

Part III

Bullying and Organizational Change

Chapter 8

Individual, Interpersonal, and Organizational Outcomes of Workplace Bullying

Ashley A. Membere, Afra S. Ahmad,
Amanda J. Anderson, Alex P. Lindsey, Isaac E. Sabat,
and Eden B. King

Workplace bullying is a pervasive issue within the American workforce. Over 35% of employees report experiencing some form of bullying within their working lives, from subtle insults to explicit forms of harassment (Lutgen-Sandvik, Tracey, & Alberts, 2007). These different forms of bullying all negatively impact the workplace as a whole. Bullying has been shown to lead to negative effects for individual targets, work teams, and organizations as a whole. Importantly, individuals with stigmatizing characteristics are much more likely to be the targets of bullying, and therefore they are more likely to experience these and other negative outcomes. Given these troubling findings, more work is needed that examines effective strategies to prevent the bullying faced by stigmatized and nonstigmatized targets. This chapter will describe the full set of outcomes caused by workplace bullying, justifying the need for more research and advocacy in combating these harmful workplace behaviors.

There has been a lack of attention on workplace bullying in scholarly literature. Much of the work on bullying focuses on school bullying with child populations (Rayner & Hoel, 1997). The literature that does examine adult bullying in the workplace is largely fragmented, with several related concepts being used to describe highly similar phenomena. Some terms that have emerged describe general forms of workplace abuse (e.g., workplace harassment, workplace mistreatment, incivility, and mobbing), whereas other terms describe more specific forms directed at certain populations (e.g., discrimination, ethnic harassment, sexual harassment, selective incivility, and interpersonal discrimination) (for a review, see Lutgen-Sandvik et al., 2007). Within the workplace, these general and specific forms of abuse often occur in tandem (Lutgen-Sandvik et al., 2007). This chapter will focus on both general and specific forms of workplace bullying.

Although it is inherently difficult to formally define what constitutes workplace bullying, a widely accepted definition is "harassing, offending, or socially excluding someone or negatively affecting someone's work task. In order for the label bullying to be applied to a particular activity, interaction, or process, it has to occur repeatedly and regularly (e.g., weekly) and over a period of time (e.g., about six months)" (Einarsen, Hoel, Zapf, & Cooper, 2010). Research has found that 35% to 50% of U.S. workers report being the targets of workplace bullying based on this strict definition. Additionally, nearly 30% of workers report experiencing two acts of workplace bullying per week (Lutgen-Sandvik et al., 2007). Importantly, individuals from minority racial (Lewis & Gunn, 2007), gender (Eriksen & Einarsen, 2004), religious (King & Ahmad, 2010), and sexual orientation (Hebl, Foster, Mannix, & Dovidio, 2002) groups are much more likely to be the targets of workplace bullying. These findings are especially troubling given the widely documented negative outcomes associated with these negative workplace behaviors. Indeed, workplace bullying negatively impacts individuals, teams, and entire organizations.

This chapter outlines the individual, interpersonal, and organizational outcomes of workplace bullying, with special focus on the ways in which stigmatized minorities are more likely to be subject to these negative outcomes. We conclude with potential strategies to curtail these bullying-related outcomes as well as a call for more research on this very important topic.

INDIVIDUAL AND INTERPERSONAL CONSEQUENCES OF BULLYING

Workplace bullying can have numerous outcomes in terms of an individual's health, affect, and behavior. For example, bullying can take its toll on an individual's work, such as lowering his or her performance and productivity. Decreases in psychological and physical health can also occur due to this phenomenon (Hansen et al., 2006; Moayed, Daraiseh, Shell, & Salem, 2006). Additionally, characteristics such as race or gender can not only affect an individual's chances of being bullied, but also the severity of experienced outcomes.

Psychological and Physical Outcomes

Workplace bullying can have a range of detrimental effects on the target's psychological health. Previous research has linked workplace bullying to outcomes such as increased depression and stress and decreased mental health (Samnani & Singh, 2012). For example, a study of full-time employees found that those who reported weekly bullying were also more likely to report experiencing more depressive symptoms compared to monthly victims and nonbullied individuals (Dehue, Bolman, Völlink, & Pouwelse, 2012). Aged care nurses also reported more depressive symptoms when they were made targets of bullying (Rodwell & Demir, 2012). Similar positive relations between workplace bullying and depression have been found in Australian, Chinese, and Japanese samples as well (Demir, Rodwell, & Flower, 2013; Giorgi, Ando, Arenas, Shoss, & Lewis, 2013; Jiang, Dong, & Wang, 2012). In addition to a decrease in their physical well-being, victims of workplace bullying have also reported a decrease in their mental health (Cooper, Hoel, & Faragher, 2004). A recent meta-analysis of cross-sectional and longitudinal studies found positive relations between bullying and mental health problems such as depression and anxiety and post-traumatic stress (Nielsen & Einarsen, 2012).

In addition to psychological outcomes, workplace bullying can have detrimental effects on the target's physical health. In a study of primary schoolteachers and administrators, targets of bullying also reported increased sleeplessness, headaches, and weight loss or gain (Fahie & Devine, 2014). Similar results have been found through interviews with bully/victims in other occupations such as nurses and police officers (Strandmark & Hallberg, 2007). Neilsen and Einarsen's (2012) meta-analysis also found a positive relation between physical health problems, strain, and somatization. In sum, these findings regarding physical and psychological outcomes suggest that workplace bullying has an adverse effect on targeted individuals outside the context of work. Additionally, it is possible that these effects on a target's physical and mental well-being could impact his or her behaviors at work and lead to negative consequences on the interpersonal and organizational levels, which will be explored in the following sections.

Work-Related Outcomes

In addition to impacting the target's affect and health, workplace bullying can have numerous work-related outcomes for the target. Mixed results exist for the effect workplace bullying has on a target's performance.

In a study of nursing graduate students, Vogelpohl, Rice, Edwards, and Bork (2013) found that students reported a decrease in their performance due to bullying. However, Neilsen and Einarsen's (2012) meta-analysis did not find any significant correlation between workplace bullying and targets' performance. Additional empirical research needs to be conducted to see if bullying leads to decreased performance and if the effects are longitudinal.

Workplace bullying has been linked to other work-related outcomes, however. A survey of U.S. workers found that bullying was negatively correlated with job satisfaction and job rating and positively correlated with job stress (Lutgen-Sandvick et al., 2007). Similar negative correlations between workplace bullying and job satisfaction were found in a sample of Chinese employees (Jiang et al., 2012). Other studies have found a positive correlation between workplace bullying and the target's absenteeism and intent to leave (Djurkovic, McCormack, & Casimir, 2008; Neilsen & Einarsen, 2012). Workplace bullying has also been shown to be related to lower organizational commitment and other job-related outcomes (Neilsen & Einarsen, 2012). These results have many implications for the target in the long run. Bullied employees who feel greater degrees of job stress may see their performance suffer in the long term and receive poor evaluations from their supervisors. Additionally, due to lower job satisfaction as a result of bullying, they may be more likely to leave their current jobs for one free from bullying. These individual outcomes also have negative implications on the interpersonal and organizational levels, which will be examined in later sections.

Factors That Affect Bullying and Outcomes

Additionally, there are different factors that can influence the severity of the outcomes of workplace bullying. These factors involve the gender and race of targets that are more susceptible to workplace bullying.

Gender

Mixed findings have been reported about gender differences for workplace bullying. Some empirical evidence exists demonstrating that women are more likely to be targets of workplace bullying compared to men (Lewis & Gunn, 2007; Salin, 2003), while other studies have found no gender differences for targets (Einarsen & Skotgstad, 1996; Leymann, 1996; Vartia & Hyyti, 2002). However, gender differences have been found in terms of severity of outcomes, types of experienced bullying behavior, and relationships between targets and perpetrators. Women have been more likely to experience sexual harassment as a component of workplace bullying (Vartia & Hyyti, 2002) and experience more post-traumatic stress symptoms compared to men (Rodríguez-Muñoz, Moreno-Jiménez, Vergel, & Hernández, 2010). Additionally, women are more likely to be bullied by both men and women, while men are more likely to be bullied by other men (Hoel, Rayner, & Cooper, 1999; Yamada, Cappadocia, & Pepler, 2014). Although more research needs to be conducted regarding gender differences for outcomes of workplace bullying, these results suggest that these outcomes might be more severe for female targets.

Race

Race or ethnicity also has an effect in terms of targets of workplace bullying. Previous research has found that racial or ethnic minority individuals experience workplace bullying more often compared to whites. In a study investigating workplace bullying in the public sector by Wales, Lewis and Gunn (2007) found that ethnic minority workers were about four times as likely to report suffering from workplace bullying compared to whites. Additionally, ethnic minority individuals reported a broader range of mistreatment, such as unfair criticisms and public humiliation, compared to their white counterparts. In terms of a U.S. sample, Fox and Stallworth (2005) found that Latino employees reported being targets of bullying more often than whites; however, no significant differences were found for reports of bullying between African Americans, Asians, and whites. Organizations should take note of ethnic differences in experiences of workplace bullying, especially in light of the evidence that these experiences also relate to organizational-related outcomes such as turnover intentions. If similar correlations between experiences of workplace bullying and turnover intentions are found for ethnic minority populations, this could possibly lead to lower employee diversity within the organization.

Effects of Bullying on Observers

Bullying is inherently a dyadic experience between the target and perpetrator that takes place in a larger organizational context. Witnesses of bullying notice the negative treatment of others. Indeed, in a survey of 800 American employees, 10% of the respondents stated witnessing workplace incivility on a daily basis (Pearson & Porath, 2005). This experience is not limited to the United States, however. A sample of 126 Canadian white-collar workers found that 25% of the respondents reported witnessing incivility daily (Pearson & Porath, 2001). Examples of witnessing bullying can include a boss rebuking a subordinate in the presence of several colleagues for wasting paperclips (Pearson & Porath, 2005) or making a rude remark directed at a target in the presence of others. Witnesses to bullying behaviors can experience similar detrimental outcomes as those experienced by the victims themselves. Empirical evidence has found that witnessing bullying influences one's performance, helping behaviors, physical and psychological health, as well as several organizational outcomes. These will be discussed in detail next.

Physical and Psychological Outcomes

Witnesses to bullying behaviors are impacted physically and psychologically themselves. In terms of physical outcomes, Hoel and Cooper (2000a) conducted a study and found that bullying related to several negative outcomes, including worse health and higher sickness absenteeism. Dupré, Dawe, and Barling (2014) found that observing workplace aggression directed at employees by customers influenced observers' psychological and physical well-being. Researchers conducted an online study on a variety of U.S. workers from different age groups and industries and found that nonbullied witnesses reported greater negativity and stress (Lutgen-Sandvik et al., 2007). A separate study found observers of bullying reported higher levels of stress compared to those who did not observe bullying (Vartia, 2001) and related to observers' reporting greater levels of worrying about the event (Pearson & Porath, 2005). Some research indicates that coworkers of victims of bullying live in fear of being targets and report higher stress levels and greater intentions to leave the workplace (Vartia, 2001). Additionally, Hornstein (1996) found negative effects of supervisory misbehavior on subordinates who were not the supervisor's direct target. Witnessing a coworker being mistreated by a superior can result in emotional trauma and create fear of being the next target. These physical and psychological stressors extend beyond the victim of bullying to witnesses as well.

Work-Related Outcomes for Observers of Bullying

Job Attitudes

Witnessing bullying also impacts many relevant organizational attitudes. Hoel and Cooper (2000b) found that witnesses to bullying also reported negative organizational outcomes, including higher turnover intentions, lower levels of productivity, as well as lower organizational satisfaction and commitment. In a separate study across a variety of industries, nonbullied witnesses reported lower job satisfaction and overall rating of their work experience (Lutgen-Sandvik et al., 2007). Rayner (1999) conducted a study with public-sector union members and found that approximately one in five reported that they considered leaving their workplace as a result of witnessing bullying. The researcher suggests the turnover intention is due to employees feeling a climate of fear in the organization where bullies had not been appropriately reprimanded (Vartia,

2001). Witnessing incivility has been found to relate to less satisfaction, motivation, and organizational commitment (Pearson & Porath, 2005). The organization needs to be aware of the importance of addressing bullying as it can create an unpleasant work environment. When the relationships among employees are negative and the management ignores the problem, then absenteeism increases and productivity decreases as workers fear the next incident (Gonthier, 2002).

In addition to employees, customers can also observe workplace bullying, which can have implications for the organization's bottom line. Porath, Macinnis, and Folkes (2010) found that when an employee mistreated or was uncivil toward another employee, customers who *witnessed* it tended to "make *negative generalizations* about others who work for the firm, the firm as a whole, and future encounters with the firm" (p. 292, emphasis in the original). These researchers found that these customers were negatively affected by being observers of incivility between employees, even beyond the incivility incident.

Performance

Witnessing bullying behavior can impede one's own cognitive functioning. Indeed, Porath and Erez (2007) found that when an experimenter made an indirect rude remark about the participant's alma mater, the participant performed worse on a routine and creative task. In their study, they found that disruption to cognitive processes fully mediated the relation between rudeness and performance. In a separate study, they found that rudeness from either an authority figure or a peer again reduced the observer's performance on routine and creative tasks, and negative affect mediated the relation between witnessing rudeness and performance (Porath & Erez, 2009). Lastly, Miron-Spektor, Efrat-Treister, Rafaeli, and Schwarz-Cohen (2011) conducted three studies and found that when participants listened to an angry customer, they were less successful in solving creative problems compared to listening to a neutral customer. Ultimately, the researchers found that displays of anger influenced observers' emotions, regulatory focus, and thinking process. Clearly, regardless of who is instigating the bullying behavior, whether it is an authority figure, peer, or customer, witnessing it can have detrimental outcomes on one's performance due to the emotions it may elicit and impairment of cognitive processes.

Helping Behaviors

Helping behaviors are impacted when individuals witness bullying. In two separate studies, Porath and Erez (2007, 2009) found that witnessing rudeness decreased helpfulness and citizenship behavior. In one study, witnesses were less helpful to a perpetrator who was being rude to someone else (not the participant) as well as less helpful to the experimenter who had no relation to the rude act (Porath & Erez, 2007). Citizenship behavior, defined as performing an extravoluntarily act to help the experimenter by participating in an short study, was reduced when participants witnessed rudeness from an authority figure or a peer (Porath & Erez, 2007). Not only are cognitive functioning and performance impacted by bullying, but the prosocial behaviors of witnesses are also influenced.

In sum, observers of bullying can be impacted on a variety of outcomes, including a reduction of their own performance, exhibiting less helpful behaviors, experiencing physical and psychological distress, and reporting negative workplace attitudes. This implies that other innocent bystanders feel the repercussions of bullying behaviors. These findings remind researchers that bullying is not just an interpersonal issue but also an organizational issue. It is important for researchers to study the interaction between bullies and targets, as well as the broader impacts of bullying. This can have important implications for the organization and how the organization deals with bullying behaviors.

ORGANIZATIONAL OUTCOMES OF BULLYING

In addition to the individual and interpersonal outcomes, bullying can also have negative outcomes that directly impact the organizations in which the bullying occurs. These consequences can emerge in the form of organizationally relevant individual outcomes (e.g., individual performance or attitudes) as well as organizational-level outcomes (e.g., firm performance) that represent the aggregation or accumulation of these effects. Such outcomes of bullying have been given less attention in the literature compared to the individual or interpersonal effects of bullying. However, research indicates that bullying can result in decreased firm performance, increased sickness absenteeism (Kivimaki, Elovainio, & Vathera, 2000), costly litigation (i.e., harassment-based lawsuits; Hoel, Einarsen, & Cooper, 2003; Martin & LaVan, 2010), decreased public opinion or reputation of the organization (Bassman, 1992), increased turnover (Djurkovic, McCormack, & Casimir, 2004), and decreased levels of employee commitment and satisfaction (Djurkovic et al., 2008). In the following section, we discuss each of the potential organizationally relevant outcomes of bullying.

Effects of Individual Outcomes on Organizations

Attitudes and Commitment

Bullied employees may perceive a discrepancy between their own values and the values tolerated in their organization. Such discrepancies can ultimately contribute to decrements in employees' job satisfaction and organizational commitment. This reasoning is also consistent with justice theory and research; perceptions of injustice are correlated with reduced satisfaction and commitment (King, Hebl, George, & Matusik, 2010). Indeed, bullying has been linked to worsened job attitudes. For example, cross-lagged analyses using panel designs with workers in Belgium found that experiences of bullying were related to reduced satisfaction six months later (Rodriguez-Munoz et al., 2010). A similar study in Latin America yielded parallel conclusions. Consensus across empirical and narrative reviews of the literature is that bullying negatively impacts job attitudes.

Turnover

The negative affective reactions to bullying can further manifest in individual withdrawal behaviors and organizational rates of employee turnover. Indeed, Hoel, Rayner, and Cooper (1999) book identifies turnover as one of the primary organizational outcomes of bullying. This conclusion is consistent with empirical findings that demonstrate a consistent relation between bullying and turnover. For example, a prospective study of health care workers showed higher rates of turnover among nurses working in units in which bullying was reported compared to nurses working in organizations with lower rates of bullying (Hoel et al., 1999). These effects were confirmed in a separate study that also suggested that organizational support can buffer the negative effects of bullying on turnover intentions (Djurkovic et al., 2004). These examples demonstrate that to the extent bullying occurs, organizations can expect higher turnover.

Absenteeism

The individual outcomes described above can have important consequences for the organizations. In particular, the negative effect of bullying on wellness and well-being can translate into a positive relation between bullying and sickness absenteeism. For example, a study using hospital staff records indicated that the sickness-related absences were 26% higher (controlling for individuals' sick leave during the previous year) among those who had been bullied compared to those who had not been bullied (Kivimaki et al., 2000). Hoel and Cooper (2000a) also found that victims of bullying took an average of seven more days of sick leave per year than those who were not bullied. Other studies show that bullying victims take extended sick leave, with almost a third (29%) being absent for 30 or more days and 13% being absent for 60 or more days (UNISON, 2000). There are significant organizational and financial costs to the organization when employees use sick leave (e.g., reallocating staff to complete the work of the absent employee, paying for time off). Future research should consider the reasons for which victims utilize sick leave (i.e., increased incidence of physical health problems or voluntary self-exclusion from the bullying environment) to determine which intervention methods may be most effective.

Broader Organizational-Level Outcomes

Performance

Some studies have linked bullying to decreased productivity at the individual and organizational levels (Hoel, Cooper, & Faragher, 2001; Hoel et al., 2003). Productivity may be impacted at the individual level by increasing anxiety regarding persistent experiences of bullying, which can diminish the cognitive resources necessary to perform job tasks (Hoel et al., 2001). Indeed, victims of bullying report lower efficiency, decreased effort, and lower product quality (McCarthy & Barker, 2000; McCarthy, Sheehan, & Kearns, 1995).

Bystanders of bullying may also experience increased anxiety about becoming victims themselves in the future (Vartia, 2001), which could also potentially impact their performance. Some scholars suggest that bullying may have a cascade effect in which bullying among senior managers may be taken out as aggression on their subordinates and so on (Tepper, Duffy, Henle, & Lambert, 2006). Following this logic, bullying at the highest levels may have the greatest impact on overall organizational productivity. In sum, bullying has negative implications for the performance of victims, bystanders, and the organization as a whole.

Legal and Financial

Although there are currently no laws in the United States to specifically prohibit workplace bullying, cases of workplace bullying are often found to be illegal under Title VII of the Civil Rights Act when they are based on gender, race, disability, or any other protected class (Martin & LaVan, 2010). Some other countries have enacted legislation specifically against bullying. For example, following an inquiry into workplace bullying, Australia enacted legislation in 2014 to make bullying conduct illegal in the workplace (as an extension of the Fair Work Act of 2009). The inquiry that drove the legislation was conducted by an Australian parliamentary committee and indicated that bullying results in up to $36 billion in costs to the Australian government and costs employers $17,000 to $24,000 per case (Australian Parliament, 2012). The cost was estimated by taking into account that victims take an average of seven additional sick days per year, are less efficient at work, and are more likely to have lower morale in addition to the associated litigation costs. In a similar analysis, Leymann (1990) estimated that a single case of bullying can cost an organization between \$30,000 and \$100,000, while a more recent estimate (Hoel et al., 2003) indicated that a single case could cost an organization approximately \$50,000 (including absenteeism, turnover, and formal investigation but excluding litigation fees). Clearly, the costs accrued from legal and other outcomes of bullying can result in a sizable financial burden to organizations.

Public Opinion

Bullying or harassment-related legal cases can often receive a great deal of public attention, which can result in the decreased reputation of the company (Bassman, 1992). A decline in organizational reputation can impact applicant perceptions and reduce the quality and quantity of applicants applying to work at the organization (Lutgen-Sandvik & McDermott, 2008). Further, negative public perceptions from publicized bullying or harassment lawsuits could impact revenue and stock prices (Goldman, Gutek, Stein, & Lewis, 2006).

REMEDIATION STRATEGIES

This section will discuss several remediation strategies that could be used to reduce the prevalence or negative effects of bullying in the workplace. This discussion will be organized around strategies that may be effective at an interpersonal level of analysis before shifting the discussion to strategies that may be effective at the organizational level of analysis. Specifically, confrontation behaviors will be discussed as a potentially effective strategy at the interpersonal level, and implementing antibullying policies as a strategy that may be effective at the organizational level. Finally, we will discuss training initiatives that could be effective in mitigating the negative effects of bullying at both levels of analysis.

Interpersonal Strategies

At the interpersonal level, confrontation behaviors may be particularly effective at reducing the prevalence and negative effects of bullying in the workplace. Work on confrontation behaviors has largely focused on prejudice confrontation, which can be defined as "verbally or nonverbally expressing one's dissatisfaction with prejudicial and discriminatory treatment to the person who is responsible for the remark or behavior" (Shelton, Richeson, & Vorauer, 2006, p. 67). We would argue that this definition could easily be extended to all instances of bullying to the degree that individuals are speaking up against uncivil treatment more generally.

We wish to note that this strategy does not necessarily involve heated en-counters. Instead, confrontation could be as simple as ignoring an inap-propriate joke or asking a perpetrator to refrain from making disparaging remarks about a given stigmatized group in the future. Importantly, con-frontation has been shown to be effective in terms of reducing subsequent expressions of prejudice when used by targets of prejudice as well as their allies (Czopp, Monteith, & Mark, 2006). Thus, to the degree that these findings extend to the study of bullying, this strategy could be useful for bystanders and targets of bullying in terms of reducing the prevalence and negative outcomes associated with bullying in the workplace.

Confrontation is particularly interesting in that it may be even more effective when coming from allies than when it is enacted by target group members. Although published empirical work has yet to support this no-tion, attribution theory indicates that it may in fact be true. When confron-tation is enacted by targets of discrimination or bullying, people may label that individual as a whiner or complainer who is only confronting be-cause he or she possesses the stigma in question or was the direct target of the bullying behavior. On the other hand, when confrontation is enacted by allies, no such external attribution can be made. Thus, individuals may be more likely to take confrontation behavior from nonstigmatized, non-bullied allies more seriously due to these attributional processes.

It should come as no surprise that both targets and allies report that they do not actually engage in confrontation behaviors as often as they think they should. This is particularly true when they do not believe their confrontation will be effective or when social costs for confronting are per-ceived (Good, Moss-Racusin, & Sanchez, 2012), which may be fairly likely in a workplace context. This lack of confrontation is both problematic and alarming, given that discrimination has negative psychological conse-quences for targets and allies alike, especially when it is not addressed. Indeed, research has demonstrated that bystanders experience emotional discomfort when witnessing discrimination without acting out against it (Schmader, Croft, Scarnier, Lickel, & Mendes, 2012). Thus, a critical emer-gent question arises: How can we encourage allies and targets to confront the discrimination and bullying they witness in the workplace?

Drawing from theory and empirical findings related to bystander inter-vention, the Confronting Prejudiced Responses model states that there are several barriers that might prevent individuals from confronting inappro-priate treatment (Schmader et al., 2012). In order to overcome these barri-ers, the authors make several recommendations, which we have adapted for our purposes: (a) increase the detection of discrimination or bullying via education, (b) help people understand that discrimination or bullying is an emergency that needs to be dealt with right away, (c) increase ac-countability and perceptions of responsibility for confronting inappropri-ate behaviors, and (d) teach people how to confront by modeling appropriate behaviors and allowing them to practice (Ashburn-Nardo et al., 2008). Behavior modeling training may be particularly important in accomplishing the last recommendation, as such training has been shown to produce an effective transfer of training via practice (Taylor, Russ-Eft, & Chan, 2005). Such training could be incorporated into diversity training initiatives, which are discussed in the next section. If these recommendations are enacted and the obstacles to confrontation are overcome, it could lead to a naturally self-regulating workplace where targets and allies create a culture in which bullying and discrimination are not tolerated.

Organizational Strategies

Although strategies that can be used by targets and allies are appealing and empowering, organizations have the opportunity, and arguably the responsibility, to develop strategies that proactively curtail discrimination and bullying toward targeted populations. Such efforts should begin at the macro organizational level with policies and practices that are explicitly developed to protect marginalized populations. Accordingly, we discuss the development and implementation of antibullying policies as a critical strategy that could help organizations do their part in improving the workplace experiences for all employees.

One strategy that can be implemented to promote the inclusion of targets of bullying and incivility is the provision of benefits and "perks" that are of particular interest to a given stigmatized or targeted group. For example, in addition to zero tolerance policies regarding harassment, having a day care center at the workplace or flexible work schedules may be of particular importance for working mothers who often function as primary caregivers in addition to full-time employees. Providing such benefits sends a clear message from the organization that these employees are valued and not to be treated poorly. When providing these benefits, it is important to promote the notion that all individuals—not just those from marginalized groups—can take advantage of the benefits. Framing policies in this way can not only reduce resentment from other employees in the workplace, but could also reduce feelings of guilt on the part of the marginalized group members for utilizing these benefits to their advantage (Heilman & Haynes, 2006).

Perhaps the most commonly implemented policy related to diversity is requiring employees to participate in diversity training. Despite the finding that 33% of managers report using diversity training in their companies, recent reviews suggest that diversity training may not be effective (Bezrukova, Jehn, & Spell, 2012) and often does not measure the most appropriate outcomes. Indeed, this latter review concluded that although diversity training may have a beneficial effect on attitudes, there is simply not enough quality research addressing whether such exercises can have beneficial effects on skill acquisition and behavior change, which should be of most interest to organizational scholars. Although these reviews also include exemplars of effective diversity training programs, more work needs to be done before general recommendations can be advanced for what makes diversity training programs effective. Importantly, recent work has shown some promise for specific training exercises such as perspective taking and goal setting in terms of improving diversity-related attitudes and behaviors in the workplace (Madera, Neal, & Dawson, 2011).

Importantly, recent work suggests that implementing such policies is more beneficial in improving the experiences of minorities to the extent that there are structures of accountability in place (Madera et al., 2011). Structures of accountability could include a specific position or office that is directly accountable for equality (e.g., a chief diversity officer) within an organization. In a longitudinal meta-analysis, results demonstrated that companies with such structures in place showed significant growth in terms of the number of minorities in managerial roles, which is theoretically indicative of better treatment in the workplace. This study also demonstrated that although minorities may benefit in less formal ways from mentoring programs and diversity training activities, these kinds of programs did not ultimately correlate with the increased diversity in managerial roles. Thus, policies and programs such as diversity training and providing benefits may only be successful in curbing discrimination and bullying toward marginalized groups to the extent that formal structures of accountability are in place to support their availability and enforcement.

CONCLUSION

Although research regarding workplace bullying has increased in recent years, additional research needs to be conducted in order to gain a full understanding of the consequences of the phenomenon. This chapter demonstrates that workplace bullying causes harm not only to its targets, but also to observers and the organization as a whole. In order to reduce the effects of workplace bullying, scholars need to continue to investigate how these outcomes differ in frequency and severity for different groups such as women and ethnic minorities. Such focused attention will enable the development of more effective strategies and policies to minimize the harm caused by workplace bullying.

REFERENCES

Australian Parliament. (2012). Fair Work Act. House of Representatives Committee bullying report. Retrieved from http://www.aph.gov.au/parliamentary _business/committees/house_of_representatives_committees?url=ee/bull ying/report.htm.

Bassman, E. (1992). *Abuse in the workplace.* Westport, CT: Quorum Books.

Bezrukova, K., Jehn, K., & Spell, C. (2012). Reviewing diversity training: Where we have been and where we should go. *Academy of Management Learning & Education, 1*(2), 207–227/

Cooper, C. L., Hoel, H., & Faragher, B. (2004). Bullying is detrimental to health, but all bullying behaviours are not necessarily equally damaging. *British Journal of Guidance & Counselling, 32*(3), 367–387.

Czopp, A., Monteith, M., & Mark, A. (2006). Standing up for a change: Reducing bias through interpersonal confrontation. *Journal of Personality and Social Psychology, 90,* 784–803.

Dehue, F., Bolman, C., Völlink, T., & Pouwelse, M. (2012). Coping with bullying at work and health related problems. *International Journal of Stress Management, 19*(3), 175–197.

Demir, D., Rodwell, J., & Flower, R. (2013). Workplace bullying among allied health professionals: Prevalence, causes and consequences. *Asia Pacific Journal of Human Resources, 51*(4), 392–405.

Djurokovic, N., McCormack, D., & Casimir, G. (2004). The physical and psychological effects of workplace bullying and their relationship to intention to leave: A test of the psychosomatic and disability hypothesis. *International Journal of Organizational Theory and Behavior, 7,* 469–497.

Djurkovic, N., McCormack, D., & Casimir, G. (2008). Workplace bullying and intention to leave: The moderating effect of perceived organisational support. *Human Resource Management Journal, 18,* 405–422.

Dupré, K. E., Dawe, K. A., & Barling, J. (2014). Harm to those who serve: Effects of direct and vicarious customer-initiated workplace aggression. *Journal of Interpersonal Violence, 29,* 2355–2377.

Einarsen, S., Hoel, H., Zapf, D., & Cooper, C. (Eds.). (2010). *Bullying and harassment in the workplace: Developments in theory, research, and practice.* Boca Raton, FL: CRC Press.

Einarsen, S., & Skogstad, A. (1996). Bullying at work: Epidemiological findings in public and private organizations. *European Journal of Work and Organizational Psychology, 5*(2), 185–201.

Eriksen, W., & Einarsen, S. (2004). Gender minority as a risk factor of exposure to bullying at work: The case of male assistant nurses. *European Journal of Work and Organizational Psychology, 13*(4), 473–492.

Fahie, D., & Devine, D. (2014). The impact of workplace bullying on primary school teachers and principals. *Scandinavian Journal of Educational Research, 58*(2), 235–252.

Fox, S., & Stallworth, L. E. (2005). Racial/ethnic bullying: Exploring links between bullying and racism in the US workplace. *Journal of Vocational Behavior, 66*(3), 438–456.

Giorgi, G., Ando, M., Arenas, A., Shoss, M. K., & Leon-Perez, J. M. (2013). Exploring personal and organizational determinants of workplace bullying and its prevalence in a Japanese sample. *Psychology of Violence, 3*(2), 185–197.

Goldman, B. M., Gutek, B. A., Stein, J. H., & Lewis, K. (2006). Employment discrimination in organizations: Antecedents and consequences. *Journal of Management, 32,* 786–830.

Gonthier, G. (2002). *Rude awakenings: Overcoming the civility crisis in the workplace.* Chicago, IL: Dearborn Trade.

Good, J. J., Moss-Racusin, C. A., & Sanchez, D. T. (2012). Why confront? Motivation for confronting prejudice on behalf of the self and others. *Psychology of Women Quarterly, 36,* 210–226.

Hansen, Å. M., Hogh, A., Persson, R., Karlson, B., Garde, A. H., & Ørbæk, P. (2006). Bullying at work, health outcomes, and physiological stress response. *Journal of Psychosomatic Research, 60*(1), 63–72.

Hebl, M. R., Foster, J. B., Mannix, L. M., & Dovidio, J. F. (2002). Formal and interpersonal discrimination: A field study of bias toward homosexual applicants. *Personality and Social Psychology Bulletin, 28,* 815–825.

Heilman, M. E., & Haynes, M. C. (2006). Affirmative action: Unintended adverse effects. In M. F. Karsten (Ed.), *Gender, race, and ethnicity in the workplace* (Vol. 2, pp. 1–24). Westport, CT: Greenwood.

Hoel, H., & Cooper, C.L. (2000a). *Destructive conflict and bullying at work.* Unpublished report, University of Manchester Institute of Science and Technology.

Hoel, H., & Cooper, C. L. (2000b). Working with victims of workplace bullying. In H. Kemsell & J. Pritchard (Eds.), *Good practice in working with victims of violence* (pp. 101–118). Philadelphia, PA: Jessica Kingsley Publishers.

Hoel, H., Cooper, C. L., & Faragher, B. (2001). The experience of bullying in Great Britain: The impact of organizational status. *European Journal of Work and Organizational Psychology, 10,* 443–465.

Hoel, H., Einarsen, S., & Cooper, C. L. (2003). Organizational effects of bullying. In S. Einarsen, H. Hoel, D. Zapf, & C. L. Cooper (Eds.), *Bullying and emotional abuse in the workplace: International perspectives in research and practice* (pp. 145–161). London: Taylor & Francis.

Hoel, H., Rayner, C., & Cooper, C. L. (1999). Workplace bullying. In C. L. Cooper & I. T. Robertson (Eds.), *International review of industrial and organizational psychology 1999* (Vol. 14, pp. 195–230). New York, NY: Wiley.

Hornstein, H. A. (1996). *Brutal bosses and their prey.* New York, NY: Riverhead.

Jiang, J., Dong, J., & Wang, R. (2012). Workplace bullying, employees' depression and job satisfaction: Moderating effect of coping strategies. *Chinese Mental Health Journal, 26*(8), 610–615.

King, E. B., & Ahmad, A. S. (2010). An experimental field study of interpersonal discrimination toward Muslim job applicants. *Personnel Psychology, 63,* 881–906.

Kivimaki, K., Elovainio, M., & Vathera, J. (2000). Workplace bullying and sickness absence of hospital staff. *Occupational and Environmental Medicine, 57,* 656–660.

Lewis, D., & Gunn, R. (2007). Workplace bullying in the public sector: Understanding the racial dimension. *Public Administration, 85*(3), 641–665.

Leymann, H. (1990). Mobbing and psychological terror at workplaces. *Violence and Victims, 5,* 119–126.

Leymann, H. (1996). The content and development of mobbing at work. *European Journal of Work and Organizational Psychology, 5*(2), 165–184.

Lutgen-Sandvik, P., & McDermott, V. (2008). The constitution of employee-abusive organizations: A communication flows theory. *Communication Theory, 18*(2), 304–333.

Lutgen-Sandvik, P., Tracy, S. J., & Alberts, J. K. (2007). Burned by bullying in the American workplace: Prevalence, perception, degree and impact. *Journal of Management Studies, 44*(6), 837–862.

Madera, J., Neal, J., & Dawson, M. (2011). A strategy for diversity training. *Journal of Hospitality and Tourism Research, 35,* 469–487.

Martin, W., & LaVan, H. (2010). Workplace bullying: A review of litigated cases. *Employee Responsibilities and Rights Journal, 22,* 175–194.

McCarthy, P., & Barker, M. (2000). Workplace bullying risk audit. *Journal of Occupational Health and Safety Australia and New Zealand, 16,* 409–418.

McCarthy, P., Sheehan, M., & Kearns, D. (1995). *Managerial styles and their effects on employees health and well-being in organisations undergoing restructuring.* Report for Worksafe Australia, Griffith University, Brisbane.

Miron-Spektor, E., Efrat-Treister, D., Rafaeli, A., & Schwarz-Cohen, O. (2011). Others' anger makes people work harder not smarter: The effect of observing anger and sarcasm on creative and analytic thinking. *Journal of Applied Psychology, 96,* 1065.

Moayed, F. A., Daraiseh, N., Shell, R., & Salem, S. (2006). Workplace bullying: A systematic review of risk factors and outcomes. *Theoretical Issues in Ergonomics Science, 7*(3), 311–327.

Nielsen, M. B., & Einarsen, S. (2012). Outcomes of exposure to workplace bullying: A meta-analytic review. *Work & Stress, 26*(4), 309–332.

Pearson, C. M., & Porath, C. L. (2001). *Effects of incivility on the target: Fight, flee or take care of "me"?* Paper presented at the annual meeting of the Academy of Management, Washington, D.C.

Pearson, C. M., & Porath, C. L. (2005). On the nature, consequences and remedies of workplace incivility: No time for "nice"? Think again. *Academy of Management Executive, 19,* 7–18.

Porath, C. L., & Erez, A. (2007). Does rudeness really matter? The effects of rudeness on task performance and helpfulness. *Academy of Management Journal, 50,* 1181–1197.

Porath, C. L., & Erez, A. (2009). Overlooked but not untouched: How rudeness reduces onlookers' performance on routine and creative tasks. *Organizational Behavior and Human Decision Processes, 109,* 29–44.

Porath, C., Macinnis, D., & Folkes, V. (2010). Witnessing incivility among employees: Effects on consumer anger and negative inferences about companies. *Journal of Consumer Research, 37,* 292–303.

Rayner, C. (1999). "A comparison of two methods for identifying targets of workplace bullying." In *Abstracts for the Ninth European Congress on Work and Organizational Psychology.* Helsinki: Finnish Institute of Occupational Health.

Rayner, C., & Hoel, H. (1997). A summary review of literature relating to workplace bullying. *Journal of Community & Applied Social Psychology, 7*(3), 181–191.

Rodríguez-Muñoz, A., Moreno-Jiménez, B., Vergel, A. I. S., & Hernández, E. G. (2010). Post-traumatic symptoms among victims of workplace bullying: Exploring gender differences and shattered assumptions. *Journal of Applied Social Psychology, 40*(10), 2616–2635.

Rodwell, J., & Demir, D. (2012). Psychological consequences of bullying for hospital and aged care nurses. *International Nursing Review, 59*(4), 539–546.

Salin, D. (2003). Ways of explaining workplace bullying: A review of enabling, motivating and precipitating structures and processes in the work environment. *Human Relations, 56*(10), 1213–1232.

Samnani, A-K., & Singh, P. (2012). 20 Years of workplace bullying research: A review of the antecedents and consequences of bullying in the workplace. *Aggression and Violent Behavior, 17*(6), 581–589.

Schmader, T., Croft, A., Scarnier, M., Lickel, B., & Mendes, W. B. (2012). Not in mixed company: Emotional reactions to observed prejudice. *Group Processes and Intergroup Relations, 15,* 379–392.

Shelton, J., Richeson, J., & Vorauer, J. (2006). Threatened identities and interethnic interactions. *European Review of Social Psychology, 17,* 321–358.

Strandmark, K. M., & Hallberg, L. R-M. (2007). The origin of workplace bullying: Experiences from the perspective of bully victims in the public service sector. *Journal of Nursing Management, 15*(3), 332–341.

Taylor, P., Russ-Eft, D., & Chan, D. (2005). A meta-analytic review of behavior modeling training. *Journal of Applied Psychology, 90,* 692–709.

Tepper, B., Duffy, M., Henle, C., & Lambert, L. (2006) Procedural injustice, victim precipitation, and abusive supervision. *Personnel Psychology, 59,* 101–123.

UNISON. (2000). *Policy staff bullying report* (No. 1777). London: UNISON.

Vartia, M. (2001). Consequences of workplace bullying with respect to well being of its targets and the observers of bullying. *Scandinavian Journal of Work, Environment, and Health, 27,* 62–69.

Vartia, M., & Hyyti, J. (2002). Gender differences in workplace bullying among prison officers. *European Journal of Work and Organizational Psychology, 11*(1), 113–126.

Vogelpohl, D. A., Rice, S. K., Edwards, M. E., & Bork, C. E. (2013). New graduate nurses' perception of the workplace: Have they experienced bullying? *Journal of Professional Nursing, 29*(6), 414–422.

Yamada, S., Cappadocia, M. C., & Pepler, D. (2014). Workplace bullying in Canadian graduate psychology programs: Student perspectives of student–supervisor relationships. *Training and Education in Professional Psychology, 8*(1), 58–67.

Chapter 9

Ally Training

Kathleen Gargan and Christa Grant

Active bystander is a familiar term that we often hear when discussing violence prevention programs on college campuses. An active bystander has the power to intervene and address conflicts or unacceptable, destructive behaviors. Building an inclusive community where all members feel welcomed, valued, and respected is a commitment Siena College, a Catholic Franciscan institution, has held since its establishment in 1937. The active bystander model provides us with the framework to reframe the ally training program and fulfill this commitment.

In the chapter of *Being an Ally* by Nancy J. Evans and Jamie Washington (2010), the four basic levels of being an ally outlined are "awareness," "knowledge/education," "skills," and "action" (p. 418), and these four elements provided us with the groundwork to develop a new ally training program. In order for an ally training program to be successful, where one can truly be able to serve as an ally, the program must incorporate these four elements. We recognized that a comprehensive ally training should not only educate participants with the basic knowledge of the lesbian, gay, bisexual, transgender, and queer/questioning (LGBTQ) community, such as terms and definitions, but also should provide participants with the concrete skill sets to become active allies by practicing the active bystander model.

According to the Research Institute of Higher Education's *State of Higher Education for Lesbian, Gay, Bisexual & Transgender People* (2010), LGBT individuals often experienced hostility and isolation on college campuses. These experiences often are contributed by "negative societal attitudes and discriminatory behaviors" (p. 25) and result in a negative campus climate. Literature shows students' learning experiences, engagement, and involvement on campus are directly correlated with the campus climate (Research Institute of Higher Education, 2010). At Siena College, we strive to create a positive and welcoming environment where everyone can live and study. We believe in treating each individual with respect and dignity, celebrating and embracing the uniqueness of each individual, as part of the Franciscan heritage. It is this reason why it is so crucial to incorporate the active bystander model in our ally training.

As part of Title IX, many institutions, by federal law, are required to provide training for students, faculty, administrators, and staff. Promoting being an active bystander to end sexual violence has become a trend in our Title IX training. The term active bystander has also become a familiar role many students can associate with. Both ally and active bystander have different meanings, nevertheless, they share the same purpose. They are prosocial behaviors, and individuals who are in both roles take steps to speak up and make a difference. The training points out the importance of providing support, confronting inappropriate behaviors, and modeling advocacy (Evans & Washington, 2010) as prosocial behaviors that allies must demonstrate to combat homophobia and heterosexism.

By completing the ally training program, participants will demonstrate the ability to utilize the active bystander model to be an effective ally. They will also be able to demonstrate and apply knowledge of prosocial behaviors that promote inclusive communities. Meanwhile, it is equally important for the individuals to be able to identify how systems of oppression and cycles of socialization impact LGBTQ people and recognize that being an ally is tied to and supported by our institution's mission and values. It is important to note that in this particular ally training program, although developed with the focus on the LGBTQ population, participants can apply the same skill sets into different situations involving other subordinated groups.

The active bystander model serves two purposes in the ally training. First, it allows an ally to identify the steps to intervene in any LGBTQ bias–related incidents including addressing derogatory remarks. Second, it allows an ally to have the ability to recognize the challenges someone who identifies as a member of the LGBTQ community may face during his or her coming out process and provide those individuals with the appropriate resources and referrals.

Fostering diversity and building an inclusive community are every-one's responsibilities. They require efforts from community members, involving students, faculty, staff, and administrators. By working together, we hope to eliminate discrimination, prejudice, and oppression and build a world that is "just, peaceable, and humane" (Siena College, 2014), as mentioned in Siena College's mission statement.

REFERENCES

Evans, N. J., & Washington, J. (2010). Becoming an ally: A new examination. In M. Adams, W. Blumenfeld, C. Castaneda, H. W. Hackman, M. l. Peters, & X. Zuniga (Eds.), *Readings for diversity and social justice* (pp. 413–421). New York. NY: Routedge.

Research Institute of Higher Education. (2010). State of Higher Education for Lesbian, Gay, Bisexual & Transgender People. (2010). Campus Pride. Retrieved from http://www.campuspride.org/wp-content/uploads/camp uspride2010lgbtreportssummary.pdf.

Siena College (2014). Mission statement of Siena College. Retrieved from https://www.siena.edu/about/mission/.

Chapter 10

How a College/University Campus Can Inform Students, Faculty, and Staff about Bullying: One Student's Perspective

Lucas Lavera

I believe that any college and university should be able to provide information about bullying, whether it is to inform students or to train faculty and staff on how to prevent bullying on or off campus. It is important to be aware of the issues implied with bullying and what negative effects it has on students, staff and faculty, administration, and community members. A campus becomes a community where all parties should be aware of the problems each member could be facing and be able to act accordingly to prevent disastrous consequences.

Bullying can be detrimental to one's character, and making sure the campus community is aware of how to react and act can improve the campus climate. Informing the campus community about bullying in a safe and respectful manner is very important. Colleges and universities can inform first-year students as part of their orientation activities by showing content specifically aimed at students to help them understand and recognize bullying in all its forms and making the students actively engage in conversations that lead students to further their knowledge on the topic. I believe it is important to at least plant the seed with first-year students. In my experience as an orientation leader, I have noticed that first-year students do not necessarily have a strong background on current events and problems involving the greater community.

The bullying climate at a high school is also very different from a higher-education setting. In college, the students are expected to handle situations on their own time and be independent. This can be problematic once a situation arises that affects the student's morale. The students begin to believe they have to handle everything on their own and that they need no outside help. Therefore, it is crucial for colleges and universities to inform students of how significant it is for students to report bullying and to guide them in the right direction toward the steps they can take to confront bullying safely.

Another way colleges and universities can inform students about bullying is through creative programming throughout the semester. Students nowadays do not feel the need to attend lectures unless it is required for a class or if there is free food. This is why it is critical to be creative with antibullying programming and campaigning so the attention of students is caught right away and they begin to question bully-like activities from their peers. Making students lead these programs is also beneficial; students are more likely to listen to their peers than to administration or staff. Supporting the formation of clubs and organizations that seek to educate and fight bullying on campus is important.

With the mindset of having clubs and organizations fighting for and promoting antibullying programming, staff and administration need to encourage these organizations to not only focus on students but also other members of the community. The college and university need to make sure that training against bullying is provided for staff, administration, and faculty and make sure that there is a focus on identifying bullying and taking action. Staff, administration, and faculty create the influence in informing the students of the campus about bullying, and it is critical for these groups to be well informed and trained.

Chapter 11

Workplace Bullying: Campus Public Safety Role and Responsibility

Ronald Matos

Campus public safety and security departments are routinely asked to respond to many different types of incidents. During any given day, safety and security personnel may respond to calls for service ranging from assisting a person that finds him- or herself in need of directions to fielding a criminal complaint. With every response, the assigned official is required to call upon his or her training in order to best handle the situation. Proper training and personnel development play a critical role in how the official responds to and resolves an issue. A properly trained member of a public safety or security department will display a greater degree of competence when handling an event, which oftentimes helps put a person in need of assistance at ease. Having the ability to place a person at ease, especially when that person is reporting a stressful event such as workplace bullying or harassment, directly helps with building good rapport, which sets the tone for the entire exchange of information. In addition to other mandatory modules, training sessions should build upon awareness of policies, procedures, and institutional responses to all aspects of campus life, including issues that affect the workplace.

A campus public safety or security department official called upon to respond to a workplace bullying complaint must remember many things. The official must first remember his or her own personal safety as well as the safety of all persons involved with the event. The official must recognize that bullying involves a pattern of behavior that may be very difficult to discuss in the setting that the official is asked to respond to. It is imperative that the official seek a "safe" place to discuss the reason for the report. Early in the response process, the public safety or security official must ask the reporting person where he or she feels most comfortable talking about the event. Again, the idea is to put the reporting person at ease so there can be a better exchange of information. Attention must be paid to the fact that bullying may involve more than one offender and may also involve a person in a position of authority (Washington State Department of Labor & Industries, 2011). These factors must be considered when the official first begins working with the reporting person. Once a "safe" place has been established, the interview may begin.

An interview conducted with a person who has been involved in an emotional or stressful situation must not be rushed. The interview should unfold at a pace that is comfortable for the reporting person. It is important that the public safety or security official demonstrate patience and empathy. The responding official must recognize that certain barriers exist for a person who is contemplating making a report of workplace bullying. In addition to the reduced self-esteem often exhibited by bullying victims, the reporting person may have fears of being humiliated, fired, and isolated as well as the fear of not being believed (Marcian & Rasmussen, 2012). Through the use of open-ended questions and two-way dialogue, the interview should focus on not only the event that prompted the call for assistance but also the history behind the bullying. The safety or security official should pay close attention to any mention of anything that can be preserved as evidence. Examples of evidence to be aware of are photographs, electronic messaging, physical injury, vandalism, and written communications. When applicable to the circumstances, the public safety or security official should work with the reporting person on the best methods to identify and preserve anything that could constitute evidence. Once the specifics are documented and the official has an understanding of the offending conduct, the reporting person should be advised of the institutional processes and potential interim measures.

In order to provide the reporting person with information regarding the resolution process and his or her options, a campus public safety or security department official must be aware of the role that other campus divisions, such as human resources or employee relations, play. The role of the campus divisions should be articulated to the reporting person and, when possible, contact information shared. In instances where the behavior associated with bullying rises to the level of a criminal act, the reporting person should be advised of his or her right to file a report with a law enforcement agency with the appropriate jurisdiction. In the event that the reporting person chooses to notify a law enforcement agency, that person should be advised by the campus safety or security official that the institution will continue to follow through with its internal processes.

After a report has been received and documented by the campus public safety or security department official, communication must be established with the person or persons designated to investigate the complaint. Prompt communication is essential to ensure that the report is investigated in the most efficient and just manner. The prompt exchange of information also ensures that the safety of all involved can be assessed and potential protective measures can be discussed. The safety assessment should look not only at the safety of the reporting person but also the workplace as a whole. If necessary, a multidisciplinary threat assessment team can be consulted to determine if protective measures are needed. Protective measures can vary greatly depending on the institution but may include restricted access, suspension, or reduced privileges. When protective measures are warranted, public safety or security personnel should be briefed on the circumstances as they may be called upon to enforce a restriction that has been instituted.

No good response happens in a vacuum. There must be a coordinated effort with community buy-in in order to address any emerging problem. Workplace bullying is no different. In order for a community, such as a college campus, to be effective at addressing the issue, a top-down approach must be embraced (Law, Dollard, Tuckey, & Dormann, 2011). The top-down approach must start with a change in attitude and culture throughout the workplace with respect to policies, awareness, training, and response. It is important that support of this approach be demonstrated to the entire institution (Law et al., 2011). Support of policies, training, and awareness campaigns should not stop with the top administration as they are the responsibility of all. Support can also be demonstrated to the community through the work of public safety and security officials. This is done when safety and security officials establish campus relationships and build trust in the same manner used in effective community-based policing models (Stopbullying, 2010). In the end, a collaborative and supportive approach adopted by campus public safety and security departments and their partners from other divisions is critical to ensure the best response to a complaint of workplace bullying.

REFERENCES

Law, R., Dollard, M., Tuckey, M., & Dorman, C. (2011). *Accident analysis and prevention psychological safety climate.* New York, NY: Elsevier.

Marciano, P., & Rasmussen, D. (2012). *Workplace bullying*. Retrieved from www
    .slideshare.net/pmarciano/workplace-bullying.
Stopbullying. (2010). *Roles of law enforcement officers in bullying prevention*. Law
    enforcement technology. Retrieved from http://www.stopbullying.gov
    /prevention/training-center/hrsa_guide_law-enforcement-officers_508v2
    .pdf.
Washington State Department of Labor & Industries. (2011). SHARP Safety &
    Health Research for Prevention. *Stop workplace bullying and disruptive behav-
    ior: What everyone needs to know*. Retrieved from www.NoBullying.Lni
    .wa.gov/safety/research/files/bullying.pdf.

Part IV

Bullying across the Lifecycle: Schoolyard Bullies Become Workplace Bullies

Chapter 12

Microaggressions: A Root of Bullying, Violence, and Victimization toward Lesbian, Gay, Bisexual, and Transgender Youth

Kevin L. Nadal and Katie E. Griffin

In the fall of 2010, six young people in various regions of the United States committed suicide. Although teen suicide in itself may not be a new phenomenon, these six individuals gained national attention because they were all reported to have committed suicide as a result of teen bullying. What was even more unique about these young people's stories was they were all reported to have been bullied because they were (or were perceived to be) gay. One of these young people was Tyler Clementi, an 18-year-old college freshman at Rutgers University, whose classmates posted an Internet video of him having sex with another man. Clementi, who was allegedly a closeted gay man, was reportedly mortified and took his own life shortly after this cyberbullying had occurred. Immediately following this event, a nationwide campaign garnered attention when

Portions of this chapter appeared in M. Paludi (Ed.). (2011). *The psychology of teen violence and victimization*, Volume 1: *From bullying to cyberstalking to assault and sexual violation* (pp. 3–21). Santa Barbara, CA: Praeger.

celebrities and laypeople alike began to create and post videos on the Internet with a message that "It Gets Better." These videos urged young lesbian, gay, bisexual, and transgender (LGBT) people to value their lives and to not view suicide as a viable option.

Following the course of these events, psychologists, educators, and other practitioners in the media began to hypothesize reasons why bullying exists and why bullying leads to potential suicide. Discussions ensued regarding the motivations of bullies and where bullies learn that such behavior is acceptable and tolerable. Others began to explore the psychological hardships of the victims of bullying, as well as the ways that educational systems were not protecting these LGBT children or creating a safe space for them. Regardless of the motivation of these discussions, all of these experts could agree that bullying needed to stop (or at least be minimized) in order to promote optimal physical safety and positive psychological health for our nation's youth. However, perhaps all of these questions would need to be examined further in order to work toward a solution.

This chapter explores how microaggressions, or subtle forms of discrimination, may potentially play a huge role in the bullying that occurs toward children and adolescents. Microaggressions are "brief and commonplace daily verbal, behavioral, or environmental indignities (whether intentional or unintentional) that communicate hostile, derogatory, or negative racial slights and insults toward members of oppressed groups" (Nadal, 2008, p. 23). Originally modeled from research on racial microaggressions (Sue et al., 2007), this type of subtle discrimination is argued to exist toward all marginalized groups, including people of color, women, LGBT persons, persons with disabilities, and religious minorities (Nadal, 2008). The cumulative nature of microaggressions is suggested to detrimentally impact mental health, particularly depression, anxiety, mood, and self-esteem.

This chapter will examine previous literature on microaggressions in an attempt to understand the influences of such discrimination on the lives of bullies, victims, and all of society. First, we will examine how the microaggressions that bullies witness in their families, communities, and media may lead to the acceptance of hate toward various groups—particularly people who identify as (or are perceived to be) LGBT. Second, we will explore how microaggressions impact the lives of victims, and how victims learn to internalize or oppress discrimination and hate. Finally, we will examine the impacts that microaggressions have on more systemic and environmental levels, advocating for the changes that need to occur in media, government, and educational systems. This first section will define microaggressions, providing an understanding of the background behind the concept, the current research involving microaggressions, and the impacts that microaggressions may have on mental health.

REVIEW OF MICROAGGRESSION LITERATURE

The existence of discrimination and prejudice has been recorded throughout all of history. Thinking back to as recently as the 20th century, one can easily recall events like the Holocaust or the racial discrimination that led to the civil rights movement. The violence and cruelty that accompanied these historical events held their basis in racial and religious hatred, in conjunction with strongly held beliefs of inequality and inferiority. The teachings of groups like the Ku Klux Klan and the Nazis were more commonplace in families, communities, and even some school systems. Thus, people in American society were much more vocal and straightforward with their biases, making racism much easier to identify.

However, in present-day society, it may be less acceptable and "politically incorrect" to maintain the same sentiments as these aforementioned extremist groups. Nowadays, people tend to hide their biases and prejudices, while many try to be "color blind" and not see or acknowledge others' races or ethnicities. As a result, explicit discrimination (such as race-based hate crimes and physical assaults) may have decreased in many parts of the United States, leading many people to believe that discrimination is extinct and a thing of the past. Despite this, blatant discrimination still occurs, albeit arguably at a lower frequency and magnitude. But many authors are now suggesting that racism manifests in a new form of subtle or covert discrimination, otherwise known as microaggressions (Sue, 2010).

In the 1970s, Pierce, Carew, Pierce-Gonzalez, and Willis first used the term "racial microaggressions" and later described it as "subtle, stunning, often automatic, and non-verbal exchanges which are 'put downs'" (p. 66). Sue, Capodilupo, and colleagues (2007) refined the term microaggressions to be "brief, everyday exchanges that send denigrating messages to people of color because they belong to a racial minority group" (p. 273). Sue, Capodilupo, and colleagues (2007) proposed a taxonomy of racial microaggressions that included nine themes:

1. Alien in own land,
2. Ascription of intelligence,
3. Color blindness,
4. Criminality/Assumption of criminal status,
5. Denial of individual racism,
6. Myth of meritocracy,
7. Pathologizing cultural values/communication styles,
8. Second-class citizen,
9. Environmental microaggressions.

An individual is a victim of a microaggression when asked where he or she is from (*alien in own land*) or when followed around in a store by an owner or clerk (*criminality/assumption of criminal status*). In the first example, the individual is being sent the message that he or she is not American and does not belong, while the individual in the second example is being sent the message that she or he must be a criminal. In both instances, the act may be unconscious or unintentional to the enactor but sends a hurtful message to the victim that she or he is different, unwelcome, or inferior in some way.

In this racial microaggression taxonomy, it was theorized that microaggressions can be categorized in three major ways: microassaults (direct, intentional statements or behaviors targeting people of color), microinsults (indirect, unintentional statements or behaviors that offend, upset, or hurt persons of color), and microinvalidations (indirect, unintentional statements or behaviors that disregard, discount, or ignore a person of color's experiences). A microassault would be most similar to "old-fashioned racism" and would reflect the types of discrimination that are often conscious and intentional. For example, someone making a racist joke or racial slur could be viewed as making a conscious action that conveys a person's true intention and bias. Nadal, Rivera, and Corpus (2010) discussed how microassaults apply to microaggressions toward LGBT people (e.g., someone using homophobic insults or who blatantly conveys their disgust or disapproval with nonheterosexual people).

Microinsults are often unintentional and the enactor is often unaware that his or her behaviors or statements may be hurtful to the people of color who experience them. For example, the aforementioned store owner who follows a person of color around in a store may not recognize that she or he only follows people of color. Moreover, if confronted, this individual may even become defensive and explain that he or she is simply trying to protect the store or that he or she follows anyone who looks suspicious, regardless of race. However, for a person of color who experiences such discrimination regularly, it may be daunting and hurtful to feel this type of communication of fear or distrust. For LGBT people, microinsults can include everything from a person glaring at same-sex couples in curiosity or disgust to a person casually saying that something is "gay" as a synonym to "bad," "weird," or "awful" (Nadal, Rivera, & Corpus, 2010).

Microinvalidations are usually statements that are demeaning; again, usually the enactor may not recognize the impact that such statements could have on people of marginalized groups. For example, when a white person tells a person of color that she or he is being paranoid and that racism does not exist anymore, the person of color's racial reality is challenged and dismissed. Similarly, when someone tells LGBT people to "get over it" or to "not be so sensitive," a message is communicated that there is something wrong with them, instead of acknowledging the heterosexism or discrimination that exists.

The taxonomy on racial microaggressions has been supported and extended by research on the experiences of black/African Americans (Sue, Capodilupo, & Holder, 2008; Sue, Nadal, Capodilupo, Lin, Torino, & Rivera, 2008), Asian Americans (Sue, Bucceri, Lin, Nadal, & Torino, 2007), and Latino/a Americans (Rivera, Forquer, & Rangel, 2010). Both qualitative and quantitative studies have supported that experiencing microaggressions on a daily, consistent basis may have an accumulating effect on those who are victims of such discrimination. Furthermore, literature has purported that microaggressions can impact many other marginalized groups including women (Nadal, 2010), religious minorities (Nadal, Issa, Griffin, Hamit, & Lyons, 2010), multiracial individuals, and LGBT people (Nadal, Rivera, & Corpus, 2010).

There has been an increase in the types of microaggressions that are experienced by LGBT individuals. Sexual orientation microaggressions can be defined as "brief and commonplace daily verbal, behavioral, and environmental indignities (whether intentional or unintentional) that communicate hostile, derogatory, or negative heterosexist and homophobic slights and insults toward gay, lesbian, and bisexual individuals, while transgender microaggressions are the verbal, behavioral, and environmental indignities that target transgender persons" (Nadal, Rivera & Corpus, 2010, p. 218). Nadal and colleagues (2010) proposed a taxonomy for sexual orientation microaggressions based on relevant literature that included nine themes:

1. Use of heterosexist terminology,
2. Endorsement of heteronormative culture/behaviors,
3. Assumption of universal LGBT experiences,
4. Exoticization,
5. Discomfort/disapproval of LGBT experiences,
6. Denial of societal heterosexism/transphobia,
7. Assumption of sexual pathology,
8. Denial of individual heterosexism/transphobia,
9. Environmental microaggressions.

LGBT individuals experience a sexual orientation microaggression when someone asks them to stop acting so gay (*endorsement of heteronormative culture/behaviors*) or when asked if they have HIV/AIDS (*assumption of sexual pathology/abnormality*). A qualitative study regarding LGBT experiences with sexual orientation discrimination supported this taxonomy, revealing the same first five themes, grouping themes six and eight together to form *Denial of the reality of heterosexism*, and adding an additional theme of *Assaults and threatening behaviors* (there were not enough examples given to support the *Environmental microaggressions* theme) (Nadal, Issa, under review).

Just as research has revealed that racial microaggressions (Sue, Bucerri, et al., 2007; Sue, Capodilupo et al., 2008; Sue, Nadal et al., 2008) and gender microaggressions (Nadal, Hamit et al., in press) have an impact on the mental health of the victims of such recurring discrimination, research focusing on the experiences of LGBT individuals shows similar results. LGBT individuals have shared the effect that their experiences of victimization have had on their daily function and their emotional and physical health (Nadal, Issa, under review; Nadal, Wong, under review; Nadal, Skolnik, & Wong, under review).

Similarly, the types of microaggressions that are related to teen bullying can fit into proposed categories of microassaults, microinsults, and microinvalidations. For example, the act of bullying itself (e.g., teasing, threatening, etc.) can be viewed as a microassault, in that the perpetrators are very aware of their actions and conscious of their biases and hatred. But, perhaps because they are not physically assaulting the person, these individuals may believe their actions to be harmless or innocuous. The types of homophobic language that is used "jokingly" may be viewed as microinsults; these include words like "faggot" or "dyke" or phrases like "That's so gay" or "Stop being a sissy." When people use such words (either toward others or casually in conversation), a communication of intolerance or disapproval toward LGBT people can create a hostile environment for young people who identify as LGBT or who are questioning their sexual or gender identities. Finally, when young victims of bullying are told to "ignore" the problem or that they are "making a big deal" of the situation, their experiences are invalidated and they may feel dismissed. Such experiences are not only psychologically damaging to these young people, but they may also send implicit messages that the bullying is tolerated and that bullying does not result in punishment.

Nadal, Skolnik, and colleagues (under review) found that transgender participants reported feeling a variety of emotional reactions in response to victimization, including anger, frustration, and disappointment. Additionally, these participants reported that these experiences have negatively impacted their interpersonal relationships with their family, friends, and intimate partners and deemed these experiences as tiresome and wearing. Coping mechanisms have also been found in the research on LGBT individuals, in that many LGBT people utilize various behavioral, emotional, and cognitive reactions to help themselves deal with discrimination (Nadal, Wong et al., under review). A type of a behavioral response may be a passive coping (e.g., the individual walks away from the perpetrator of the microaggression). A type of an emotional response may be anger or frustration. Finally, a cognitive response may include acceptance and conformity, which may be exemplified by an LGBT individual who may act more "straight" in a job interview so as to up his or her chances of being hired (Nadal, Wong et al., under review). Victims of sexual orientation microaggressions, therefore, have necessarily found ways to cope with such experiences but still report feeling taxed and exhausted by these happenings and by their attempts to deal with them (Nadal, Wong et al., under review).

LGBT TEENS' EXPERIENCES WITH MICROAGGRESSIONS

Now that we have examined the history of microaggressions and the various types of microaggressions that may manifest toward LGBT people, this section will focus specifically on the microaggressions that are experienced by LGBT teens. As aforementioned, teen bullying may be a type of microaggression in itself, while the verbal and nonverbal microaggressions that create or maintain an unsafe environment may permit the bullying to continue. Thus, it is important to examine the types of bullying that may be considered microaggressive in nature, the various environments where LGBT teens may experience such bullying and other types of microaggressions, and the unintentional and unconscious behaviors that promote dangerous environments, thus allowing microaggressions to perpetuate and thrive.

Although previous research on sexual orientation microaggressions has recruited adult participants to share their experiences, many of the examples given by these adults had occurred when they were adolescents (Nadal, Issa et al., under review). Because teenagers tend not to have reached their highest levels of emotional, psychological, and cognitive development, they can be particularly susceptible to the perpetration of microaggressions by their peers. Moreover, because adolescence is a time in which individuals may feel especially sensitive, the experience of microaggressions may be damaging to their self-esteem and mental health.

Furthermore, it is often during adolescence that LGBT individuals are in various stages of their sexual identity development in that they may be questioning, denying, hiding, or coming to terms with their sexual orientation, making this an often fragile period of their lives. Research has found that sexual minorities are more likely to report physical and sexual abuse than their heterosexual counterparts (Saewyc et al., 2006). Additionally, sexual minorities report more difficulties with their peers and families as well as increased levels of psychological distress (Ueno, 2005). Some of the protective factors that aid in combating against the effects of such discrimination are social connectedness and family connectedness; however, sexual minorities, and bisexual individuals specifically, report less protective factors than do heterosexual individuals (Saewyc et al., 2009). Adolescents, therefore, may be targets of all kinds of sexual orientation–based discrimination and microaggressions; these may occur at school, in their peer groups, and even in their families.

Microaggressions within Schools or Educational Systems

Teens spend about half of their day in school, throughout which they are immersed in a social as well as educational atmosphere. As a result, adolescents may become victims of bullying or microaggressions in the hall between classes, in the lunchroom, and even in the classroom itself. Although little research has been done on sexual orientation microaggressions experienced through classroom interactions, one study looked at the opinions of students regarding sexual orientation and the rights and safety of LGBT individuals. Horn, Szalacha, and Drill (2008) found that students could separate their own beliefs about homosexuality and their opinions regarding the rights of these individuals. Although these participants reported that LGBT individuals have a right to feel safe in school, students who endorsed conventional reasoning or based on social norms in addition to homosexuality as personal choice were more likely to judge the exclusion and teasing of others as acceptable behaviors. Thus, although other students may report that everyone has the right to be protected and feel safe at school, they may still behave in such a way that has the opposite effect.

Another way in which LGBT teens may experience microaggressions at school is in the classroom as a result of student–teacher interactions. In a study on racial microaggressions, researchers found that such instances in the classroom can lead to a resultant dialogue on race (Sue, Lin, Torino, Capodilupo, & Rivera, 2009). Although a discussion on race stemming from a racial microaggression has the potential to be constructive and could have a positive impact on the whole class, the discussion, if handled poorly by the teacher, also has the potential of having detrimental consequences. As research has shown that such an occurrence can happen in response to racial microaggressions, one would assume the same could happen due to the commitment of a sexual-orientation microaggression in the same setting. Therefore, LGBT teens may have these experiences in the school setting, which may lead to events that further exacerbate the issue.

Microaggressions from Peers

Another source of sexual orientation microaggressions for adolescents is their peers. Sexual minorities have reported more sexual harassment and bullying from their peers than their heterosexual counterparts (Williams, Conolly, Pepler, & Craig, 2005). Although both LGBT and heterosexual individuals experience dating violence, bisexual males are more likely to report all types of abuse than heterosexual males, and bisexual females report more sexual abuse than heterosexual females (Freedner, Freed, Yang, & Austin, 2002). Furthermore, Freedner and colleagues (2002) found that lesbians reported feeling more scared about their own safety than heterosexual females, and bisexuals experience more threats of outing than gay males and lesbians. A study examining the basis for peer acceptance found that among 10th- and 12th-graders, not only was sexual orientation taken into account, but so was gender conformity (Horn, 2007). This finding suggests that if a sexual minority teen does not conform to gender norms, she or he may be more susceptible to bullying, microaggressions, or other victimization from his or her peers.

Teens may have peer-related protective factors that help them to deal and cope with sexual orientation microaggressions; however, LGBT teens may lack the necessary protective factors to shield themselves from the effects of such discrimination. Williams and colleagues (2005) found that the relation between social support and externalizing behaviors was mediated by peer victimization and that the relation between sexual orientation and psychosocial symptoms was mediated by both peer victimization and social support. Furthermore, the results of the study revealed that sexual minority adolescents reported less companionship with their best friends than did their heterosexual counterparts (Williams et al., 2005). Saewyc and colleagues (2009) found that bisexual adolescents reported lower levels of school connectedness than heterosexual adolescents. Ueno (2005) suggested that bonding with other teens who have common social backgrounds is a protective factor for adolescents; however, while heterosexuals often form these bonds, this is less likely to happen for LGBT individuals. When these bonds do form, LGBT individuals report lower psychological distress than those without this protective factor (Ueno, 2005). Therefore, LGBT teens are likely to experience sexual orientation microaggressions from other peers and may lack a social support peer group to assist them in countering the negative effects of these events.

Microaggressions within the Family

Just as peer groups can serve as a protective factor as well as a source of sexual orientation microaggressions, so too can one's family. With family support, an LGBT teen may have a better coming out experience and may be better able to cope with other sources of such discrimination. Unfortunately, it is often the case that coming out to one's parents is a very stressful experience and leads to altered parent–child relationships (Saltzburg, 2004). Saewyc and colleagues (2009) found that bisexual individuals reported lower levels of family connectedness than their heterosexual counterparts, thereby reducing the existence of this protective factor. Additionally, Williams and colleagues (2003) found that sexual minorities reported less closeness with their mothers than their heterosexual peers. In Saltzburg's (2004) study looking at the experience of parents after their child has come out to them, parents reported feeling various emotions including disappointment, confusion, and fear of es-trangement. Many of the parents in the study reported feeling as though they had lost their child, and all their hopes for what their child's life could be were crushed (Saltzburg, 2004). Throughout this process, a child may lose connectedness with his or her parents as both may feel as though they are so different as to not be able to relate to each other (Saltzburg, 2004). When this is the case or, worse, if the parent disowns the child, the LGBT teen loses a major protective factor and becomes more susceptible to the negative impact of discrimination.

In terms of microaggressions specifically, some studies found that un-like racial microaggressions, LGBT individuals often experience subtle discrimination within their own families (Nadal, Issa et al., under review; Nadal, Skolnik et al., under review). Although the experience of outward rejection by one's family (particularly one's parents) can be distressing, so too can be the implicitly disapproving behaviors and statements. For ex-ample, lesbian, gay, and bisexual people are often told "not to act so gay" or to "tone it down," and parents of transgender people may have difficult referring to them using their preferred gender names or pronouns. Thus, even if family members may believe they are being accepting, their subtle behaviors may indicate unconscious desires for their children to be het-erosexual. And because families may not be aware of their microaggres-sive statements or behaviors, they may not recognize the lack of support they are conveying to their children.

Microaggressions Based on Intersectional Identities

When LGBT teens hold multiple identities, the experiences of microag-gressions, bullying, and other forms of discrimination may be even more complex, damaging, or both. When LGBT teens of color (i.e., African Americans, Latina/os, Asian Americans, etc.) are the victims of bullying or hate crimes, one may wonder if the experience is due to their sexual orientations (or perceived sexual orientations), because of their racial and ethnic backgrounds, or both. In 2003, Sakia Gunn, a 15-year-old African American, was murdered as a result of a hate crime in New Jersey (Smith, 2004). Some of her friends said she identified as a lesbian, while others suggested she may have identified as a transgender man. Regardless of her sexual identity, the lack of media attention that was paid to Sakia's death demonstrates how the media may pay little attention to hate crimes that target LGBT of color. Just a few years prior, the murder of Matthew Shepard, a young white male in Wyoming, became a national topic of in-terest that eventually led to greater awareness about hate crimes toward LGBT people. However, when a similar crime occurs toward an LGBT person of color, it did not (and still may not) have as much of an impact as a crime that targets a gay white man.

Similar experiences occur with LGBT people of color who may not necessarily be victims of overt racism, heterosexism, or hate crimes. Tyra Hunter, an African American transgender woman, died after she was struck by a car in Washington, D.C. When paramedics arrived on the scene, she was found to be seriously injured. While onlookers pleaded for them to help her, the paramedics who responded to the call stood back and ridiculed her. Some argue it was because of her transgender identity, her gender presentation, her race, or some combination of all of these things. Although they eventually took her to the hospital, the delay in assistance eventually resulted in her death. Her injuries were serious, but they were not life-threatening; therefore, her death was preventable (Remembering Our Dead, 1995). A jury later awarded her family $2.9 million in an action against the D.C. Fire Department and D.C. General Hospital for withholding treatment and for medical malpractice. Again, perhaps these paramedics were not the assailants of the hate crimes themselves. But because of their prejudices and discriminatory behaviors, they eventually caused the untimely death of a transgender woman who could have survived. It is unclear whether such an event was due to her race, gender identity, or both, but it is clear that discrimination (even such experiences that appear to be innocuous) can potentially result in detrimental or mortal consequences.

THE IMPACTS OF MICROAGGRESSIONS ON LGBT ADOLESCENTS' MENTAL HEALTH

Throughout this chapter, we have discussed some of the negative impacts that bullying, microaggressions, and other forms of discrimination may have on the lives of LGBT youth. Perhaps the most important reason for examining these experiences is because there have been many studies that have reported the many disparaging mental health experiences of LGBT youth, particularly in comparison to their heterosexual counterparts. Studies have revealed that LGBT youth tended to be much more depressed than their heterosexual counterparts, and they were more likely to report suicidal ideation and self-harm (Almeida, Johnson, Corliss, Molnar, & Azrael, 2009). Another study found that in a sample with both urban and rural LGBT youth that 42% of the urban sample and 32% of the rural sample attempted suicide at least once (Waldo, Hesson-McInnis, & D'Augelli, 1998). Literature has pointed out that LGBT individuals may be susceptible to developing social anxiety (Safren & Pantalone, 2005), and that LGBT individuals are more likely to develop substance abuse problems in comparison to their heterosexual counterparts (Marshal et al., 2008). Finally, one report revealed that LGBT persons are at higher risk of suffering from mental health problems (e.g., depression and substance abuse disorders) and physical health problems (e.g., high blood pressure) (Cochran, 2001; Meyer, 2003).

A substantial amount of research has reported that overt and covert discrimination has a significant impact on the mental health of LGBT individuals (Burn, Kadlec, & Rexer, 2005; Herek, 2000, 2007; Hill & Willoughby, 2005; Meyer, 1995, 2003; Walls, 2008). One study reported that LGBT youth who were victimized were more likely to hold suicidal thoughts, particularly if they were questioning or unsure of their sexual identities (Poteat, Aragon, Espelage, & Koenig, 2009). Some authors have cited that the harassment of gays during adolescence can be linked to the exceptionally high rate of suicide among LGBT youth (D'Augelli, 1992). Another study found that hate crimes toward LGBT individuals may result in more severe psychological consequences, such as depression, anxiety, posttraumatic stress disorder, and other mental health disparities in victims (Herek & Capitanio, 1999). Finally, studies have reported that experiences of discrimination and stigmatization may lead to lower self-esteem, fears of rejection, or consistent hiding or concealing of identities (Burn et al., 2005; Rostosky, Riggle, Gray, & Hatton, 2007). Given all of these, it is important to recognize that all forms of discrimination, including bullying, hate crimes, assaults, and microaggressions, need to decrease in order to promote more favorable mental health outcomes for LGBT people, especially LGBT youth.

RECOMMENDATIONS FOR ADDRESSING TEEN BULLYING AND MICROAGGRESSIONS

Throughout this chapter, we have highlighted the multitude of reasons of why it is important to reduce or eliminate microaggressions in order to provide safer and more accepting environments for LGBT youth. Perhaps in creating these safer spaces, bullying toward LGBT youth will decrease and an environment of acceptance can be created. Because of this, Nadal, Hamit, and Issa (2010) discussed various ways that microaggressions can be prevented or dealt with in order to create more welcoming and accepting spaces. These include the following:

1. Talking about microaggressions openly when they occur (e.g., confronting others when one observes a microaggression, or if appropriate or safe, confronting others when one is the victim of a microaggression).
2. Having dialogues in families, workplace environments, and other systems about discrimination, prejudice, and diversity, as well as the ways that race and culture impact various aspects of our lives.
3. Being a support system or resource for victims of microaggressions, particularly by validating others' experiences.
4. Educating others about the term "microaggressions" so that individuals are aware that discrimination may take more subtle forms,

which in turn may make some situations easier to identify or manage.

Because these suggestions focus on microaggressions in general, perhaps it may be beneficial to apply these suggestions and provide specific guidelines for addressing bullying toward LGBT youth.

First, it is important for individuals to acknowledge this bullying when it occurs. It is very easy for individuals to turn a "blind eye" to bullying because of our fears of dealing with conflict or because of our rationalization that "kids will be kids." However, when school systems, parents, and other individuals fail to address bullying, the levels of victimization may exacerbate, which may lead to the multitude of psychosocial and mental health problems that have been discussed throughout the chapter. As a result, it is important for bullying to be tackled immediately in order to convey the lack of tolerance toward victimizing others, as well as to prevent the victimization from becoming more painful or intolerable.

Second, it is necessary for dialogues to occur in various groups and systems in order to prevent bullying from occurring. Perhaps parents need to discuss the importance of equality and respect with their children from an early age. And perhaps teachers and school systems need to emphasize the same. Sometimes children and adolescents are unaware that their behavior may be considered bullying; other times these young people may continue with their behaviors because they are not corrected, are not punished, or both. Perhaps one helpful approach may be to talk about the influx of teen suicides as a result of bullying. Adolescents who bully others may not recognize that their actions may lead to others' self-harm or even deaths. Perhaps in having these conversations, adolescents may recognize that they would not want to live the rest of their lives knowing they may have directly or indirectly caused someone to take his or her own life.

Third, being a support and resource for all adolescents, particularly LGBT teens who may be struggling with their identities, may be another approach to preventing the detrimental psychological consequences of bullying. Perhaps these teens may develop low self-esteem or social anxiety because they have not learned to accept or love themselves. And it is conceivable that the lack of role models or support systems may be one reason for this outcome. One simple way for showing this support is by talking with youth about their problems, instead of assuming that everything is okay. For example, it is very common for parents to avoid conversations with their children about adolescence and sexuality because they may feel awkward or uncomfortable in discussing such sensitive topics. Moreover, because many parents have developed heteronormative perspectives, oftentimes they may assume that their child is heterosexual. Therefore, they may not consider that their daughter or son may be struggling with sexual identity issues or victimization in schools. Because of this, it is important for open dialogue and communication to ensue (with parents, older siblings, grandparents, uncles, aunts, teachers, coaches, etc.), so that young people do not internalize their problems or turn to suicide as an option. It is also important for parents (and others) to be open to the possibility that their child may be LGBT. In doing so, they may be more alert to potential symptoms of bullying and may be able to provide them with the support and guidance they need.

Finally, identifying and acknowledging the spectrum of microaggressions that may lead to bullying are important steps to creating safer environments for LGBT youth and for all youth in general. Disallowing anyone from using heterosexist or homophobic remarks (whether intentional or unintentional) is one step toward promoting equality and preventing discrimination or hatred. Not assuming that everyone is heterosexual and celebrating the various experiences of LGBT people can help to normalize those LGBT teens who may feel different, while teaching heterosexual teens about acceptance, open-mindedness, and social justice for all.

Furthermore, there are myriad ways that systemic changes can help to decrease microaggressions, which in turn can assist in decreasing the amount of bullying toward LGBT teens. First, perhaps all professional and governing organizations must take steps similar to the American Psychological Association or American Medical Association, which advocate that competently working with LGBT clients is an ethical responsibility in being an effective practitioner. Perhaps one reason why many practitioners may not perceive LGBT issues as being salient or relevant is because of the lack of emphasis in their professional training. Thus, incorporating LGBT issues into cultural competence guidelines may result in more positive outcomes for LGBT students, clients, and patients.

Changes in the media, government, and educational systems may also help to decrease microaggressions, which could help in decreasing LGBT teen bullying and victimization. An increase in positive LGBT images can potentially enhance the acceptance of LGBT people in American society. Perhaps hatred toward LGBT people exists because of the lack of visibility in the media or because of the presence of disparaging and stereotypical images of them. Adolescents who are able to view LGBT people as being normal and successful role models may help them to view such individuals as human. Moreover, this greater exposure of LGBT individuals in the media should include all people in the LGBT community, ranging from LGBT people of color (e.g., African Americans, Asian Americans, Latina/ os, Arab Americans, multiracial people, Pacific Islanders, etc.) to bisexual and transgender people. Because these groups are often invisible or marginalized in the LGBT community itself, LGBT youth who identify in these ways may feel a double burden, which may negatively influence their self-esteem and mental health. Thus, perhaps more media presence, visibility, and normalization can help to ameliorate some of these negative outcomes.

A series of amendments in the government and legal systems may also lead to a reduction in LGBT microaggressions, bullying, and victimization. When governments uphold laws that ban or prevent same-sex marriage or disallow LGBT people from serving in the military, a societal message is communicated that LGBT people are second-class citizens in this country. When LGBT people are not allowed to visit their partners in hospitals or when LGBT people are denied health care, their basic rights as humans are compromised. On the contrary, when LGBT people are protected and considered in laws, a societal message is communicated that they are valued human beings in our society. Thus, it is important for government to pass laws that promote equal rights and opportunities for LGBT people. In doing so, messages of acceptance will be transmitted throughout all of society, consequently resulting in a decrease in microaggressions and perhaps a decrease in teen bullying.

Finally, because bullying toward LGBT teens occurs most often in school systems, it is necessary for educational policies to promote the physical and psychological safety of LGBT youths. First, curriculum should include and implement diversity in all subjects—from the influences of LGBT people in world history to the inclusion of LGBT issues in psychology to the teaching of LGBT works in American literature. Second, harassment and bullying policies should be created and enforced, including special clauses that protect the rights of LGBT students. By developing an atmosphere that does not tolerate hateful behaviors, LGBT students will feel safer and heterosexual students will learn about equality and social justice. Finally, promotion of egalitarianism and diversity should be incorporated into all aspects of student life—from the encouragements of gay–straight alliances to the hiring of LGBT teachers to the allowing of same-sex prom dates.

If school systems, the government, families, and the media really do care about the lives of LGBT youth, some or all of these recommendations can be implemented in so many simple ways. Perhaps if these LGBT affirmative environments had existed in the past, the number of LGBT teen suicides would not have been as substantial as they are (and have been). If we want to see our children survive and live healthy lives, we cannot just tell them that "It Gets Better." Rather, we have to show them that we are doing our parts to "Make It Better" for them today.

REFERENCES

Almeida, J., Johnson, R. M., Corliss, H. L., Molnar, B. E., & Azrael, D. (2009). Emotional distress among LGBT youth: The influence of perceived discrimination based on sexual orientation. *Journal of Youth Adolescence, 38,* 1001–1014.

Burn, S. M., Kadlec, K., & Rexer, R. (2005). Effects of subtle heterosexism on gays, lesbians, and bisexuals. *Journal of Homosexuality, 49*(2), 23–38.

Cochran, S. D. (2001). Emerging issues in research on lesbians' and gay men's mental health: Does sexual orientation really matter? *American Psychologist, 56*, 932–947.

D'Augelli, A. R. (1992). Lesbian and gay male undergraduates' experiences of harassment and fear on campus. *Journal of Interpersonal Violence, 7*, 383–395.

Freedner, N., Freed, L. H., Yang, Y. W., & Austin, B. (2002). Dating violence among gay, lesbian, and bisexual adolescents: Results from a community survey. *Journal of Adolescent Health, 31*, 469–474.

Herek, G. M. (2000). The psychology of sexual prejudice. *Current Directions in Psychological Science, 9*, 19–22.

Herek, G. M. (2007). Confronting sexual stigma and prejudice: Theory and practice. *Journal of Social Issues, 63*(4), 905–925.

Herek, G. M., & Capitanio, J. P. (1999). Sex differences in how heterosexuals think about lesbians and gay men: Evidence from survey context effects. *Journal of Sex Research, 36*, 348–360.

Hill, D. B., & Willoughby, B. L. B. (2005). The development and validation of the genderism and transphobia scale. *Sex Roles, 53*(7–8), 531–544.

Horn, S. S. (2007). Adolescents' acceptance of same-sex peers based on sexual orientation and gender expression. *Journal of Youth and Adolescence, 36*, 363–371.

Horn, S. S., Szalacha, L. A., & Drill, K. (2008). Schooling, sexuality, and rights: An investigation of heterosexual students' social cognition regarding sexual orientation and the rights of gay and lesbian peers in school. *Journal of Social Issues, 64*(4), 791–813.

Marshal, M. P., Friedman, M. S., Stall, R., King, K. M., Miles, J., Gold, M. A., . . . Morse, J. Q. (2008). Sexual orientation and adolescent substance use: A meta-analysis and methodological review. *Addiction, 103*, 546–556.

Meyer, I. H. (1995). Minority stress and mental health in gay men. *Journal of Health and Social Behavior, 36*, 38–56.

Meyer, I. H. (2003). Prejudice, social stress, and mental health in lesbian, gay, and bisexual populations: Conceptual issues and research evidence. *Psychological Bulletin, 129*(5), 674–697.

Nadal, K. L. (2008). Preventing racial, ethnic, gender, sexual minority, disability, and religious microaggressions: Recommendations for promoting positive mental health. *Prevention in Counseling Psychology: Theory, Research, Practice and Training, 2*(1), 22–27.

Nadal, K. L. (2010). Gender microaggressions and women: Implications for mental health. In M. A. Paludi (Ed.), *Feminism and women's rights worldwide*. Vol. 2: *Mental and physical health* (pp. 155–175). Westport, CT: Praeger.

Nadal, K. L., Hamit, S., & Issa, M. A. (2010). Overcoming gender and sexual orientation microaggressions. In M. A. Paludi & F. M. Denmark (Eds.), *Victims of sexual assault and abuse: Resources and responses for individuals and families*. Westport, CT: Praeger.

Nadal, K. L., Issa, M-A., Griffin, K., Hamit, S., & Lyons, O. (2010). Religious micro-aggressions in the United States: Mental health implications for religious minority groups. In D. W. Sue (Ed.), *Microaggressions and marginality: Manifestation, dynamics, and impact* (pp. 287–310). New York, NY: Wiley.

Nadal, K. L., Issa, M. A., Leon, J., Meterko, V., Wideman, M., & Wong, Y. (Under review). Sexual orientation microaggressions: Perspectives of lesbian, gay, and bisexual people.

Nadal, K. L., Rivera, D. P., & Corpus, M. J. H. (2010). Sexual orientation and trans-gender microaggressions in everyday life: Experiences of lesbians, gays, bi-sexuals, and transgender individuals. In D. W. Sue (Ed.), *Microaggressions and marginality: Manifestation, dynamics, and impact* (pp. 217–240). New York, NY: Wiley.

Nadal, K. L., Skolnik, A., & Wong, Y. (Under review). Interpersonal and systemic microaggressions: Psychological impacts on transgender individuals and communities.

Nadal, K. L., Wong, Y., Issa, M. A., Meterko, V. M., Leon, J., & Wideman, M. (Under review). Sexual orientation microaggressions: Processes and coping mecha-nisms for lesbian, gay, and bisexual individuals.

Pierce, C., Carew, J., Pierce-Gonzalez, D., & Willis, D. (1978). An experiment in rac-ism: TV commercials. In C. Pierce (Ed.), *Television and education* (pp. 62–88). Beverly Hills, CA: Sage.

Poteat, V. P., Aragon, S. R., Espelage, D. L., & Koenig, B. W. (2009). Psychosocial concerns of sexual minority youth: Complexity and caution in group differ-ences. *Journal of Counseling and Clinical Psychology, 77*(1), 196–201.

Rivera, D. P., Forquer, E. E., & Rangel, R. (2010). Microaggressions and the life expe-rience of Latina/o Americans. In D. W. Sue (Ed.), *Microaggressions and margin-ality: Manifestation, dynamics, and impact* (pp. 59–83). New York, NY: Wiley.

Rostosky, S. S., Riggle, E. D. B., Gray, B. E., & Hatton, R. L. (2007). Minority stress experiences in committed same-sex couple relationships. *Professional Psychology: Research and Practice, 38*(4), 392–400.

Saewyc, E. M., Homma, Y., Skay, C. L., Bearinger, L. H., Resnick, M. D., & Reis, E. (2009). Protective Factors in the lives of bisexual adolescents in North America. *American Journal of Public Health, 99*(1), 110–117.

Saewyc, E. M., Skay, C. L., Pettingell, S. L., Reis, E. A., Bearinger, L., Resnick, M., . . . Combs, L. (2006). Hazards of stigma: The sexual and physical abuse of gay, lesbian, and bisexual adolescents in the U.S. and Canada. *Child Welfare, 55*(2), 195–213.

Safren, S. A., & Pantalone, D. W. (2005). Social anxiety and barriers to resilience among lesbian, gay, and bisexual adolescents. In A. M. Omoto & H. S. Kurtzman (Eds.), *Sexual orientation and mental health: Examining identity and development in lesbian, gay, and bisexual people* (pp. 55–71). Washington, DC: American Psychological Association.

Saltzburg, S. (2004). Learning that an adolescent child is gay or lesbian: The parent experience. *Social Work, 49*(1), 109–118.

Smith, S. D. (2004). Sexually underrepresented youth: Understanding gay, lesbian, bisexual, transgendered, and questioning (GLBT-Q) youth. In J. L. Chin (Ed.), *Psychology of prejudice and discrimination: Bias based on gender and sexual orientation* (Vol. 3, pp. 151–199). Westport, CT: Praeger.

Sue, D. W. (2010). *Microaggressions in everyday life: Race, gender, and sexual orientation.* New York, NY: Wiley.

Sue, D. W., Bucerri, J. M., Lin, A. I., Nadal, K. L., & Torino, G. C. (2007). Racial microaggressions and the Asian American experience. *Cultural Diversity and Ethnic Minority Psychology, 13*(1), 72–81.

Sue, D. W., Capodilupo, C. M., & Holder, A. M. B. (2008). Racial microaggressions in the life experience of black Americans. *Professional Psychology: Research and Practice, 39,* 329–336.

Sue, D. W., Capodilupo, C. M., Torino, G. C., Bucceri, J. M., Holder, A. M. B., Nadal, K. L., & Esquilin, M. (2007). Racial microaggressions in everyday life: Implications for clinical practice. *American Psychologist, 62,* 271–286.

Sue, D. W., Lin, A. I., Torino, G. C., Capodilupo, C. M., & Rivera, D. P. (2009). Racial microaggressions in the classroom. *Cultural Diversity and Ethnic Minority Psychology, 15,* 183–190.

Sue, D. W., Nadal, K. L., Capodilupo, C. M., Lin, A. I., Torino, G. C., & Rivera, D. P. (2008). Racial microaggressions against black Americans: Implications for counseling. *Journal of Counseling & Development, 86,* 330–338.

Ueno, K. (2005). Sexual orientation and psychological distress in adolescence: Examining interpersonal stressors and social support processes. *Social Psychology Quarterly, 68*(3), 258–277.

Waldo, C. R., Hesson-McInnis, M. S., & D'Augelli, A. R. (1998). Antecedents and consequences of victimization of lesbian, gay, and bisexual young people: A structural model comparing rural university and urban samples. *American Journal of Community Psychology, 26*(2), 307–334.

Walls, N. E. (2008). Toward a multidimensional understanding of heterosexism: The changing nature of prejudice. *Journal of Homosexuality, 55*(1), 20–70.

Williams, T., Connolly, J., Pepler, D., & Craig, W. (2005). Peer victimization, social support, and psychosocial adjustment of sexual minority adolescents. *Journal of Youth and Adolescence, 24*(5), 471–482.

Chapter 13

Bullying in Middle School: What Does It Look Like, Why Does It Happen, and Who Does It Hurt?

Christine M. Wienke Totura and
Carol MacKinnon-Lewis

On a brisk Colorado morning in late April 1999, two young gunmen entered their school and opened fire, killing 13 people and then themselves. The reason for this massacre? In addition to reportedly suffering multiple emotional and psychological problems, the gunmen allegedly struggled for years in a school climate that condoned bullying and victimization (Block, 2007). Eric Harris and Dylan Klebold initiated one of America's most notorious and deadly mass shootings, and as a result, it blew the research on school violence wide open and forever changed the way the world views bullying. This infamous moment at Columbine High School has served as a marker for how cultures define, anticipate, and deal with the consequences of peer aggression.

Columbine is an extreme case of what could happen if bullying goes unchecked. Although most youths who either perpetrate bullying or are

Portions of this chapter appeared in M. Paludi (Ed.). (2011). *The psychology of teen violence and victimization*, Vol. 1: *From bullying to cyberstalking to assault and sexual violation* (pp. 105–125). Santa Barbara, CA: Praeger.

victims of it will not become violent, the pervasive and negative impacts of bullying remain a critical issue for researchers, practitioners, and parents alike. Estimated trends show that bullying occurs at all age levels, but tends to peak during early adolescence, ages 11 to 13 (Scheithauer, Hayer, Petermann, & Jugert, 2006). Therefore, middle school is a particularly prominent time to focus on the emotional and social impacts of bullying and victimization. Most studies conducted over the years have demonstrated that exposure to bullying is a significant risk factor to healthy psychological and physical development for youths, as well as to effective school climates (Haynie et al., 2001; Totura Wienke, MacKinnon-Lewis et al., 2009). Of particular importance for school districts is the consistent finding that bullying disrupts the classroom learning environment—victimization has been linked to declines in student academic motivation, grades, and test scores (Schwartz & Gorman, 2003).

Multiple individual and environmental factors influence the frequency of bullying and victimization, as well as the likelihood of youths becoming bullies or victims of bullying (Nansel et al., 2001; Totura Wienke, MacKinnon-Lewis et al., 2009). This chapter provides an overview of the long-standing issues associated with how bullying is defined and classified, how boys and girls in middle school differentially experience bullying, the contexts and consequences of peer aggression, and finally gives suggestions for building upon the existing prevention and intervention efforts. It is important to examine these variables and the relation among them in order to provide schools with feasible approaches that can be used to improve their environments.

BULLYING: A FAR-REACHING PROBLEM

Bullying is a well-documented national and international problem. Estimates of bullying problems vary from study to study and place to place. Worldwide averages estimate that roughly 35% of adolescents aged 11 to 15 report involvement in bullying, with percentages of regular bullying and victimization ranging from 2% in Sweden to almost 50% in Lithuania (Craig & Harel, 2004). Within the United States, researchers estimate that 30% of 6th- through 10th-grade students were involved in moderate to frequent bullying (Nansel et al., 2001). Of those students, 13% were classified as bullies, 11% as victims, and 6% as both bullies and victims. Other studies find higher estimates among rural youths, with 82% reportedly experiencing victimization (Dulmus, Theriot, Sowers, & Blackburn, 2004). When considering the rapid adoption of technology among youths, such as cell phones and social networking websites, national prevalence rates of cyberbullying show that 30% of adolescents report regular involvement (Raskauskas & Stoltz, 2007), with a dramatic increase in online victimization observed since 2000 (David-Ferdon &

Hertz, 2007). Despite variability in estimates, it appears that bullying is more prevalent and more severe than many people believe it is (Benbenishty & Astor, 2005). The inconsistency in bullying and victimization estimates is likely attributable to how bullying is defined and observed.

WHAT IS BULLYING?

Researchers have spent years trying to find the best ways to identify bullying and victimization among adolescents. Despite so much focus, no single definition of bullying has emerged as the gold standard. One of the more recent and most widely recognized definitions used to guide identification and assessment of bullying was developed by Olweus (2003). This definition combines several concepts established in earlier bullying definitions and clearly outlines the common characteristics: bullying is (a) a social form of aggression that takes place among youths who encounter one another regularly; (b) physical, verbal, or psychological aggression intended to hurt others and cause distress in a victim; (c) aggression involving the existence of a power differential between the bully and victim; and (d) not a response to aggressive acts (Cook, Williams, Guerra, Kim, & Sadek, 2010). Olweus's (2005) more recent definition has been used to guide assessments for the model Blueprints Bullying Prevention Program. To complicate matters further, bullying has also been categorized as either *direct* or *indirect*. This distinction between direct and indirect behaviors has had tremendous implications for estimates of bullying and victimization (Totura Wienke, Green, Karver, & Gesten, 2009).

The Many Types of Bullying Behavior

Based on definitions of bullying commonly used in the field, researchers have been able to categorize aggression into two specific types of behavior: direct and indirect. *Direct* bullying is as it sounds—the victim has direct interaction with a bully. This mode of bullying generally has two types: physical and verbal. *Physical* forms of bullying include behaviors such as hitting, kicking, pushing, punching, slapping, and spitting on others. These are visibly aggressive behaviors that are universally recognized as bullying by both adults and youths (see Berger, 2007, for a review). *Verbal* bullying involves making negative and hurtful comments about another. This could include name calling, insults, hurtful teasing, or nasty remarks. As youths enter adolescence, this type of bullying becomes more prevalent than physical aggression (Berger, 2007; Tapper & Boulton, 2005).

Indirect bullying, on the other hand, is covert in nature. The victim is not fully aware of who his or her attacker is because these behaviors are hard to detect and do not occur face to face. This type of bullying takes on two forms: relational and cyberbullying. *Relational* aggression is a form of bullying that also becomes more frequent among early adolescents as they develop instrumental social skills and a reliance on peer approval. Relational aggression involves rumor spreading, manipulation of friendships, and purposeful social isolation of others (Crick & Grotpeter, 1995; Xie, Swift, Cairns, & Cairns, 2002).

Cyberbullying is a relatively new form of indirect aggression among youths in which electronics and technology (computers, weblogs, texts, social networking websites, etc.) are used as the media for intentionally harming others through taunting, threatening, harassment, and intimidation (Berger, 2007; Williams & Guerra, 2007). The viral or rapid-spread nature of this type of aggression can make cyberbullying especially far-reaching and damaging for adolescents who rely heavily on their social networks for guidance and approval.

Bullying Roles: Profiling the Bullies, the Victims, and Those Caught in Between

Youths can experience bullying in a number of roles, each associated with unique emotional and behavioral profiles (Olweus, 2003). It is important to examine these profiles to get a picture of the context for bullying and to unlock clues that could help parents and school personnel prevent, as well as intervene, when problems arise.

Bullies

Adolescents who bully others tend to have a harder time overall in social situations (Haynie et al., 2001). Widespread theories affirm that bullies can be poor at reading social cues and accurately interpreting interactions with peers (Crick & Dodge, 1994). As a result, they are not as likely to identify prosocial solutions to what they misperceive as hostility or threats from others. Bullies, in addition to aggression, often display other problem behaviors, such as hyperactivity, attention difficulties, anger, and rule-breaking behaviors (Haynie et al., 2001). Bullies also tend to associate with friends who are similar to them—they exhibit a greater frequency of problematic behaviors and greater acceptance of misconduct than other youths (Nansel et al., 2001). Interestingly, despite studies that suggest bullies do not express much emotionality, they tend to have more symptoms of anxiety and depression than students who are not involved in bullying (Haynie et al., 2001; Nansel et al., 2001). These levels, however, are not as high as that of victims. Finally, bullying has been associated with distraction from schoolwork and poorer academic outcomes, findings that are especially important for teachers who may find themselves spending a lot of energy on classroom management instead of instruction (Graham, Bellmore, & Mize, 2006).

Studies have shown that many bullies view their behavior as reasonable and use skilled methods to exert their control over others (Rose, Swenson, & Waller, 2004). Those who know how to use these skills avoid the peer rejection that less-skilled bullies often experience. Indeed, middle school bullies can be popular among their classmates (Keisner & Pastore, 2005), although as they progress into high school, bullies become less popular compared to their more socially skilled peers.

Victims

Victims can be classified in two types: passive and reactive. *Passive* victims are those who receive bullying and tend to present as defenseless and submissive to aggressors (Berger, 2007). Conversely, *reactive* victims are not defenseless. These youths will respond to bullying with aggression, rather than becoming isolated and withdrawn. Victims often have individual characteristics that make them an easy target (Carney & Merrell, 2001). Psychologically, they are more anxious, depressed, and withdrawn and have lower self-esteem than those who are not bullied (Haynie et al., 2001). As they get older, adolescents are more often harassed and bullied for their suspected or known sexual orientation (Berlan, Corliss, Field, Goodman, & Austin, 2010). Victims, especially those who are withdrawn and shy, are generally less popular in school or bonded with classmates than other students, including bullies (Haynie et al., 2001). Victimization can also be associated with school avoidance, potentially resulting in greater incidences of truancy, which can have a negative impact on academic performance (Kochenderfer & Ladd, 1996). Interestingly, victims can also display behavior problems, such as delinquency, substance use, and acceptance of misconduct, although often not to the same degree as bullies (Sullivan, Farrell, & Kliewer, 2006).

Bully/Victims

Recent studies have found that bully/victims (youths that both bully others and are bullied) represent a distinct group, although typically much smaller in size and frequency than bullies and victims (Haynie et al., 2001; Nansel et al., 2001). Bully/victims, also known as *aggressive victims* or *provocative victims*, are not to be mistaken for reactive victims. Their bullying behavior is not a reaction to an incident of victimization, but rather is a separate and purposeful bullying act (Pelligrini & Long, 2002). These youths are considered the most at-risk bullying group—they tend to have more overall behavioral and emotional problems and poorer social abilities than other youths (Totura Wienke, Green et al., 2009). Academically, bully/victims also have the poorest performance, likely a result of poor adjustment and bonding with school, teachers, and classmates (Haynie et al., 2001; Nansel et al., 2001). Often at a greater rate than bullies, bully/victims display deviant and defiant behavior, including cigarette and alcohol use and truancy, as well as verbal and physical aggression (Nordhagen, Neisen, Stigun, & Kohler, 2005). Unlike bullies who tend to progress from physical to indirect forms of bullying as they age, bully/victims primarily engage in physical aggression throughout childhood and adolescence (Unnever, 2005).

The Peer Group Observers

Bystanders are peers who observe victimization and either pretend to ignore it or downplay it, inadvertently contributing to an environment that tolerates youth aggression. Demonstrated intervention efforts have worked toward transitioning bystanders from passive observers to active defenders of victims (Salmivalli, 2001). These efforts capitalize on environmental approaches to changing the context in which bullying occurs, rather than focusing solely on changing the behavior of bullies or victims' coping abilities. *Henchmen/contributors* are peers who serve as contributors to bullies and also help to create an environment in which bullying is tolerated, but in a much more active manner. These youths are observers who engage in teasing, taunting, or other forms of indirect aggression alongside the primary bully. Henchmen are part of a network of peers who assist bullies in establishing dominance and power over others (see Berger, 2007, and Olweus, 2003, for reviews). *Defenders*, although less common than other observer groups, are youths who buck the common trend of contributing to or passively observing bullying situations by stepping up to support and defend victims. These youths are instrumental in taking a stand to shift the peer culture that may tolerate bullying and can be key players in school prevention and intervention efforts (Salmivalli, 2001).

CULTURAL DIFFERENCES IN EXPRESSIONS OF BULLYING

There are a range of bullying roles adolescents may take and peer contexts that are conducive to bullying; however, in order to better understand the experiences of bullying, it is important to consider cultural variations in the prevalence and expression of bullying. Research has identified a number of factors that can influence bullying roles and behaviors, notable among them are gender, race, and ethnicity.

Evidence on gender differences in bullying has evolved but is still somewhat inconclusive. Early research reported that more boys are bullies and victims than girls and that bullying decreases with age (Berger, 2007). More recently, research confirmed that boys are more often bullies and that physical aggression decreases with age, but that other forms of aggression (e.g., relational, social) reported to be more prevalent among girls increase during the middle school years (Malecki, 2003; Williams & Guerra, 2007). Physical and verbal aggression, as well as cyberbullying, tend to be more common among middle school boys and relational aggression more typical of girls (Crick & Werner, 1998; Giles & Heyman, 2005; Kowalski & Limber, 2007). Interestingly, even though boys and girls appear to be at equal risk of being bullied, middle school boys are more frequently victimized (Olweus, 2003). Both boys and girls tend to be crueler to their same-sex peers than to the opposite sex (Ladd, 2005). However, when there is gender crossover, boys tend to bully girls more than vice versa (Moffitt, Caspi, Rutter, & Silva, 2001).

Researchers both nationally and internationally have examined variations in bullying and victimization by race and ethnicity. For instance, African American youths are more often identified as bullies than victims, as compared to white and Hispanic youths (Graham & Juvonen, 2002). Although ethnic bullying has become problematic in some communities among boys and girls, particularly if students have not been exposed to cultural diversity issues, evidence suggests that race or ethnicity does not necessarily put youths at risk of peer aggression. Bullying appears to be more prevalent within ethnic or racial groups than between them (Bellmore, Witkow, Graham, & Juvonen, 2004; Berger, 2007). In fact, a large-scale study found that only a small proportion of adolescents felt their race or ethnicity was a factor in their bullying (Nansel et al., 2001).

Although some cultural trends have emerged in the incidence of bullying, gaps in the research preclude definitive conclusions. Indeed, there is much to be learned about the gender, racial, and ethnic variants of bullying among adolescents. These effects need to be examined further to gain a better understanding of how culture impacts the significance, consequences, and prevention of bullying.

CONSEQUENCES: WHAT HAPPENS TO BULLIES, VICTIMS, AND BULLY/VICTIMS?

By all counts, aggression in middle school has future negative outcomes. By high school, bullies find that their overtly aggressive behavior is less the norm among peers and that youths they used to pick on often find friends (Laursen, Finkelstein, & Betts, 2001). Many bullies do not learn adaptive social skills for negotiating difficult peer interactions and thus become increasingly unpopular as they get older. At a minimum, bullying is associated with other disruptive behaviors, both inside and outside of school, such as delinquency, alcohol and drug use, and adjustment problems (Nansel, Overpeck, Saluja, & Ruan, 2004; Prinstein, Boergers, & Vernberg, 2001). More seriously, bullying has also been linked to violent behaviors, including weapon carrying, frequent fighting, and violence-related injuries (Nansel et al., 2001). Given these behaviors, future criminal behavior in adulthood is a greater likelihood as well (Olweus, 1999). Aggressive girls suffer from unique problems, including dating violence and teenage pregnancy (Putallaz & Bierman, 2004). Perhaps most problematic among bullies is the potential for suicidal thoughts and intentions. Studies have found that older adolescents, especially boys, have a fourfold greater incidence of suicidal thoughts than other youths (Kaltiala-Heino, Rimpela, Marttunen, Rimpela, & Rantanen, 1999).

Victims, as well, experience significant disruptions to their developmental course, especially if victimization is chronic and involves multiple types (e.g., "ploy-victimization"; Finkelhor, Ormrod, Turner, & Hamby, 2005). Victimized youths feel anxious about attending school and often try to avoid going, which has a negative impact on future educational achievement and job attainment (Macmillan & Hagan, 2004). Bullying, especially severe and chronic, has been a factor in several recent suicides among youths and young adults. Peer aggression appears to be doubly impactful for youths who are gay or lesbian (Rivers, 2001), or even perceived to be so by their peers, thereby contributing to ongoing trauma and potentially suicide (Friedman, Koeske, Silvestre, Korr, & Sites, 2006). When considering the rarity of homicide among youths, such as the Columbine tragedy, a common factor threading incidents together has been a repetitive and long-standing bully–victim cycle. In many of the past two decades' school shootings, the perpetrator(s) was often a teenager who had hit the limit of teasing, ridicule, and torment from classmates (Vossekuil, Fein, Reddy, Borum, & Modzeleski, 2002). For those who are not pushed to the fatal acts of suicide or homicide, victimization has long-term consequences. These adolescents grow up with progressively worsening anxiety and depression along with fears of social interactions. These fears often lead to isolation from others and potentially future victimization into adulthood (Troop-Gordon & Ladd, 2005). Young adolescents who experience both bullying and victimization are by far the most troubled among their peers. These youths are likely to have the poorest trajectories into adulthood because even when they try to improve their social skills, they remain rejected by surrounding social supports among peers, at school, and at home (Bierman, 2004).

Given what is known about the long-term impact of bullying, it is easy to see why preventing it should be a priority among schools, parents, and teenagers. It is important to consider where the bully–victim cycle starts in order to identify early risk factors that make some youths vulnerable to bullying and victimization, as well as factors that can protect them.

RISK FACTORS: WHAT CONTRIBUTES TO BULLYING AND VICTIMIZATION?

Although not an exhaustive list, researchers have looked at risk factors such as physical appearance and demeanor, genetic predispositions, and certain contextual factors in homes and schools that increase the likelihood that youths will become bullies or bullied. Interestingly, many consequences of bullying have also been found to be predictors of it, creating a sort of "chicken and egg" scenario of peer aggression that researchers and practitioners are still trying to disentangle.

Several studies examined the relation between bullying and victimization and the adjustments among adolescent boys and girls. In terms of physical appearance and presentation, bullies and victims are more often boys than girls (Olweus, 2003). However, with more and more research accumulating on the effective assessment of relational and indirect aggression, girls bully more than expected, but most research still finds that boys bully more than girls (Berger, 2007). Victims and bully/victims differ from other youths in that they are frequently younger adolescents, in the first year of middle school, with lower self-esteem. Additionally, youths with a physical or learning disability may be at risk for victimization, especially in school climates that tolerate bullying (de Monchy, Pijl, & Zandberg, 2004). A recent review concluded that physical size and perceived "power" are important risk factors, especially for boys—bigger kids victimize smaller kids and stronger kids pick on kids they see as weaker (Berger, 2007). It is important to note that "power" can mean physical strength, but also social stature, a characteristic particularly salient for adolescent girls (Casey-Cannon, Hayward, & Gowen, 2001). Expression of anger, while a consequence of bullying, is also a powerful predictor of it (Bosworth, Espelage, & Simon, 1999).

Researchers have recently begun looking at genetic precursors to bullying and victimization. Some characteristics, such as temperament and predispositions to anger, do have genetic components. However, these characteristics do not manifest and result in aggression in isolation (Van Goozen, 2005). Studies have shown that babies with difficult temperaments do not automatically become angry and aggressive or highly fearful youths (Kagan & Snidman, 2004). Whatever the genetic foundation, emotional and behavioral risk factors of bullying and victimization reach their potential when they are triggered by an environment that fosters aggression (Van Goozen, 2005).

Environments That Make a Difference

Adolescents come in contact with many environments on a daily basis. Naturally, it is important to examine the characteristics of these environments in combination with youths' individual characteristics to better identify what puts them at risk for bullying and victimization. For the purposes of this chapter, the focus will be on the two common contexts that youths experience: home and school.

Family Context

Much work has been done on the relation between parenting and peer aggression. Parents can influence their children's social development both directly (e.g., modeling and social reinforcement for aggression) and indirectly (e.g., shaping of perceptions and attitudes about aggression). Ambivalent family connections, harsh discipline practices, and inconsistent and demanding parenting styles are associated with bullying, while overprotective or coercive parenting is associated with victimization. Additionally, many parents of bullies usually provide minimal supervision and typically lack empathy and effective problem-solving skills (Curtner-Smith, 2000; Duncan, 2004). Simply put, these parents are not good role models for learning how to get along with others and solve problems (Walden & Beran, 2010). Conversely, some victimized youths have parents who are rather involved in their daily lives, but this involvement may not be emotionally supportive (Haynie et al., 2001).

Much work has shown that negative family environments can be detrimental to youths' social development. On the other hand, good parenting has a protective effect—it can prevent future problem-solving difficulties among at-risk youths (Simons-Morton, Hartos, & Haynie, 2004). When parents are able to model prosocial behavior and effective solutions to social difficulties, they decrease the likelihood that their children will engage in bullying or become bullied.

School Climate

The prevalence of bullying is an important consideration for school administrators—bullying and group norms that favor bullying contribute to a lack of engagement in academic activities and lower overall achievement (Brody, Kim, Murry, & Brown, 2005). Early adolescents experience unique environmental changes as they move from elementary to middle schools. Middle school student bodies tend to be larger and more diverse than those in elementary school, and students transition frequently throughout the day among multiple classrooms and teachers. A school's social-emotional climate can facilitate or deter bullying (Espelage, Holt, & Henkel, 2003). Teachers play a critical role in shaping the structure and values of school ecologies (Rodkin & Hodges, 2003). Schools in which aggressive behavior is tolerated by teachers and students can cultivate a climate that is associated with higher rates of bullying (Espelage et al., 2003).

In contrast, the protective effect of a positive school climate can assuage bullying and victimization for middle school students (Kuperminc, Leadbeater, & Blatt, 2001). Quality friendships and supportive relationships at school go a long way toward protecting adolescents from the negative outcomes of bullying and victimization (Schwartz, Dodge, Pettit,

Bates, & the Conduct Problems Prevention Group, 2000). Also, students who are engaged, and in a sense "fit," within their school environment are less likely to experience aggression and bullying (Nansel, Haynie, & Simons-Morton, 2003). These findings highlight the pivotal role that a supportive school environment plays on adolescents' social-emotional development.

Prevention and Intervention: What Can Be Done?

It is clear that bullying is a big problem for youths, parents, and schools—now what? Research over the past couple of decades has laid the groundwork for figuring out what works and what does not to prevent bullying. Many theories have guided the development and evaluation of programs designed to reduce aggressive behavior. One of the most well-founded theories, social-information processing (SIP), indicates that programs should target children's attributional (beliefs about intent) and affective (emotional) deficits (Crick & Dodge, 1994). These theories suggest that how youths process social cues impacts whether they will respond to situations in an aggressive or nonaggressive manner (MacKinnon-Lewis, Lamb, Hattie, & Baradaran, 2001). One aspect of SIP shown to be particularly important for understanding aggression is the "hostile attribution bias" (Crick & Dodge, 1994). Researchers have shown that in situations where a peer's intent is vague, youths with a hostile attribution bias are inclined to believe the peer intended harm and will respond aggressively (Orobio de Castro, Merk, Koops, Veerman, & Bosch, 2005). Early research focused on looking at attributional biases and physical aggression, but more recent work demonstrates the applicability of the SIP model with relational aggression as well (Crick et al., 2002). Affective, or emotional, aspects of the SIP model are also important for decreasing aggression, by focusing on the ability to accurately interpret emotional cues, especially anger, and regulate (or control) emotional responses (Crick & Dodge, 1994). As such, emotion regulation techniques, in addition to addressing attributional biases, are important components included in interventions aimed at reducing physical (e.g., Anger Coping Program; Lochman, 1992) and relational aggression (Crick, Grotpeter, & Bigbee, 2002).

It is important to note that not all youths who bully others suffer from attributional biases or emotional regulation difficulties. Some youths use aggressive means instrumentally to control others because they (a) lack more effective social skills for negotiating relationships, or (b) are rewarded for using aggression to manipulate peers in seeking approval or popularity (Rose et al., 2004). This is where bystanders of bullying can play a key role in either reinforcing or dissuading aggression (Salmivalli, 2001), an important consideration for schools because they play a critical role in modeling appropriate interactions and creating an environment that rewards positive behavior rather than bullying.

WHAT WORKS AND WHAT DOES NOT WORK?

Scores of programming and techniques, some well researched and some not, have been devoted to reduce bullying and victimization among adolescents. A few select evidence-based programs will be described in this section, followed by recommendations for program enhancement. Starting with early prevention among youths, the Roots of Empathy program has been shown to have a dramatic effect in reducing aggression by developing empathy for others' experiences (Gordon & Green, 2008). Designed for kindergarten to grade eight, a neighborhood infant (accompanied by a parent) serves as the "lever" to teach children perspective-taking skills as well as fostering the development of empathy. The program, which began in Canada, has expanded to other countries including the United States, United Kingdom, and New Zealand. Among first- to third-grade program participants, proactive aggression was found to be reduced by 88%, with similar reductions in both proactive and relational aggression among fourth- through seventh-graders (Schonert-Reichl, 2007).

Incredible Years is another early prevention program with demonstrated effects in reducing the cycle of youth aggression, a contributor to later bullying behavior (Webster-Stratton et al., 2001). By working with families of preschool and early elementary children, both parents and at-risk youths learn prosocial problem-solving skills. This successful program has been extended to schools in which teachers are taught effective behavior management skills to be applied universally within classrooms.

Several programs have also been employed with older children and adolescents to intervene with existing bullying problems in schools. Using a variety of intervention strategies, Second Step Violence Prevention has been successful in reducing the incidence and tolerance for both relational and physical aggression and improving youths' social skills (Frey, Nolan, Van Schoiack Edstrom, Hirschstein, 2005). The program focuses on changing maladaptive attitudes about aggression by increasing empathy, perspective taking, problem-solving skills, and anger management abilities among elementary and middle school students. Further, the Anger Coping (Lochman, 1992) and BrainPower (Hudley, 1994) programs have successfully taught physically aggressive youths emotional regulation and to more accurately evaluate the intentions of others in social situations. Moreover, Leff and colleagues' (2009) Friend to Friend program, an adaptation of the Anger Coping and BrainPower programs, specifically targets relational aggression and has been shown to be effective at reducing hostile attributional biases, as well as relational and physical aggression among highly relationally aggressive girls.

One of the most effective programs developed to date is the Olweus Bullying Prevention program (Olweus, 2005). This Blueprints for Violence Prevention model program uses a whole-school approach to decrease bullying and victimization by improving awareness of these behaviors among teachers, students, and parents. Core components of the program are directed toward restructuring the existing school environment to reduce opportunities and rewards for bullying at the school, classroom, and individual student levels. Longitudinal data from students and teachers have shown the program to be remarkably effective in substantially reducing, by almost 50%, the incidences of bullying and victimization. Although the Bullying Prevention program primarily targets physical forms of aggression, its emphasis on promoting awareness among teachers, students, and parents, along with strategies for behavior management, may be effective in reducing other forms of aggression and victimization.

Despite the promising outcomes described above, preventions and interventions are less effective in environments in which aggression is tolerated (Aber, Jones, Brown, Chaundry, & Samples, 1998). Effective structure and monitoring of student behavior by school staff have positive implications for how adolescents learn to get along and form peer relationships. Accordingly, one of the first goals of any school-based program should be to educate students, teachers, and other school staff about the negative consequences of aggression with the goal of creating a more positive school climate. Broadly applying zero-tolerance policies, peer mediation, or simply suggesting victimized youths take a stand against bullying are ineffective prevention strategies (Fox, Elliott, Kerlikowske, Newman, & Christeson, 2003). Zero-tolerance policies typically result in bullies receiving suspensions and unsupervised time at home, rather than providing an opportunity to truly understand the causes of bullying. Encouraging victims to stand up to bullies may actually put them at greater risk of future bullying. Finally, peer mediation does nothing to address the power that bullies have over victims and could lead to further emotional damage by assuming victims have accountability in the aggression perpetrated against them.

Lessons Learned

As a result of developmental research, much has been learned about bullies and victims, although intervention strategies have met with somewhat limited success (Rigby, 2005). However, researchers have continued to develop and refine preventive interventions to address bullying behavior, many of which are school based. Unfortunately, few school interventions have undergone scientific evaluation (Berger, 2007), a shortcoming that must be rectified. Moreover, much of the field's past prevention and intervention research focused on boys' physical aggression (Crick & Zahn-Waxler, 2003). Because research shows that both boys and girls can be physically and relationally aggressive, attention to how gender differences translate into the expression of aggression will lead to more sensitive and effective interventions (Ostrov et al., 2009).

Although much progress is left to be realized, effective programming has demonstrated some common elements: (a) programs targeting youths' social-information processes and the connections between thoughts, feelings, and behaviors are the most promising; (b) effective programs work on both the individual and environmental levels and involve multiple components (e.g., teacher training, parent consultation, youths' social skills training); (c) programs that are successful across genders are specifically addressing female culture and relational aggression; (d) well-implemented school-based programs deal with school systemic issues that can pose challenges, such as leadership buy-in, demands on teachers' time, teachers' perceptions of student bullying, and available resources.

Despite some universal emphasis on these common elements across programs with empirical evidence, outcomes from many prevention and intervention efforts have been less than promising. Bullying is a multifactor, complex problem that involves effectively intervening with tightly intertwined developmental and social processes—doing this well is very difficult. The resulting lack of robust change in the rates of bullying and victimization underscores the need to ensure that programs are firmly planted in sound behavior-change theory and are embraced by all key players who have a stake in their success. By utilizing a social-ecological framework, in which efforts are targeted at youths and take into account the contextual factors that shape their lives, program developers can adopt a holistic approach to involving the people and environments that impact youths' behavior (Swearer, Espelage, Vaillancourt, & Hymel, 2010).

FUTURE DIRECTIONS FOR RESEARCH AND PRACTICE: WHERE DO WE GO FROM HERE?

With youths becoming increasingly tech savvy and more and more bullying occurring in virtual formats, prevention and intervention programming must remain as innovative as the technologies adolescents are using to victimize their peers (Berger, 2007; Raskauskas & Stoltz, 2007). Over the years, studies have increasingly incorporated technology into assessments and observations of youths' behavior as it occurs, including use of devices such as pagers, cell phones, video cameras, and digital recorders (Tapper & Boulton, 2005). Not only does this provide a wealth of information about peer relationships, but the information is also collected in real time without reliance on traditional observation, nomination, or survey techniques. This is a natural phenomenon—as time goes on, technology becomes more advanced and available and youths are inherently the first market to be fully dialed into these advances. Thus, it seems a logical progression that technology would come to the forefront of prevention and intervention as well, in addition to its successful utility in the assessment of youths' behaviors.

As it happens, limited success of many behavior-change intervention programs has prompted some to question whether new strategies are needed to effectively reach youths (Baranowski, Buday, Thompson, & Baranowski, 2008). Initial evidence, although rare, suggests that computer-based applications hold great promise as an effective channel for targeting youths' behavior change, primarily because adolescents find them to be engaging and they are already being used for social, entertainment, and educational purposes (Bers, 2006). Wilkinson, Ang, and Goh (2008), in their comprehensive review of the history and emergence of the Internet and video game literature, explored how recent technological and cultural innovations can be used to treat a host of mental health challenges. Despite an initial backlash by some scholars with concerns about the possible harmful effects of video games for therapeutic purposes, several program developers are identifying methods for harnessing youths' attraction to video games and the communicative possibilities of the Internet in treating aggression (Bosworth, Espelage, DuBay, Daytner, & Karageorge, 2000). These pioneering efforts are opening new doors for innovative preventive interventions that have not previously been considered. Future researchers should consider how innovative technological approaches might be used in the dissemination and implementation of preventive interventions targeting bullying behavior.

REFERENCES

Aber, J. L., Jones, S. M., Brown, J. L., Chaundry, N., & Samples, F. (1998). Resolving conflict creatively: Evaluating the developmental effects of a school-based violence prevention program in neighborhood and classroom context. *Development and Psychopathology, 10*, 187–213.

Baranowski, T., Buday, R., Thompson, D., & Baranowski, J. (2008). Playing for real: Video games and stories for health-related behavior change. *American Journal of Preventive Medicine, 34*, 74–82.

Bellmore, A. D., Witkow, M. R., Graham, S., & Juvonen, J. (2004). Beyond the individual: The impact of ethnic context and classroom behavioral norms on victim's adjustment. *Developmental Psychology, 40*, 1159–1172.

Benbenishty, R., & Astor, R. A. (2005). *School violence in context.* New York, NY: Oxford University Press.

Berger, K. (2007). Update on school bullying at school: Science forgotten? *Development Review, 27*, 90–126.

Berlan, E. D., Corliss, H. L., Field, A. E., Goodman, E., & Austin, S. B. (2010). Sexual orientation and bullying among adolescents in the Growing Up Today Study. *Journal of Adolescent Health, 46*, 366–371.

Bers, M. (2006). The role of new technologies to foster positive youth development. *Applied Developmental Science, 10*, 200–219.

Bierman, K. L. (2004). *Peer rejection.* New York, NY: Guilford.

Block, J. J. (2007). Lessons from Columbine: Virtual and real rage. *American Journal of Forensic Psychiatry, 28*, 1–27.

Bosworth, K., Espelage, D., DuBay, T., Daytner, G., & Karageorge, K. (2000). Preliminary evaluation of a multimedia violence prevention program for adolescents. *American Journal of Health Behavior, 24*, 268–280.

Bosworth, K., Espelage, D.L., & Simon, T.R. (1999). Factors associated with bullying behavior in middle school students. *Journal of Early Adolescence, 19*, 341–362.

Brody, G. H., Kim, S., Murry, V. M., & Brown, A. C. (2005). Longitudinal links among parenting, self-presentations to peers, and the development of externalizing and internalizing symptoms in African American siblings. *Development and Psychopathology, 17*, 185–205.

Carney, A. G., & Merrell, K. W. (2001). Bullying in schools: Perspectives on understanding and preventing an international problem. *School Psychology International, 22*, 364–382.

Casey-Cannon, S., Hayward, C., & Gowen, K. (2001). Middle-school girls' reports of peer victimization: Concerns, consequences, and implications. *Professional School Counseling, 5*, 135–147.

Cook, C. R., Williams, K. R., Guerra, N. G., Kim, T. E., & Sadek, S. (2010). Predictors of bullying and victimization in childhood and adolescence: A meta-analytic investigation. *School Psychology Quarterly, 25*, 65–83.

Craig, W. M., & Harel, Y. (2004). Bullying, physical fighting, and victimization. In C. Currie, C. Roberts, A. Morgan, R. Smith, W. Settertobulte, & O. Samdal (Eds.), *Young people's health in context* (pp. 133–144). Geneva, Switzerland: World Health Organization.

Crick, N. R., & Dodge, K., A. (1994). A review and reformulation of social information-processing mechanisms in children's social adjustment. *Psychological Bulletin, 115*, 74–101.

Crick, N. R., & Grotpeter, J. K. (1995). Relational aggression, gender, and social-psychological adjustment. *Child Development, 66*, 710–722.

Crick, N. R., Grotpeter, J. K., & Bigbee, M. A. (2002). Relationally and physically aggressive children's intent attributions and feelings of distress for relational and instrumental peer provocations. *Child Development, 73*, 1134–1142.

Crick, N. R., & Werner, N. E. (1998). Response decision processes in relational and overt aggression. *Child Development, 69*, 1630–1639.

Crick, N. R., & Zahn-Waxler, C. (2003). The development of psychopathology in females and males: Current progress and future challenges. *Development and Psychopathology, 15*, 719–742.

Curtner-Smith, M. E. (2000). Mechanisms by which family processes contribute to school-age boys' bullying. *Child Study Journal, 30*, 169–186.

David-Ferdon, C., & Hertz, M. F. (2007). Electronic media, violence, and adolescents: An emerging public health problem. *Journal of Adolescent Health, 41*, S1–S5.

de Monchy, M., Pijl, S. J., & Zandberg, T. (2004). Discrepancies in judging social inclusion and bullying of pupils with behavior problems. *European Journal of Special Needs Education, 19*, 317–330.

Dulmus, C. M., Theriot, M. T., Sowers, K. M., & Blackburn, J. A. (2004). Students reports of peer bullying victimization in a rural school. *Stress, Trauma, and Crisis: An International Journal, 7*, 1–16.

Duncan, R. D. (2004). The impact of family relationships on school bullies and victims. In D. L. Espelage & S. M. Swearer (Eds.), *Bullying in American schools: A social-ecological perspective on prevention and intervention* (pp. 227–244). Mahwah, NJ: Erlbaum.

Espelage, D. L., Holt, M. K., & Henkel, R. R. (2003). Examination of peer-group contextual effects on aggression during early adolescence. *Child Development, 74*, 205–220.

Finkelhor, D., Ormrod, R. K., Turner, H. A., & Hamby, S. L. (2005). Measuring poly-victimization using the Juvenile Victimization Questionnaire. *Child Abuse and Neglect, 29*, 1297–1312.

Fox, J. A., Elliott, D. S., Kerlikowske, R. G., Newman, S. A., & Christeson, W. (2003). *Bullying prevention is crime prevention: A report by Fight Crime: Invest in Kids.* Fight Crime. Retrieved from http://www.fightcrime.org/sites/default/files/reports/BullyingReport.pdf.

Frey, K. S., Nolen, S. B., Van Schoiack Edstrom, L., & Hirschstein, M. K. (2005). Effects of a school-based social-emotional competent program: Linking children's goals, attributions, and behavior. *Applied Developmental Psychology, 26*, 171–200.

Friedman, M. S., Koeske, G. F., Silvestre, A. J., Korr, W. S., & Sites, E. W. (2006). The impact of gender-role nonconforming behavior, bulling, and social support on suicidality among gay male youth. *Journal of Adolescent Health, 38*, 621–623.

Giles, J. W., & Heyman, G. D. (2005). Young children's beliefs about the relationship between gender and aggressive behavior. *Child Development, 76*, 107–121.

Gordon, M., & Green, J. (2008). Roots of Empathy: Changing the world child by child. *Education Canada, 48*, 34–36.

Graham, S., Bellmore, A. D., & Mize, J. (2006). Peer victimization, aggression, and their co-occurrence in middle school: Pathways to adjustment problems. *Journal of Abnormal Child Psychology, 34*, 363–378.

Graham, S., & Juvonen, J. (2002). Ethnicity, peer harassment, and adjustment in middle school: A exploratory study. *Journal of Early Adolescence, 22*, 173–199.

Haynie, D. L., Nansel, T., Eitel, P., Crump, A. D., Saylor, K., Yu, K., & Simons-Morton, B. (2001). Bullies, victims, and bully/victims: Distinct groups of at-risk youth. *Journal of Early Adolescence, 21*, 29–49.

Hudley, C. (1994). The reduction of childhood aggression using the BrainPower Program. In M. Furlong & D. Smith (Eds.), *Ander, hostility and aggression: Assessment, prevention, and intervention strategies for youth* (pp. 313–344). Brandon, VT: Clinical Psychology Publishing.

Kagan, J., & Snidman, N. C. (2004). *The long shadow of temperament.* Cambridge, MA: Belknap.

Kaltiala-Heino, R., Rimpela, M., Marttunen, M., Rimpela, A., & Rantanen, P. (1999). Bullying, depression, and suicidal ideation in Finnish adolescents: School survey. *British Medical Journal, 319*, 348–351.

Keisner, J., & Pastore, M. (2005). Difference in the relations between antisocial behavior and peer acceptance across contexts and across adolescence. *Child Development, 76*, 1278–1293.

Kochenderfer, B. J., & Ladd, G. W. (1996). Peer victimization: Cause of consequence of school maladjustment. *Child Development, 67*, 1305–1317.

Kowalski, R. M., & Limber, S. P. (2007). Electronic bullying among middle school students. *Journal of Adolescent Health, 41*, 22–30.

Kuperminc, G. P., Leadbeater, B. J., & Blatt, S. J. (2001). School social climate and individual differences in vulnerability to psychopathology among middle school students. *Journal of School Psychology, 39*, 141–159.

Ladd, G. W. (2005). *Children's peer relations and social competence.* New Haven, CT: Yale University Press.

Laursen, B., Finkelstein, B. D., & Betts, N. T. (2001). A developmental meta-analysis of peer conflict resolution. *Developmental Review, 21*, 423–449.

Leff, S. S., Gullan, R. L., Paskewich, B. S., Abdul-Kabir, S., Jawad, A. F., Grossman, M., . . . Power, T. J. (2009). An initial evaluation of a culturally-adapted social problem solving and relational aggression prevention program for urban African American relationally aggressive girls. *Journal of Prevention and Intervention in the Community, 37*, 1–15.

Lochman, J. E. (1992). Cognitive-behavioral intervention with aggressive boys: Three-year follow-up and preventive effects. *Journal of Consulting and Clinical Psychology, 60*, 426–432.

MacKinnon-Lewis, C., Lamb, M., Hattie, J., & Baradaran, L. P. (2001). A longitudinal examination of the associations between mothers' and sons' attributions and their aggression. *Development and Psychopathology, 13*, 69–81.

Macmillan, R., & Hagan, J. (2004). Violence in the transition to adulthood: Adolescent victimization, education, and socioeconomic attainment in later life. *Journal of Research on Adolescence, 14*, 127–158.

Malecki, C. K. (2003). Perceptions of the frequency and importance of social support by students classified as victims, bullies, and bully/victims in an urban middle school. *School Psychology Review, 32*, 471–489.

Moffitt, T. E., Caspi, A., Rutter, M., & Silva, P. A. (2001). *Sex differences in antisocial behavior: Conduct disorder, delinquency, and violence in the Dunedin longitudinal study.* Cambridge, UK: Cambridge University Press.

Nansel, T. R., Haynie, D. L., & Simons-Morton, B. G. (2003). The association of bullying and victimization with middle school adjustment. *Journal of Applied School Psychology, 19,* 45–61.

Nansel, T. R., Overpeck, M. D., Pilla, R. S., Ruan, W. J., Simons-Morton, B., & Scheidt, P. (2001). Bullying behavior among US youth: Prevalence and association with psychosocial adjustment. *Journal of the American Medical Association, 285,* 2094–2100.

Nansel, T. R., Overpeck, M. D., Saluja, G., & Ruan, W. J. (2004). Cross-national consistency in the relationship between bullying behaviors and psychosocial adjustment. *Archives of Pediatrics and Adolescent Medicine, 158,* 730–736.

Nordhagen, R., Neisen, A., Stigum, H., & Kohler, L. (2005). Parental reported bullying among Nordic children. *Child: Care, Health, and Development, 31,* 693–701.

Olweus, D. (1999). Sweden. In P. K. Smith, Y. Morita, J. Junger-Tas, D. Olweus, R. F. Catalano, & P. T. Slee (Eds.), *The nature of school bullying* (pp. 8–27). London: Routledge.

Olweus. D. (2003, March). The profile of bullying at school. *Educational Leadership,* 12–17.

Olweus, D. (2005). A useful evaluation design, and effects of the Olweus Bullying Prevention Program. *Psychology, Crime, & Law, 11,* 389–402.

Orobio de Castro, B., Merk, W., Koops, W., Veerman, J. W., & Bosch, J. D. (2005). Emotions in social information processing and their relations with reactive and proactive aggression in referred aggressive boys. *Journal of Clinical Child and Adolescent Psychology, 34,* 105–116.

Ostrov, J. M., Massetti, G. M., Stauffacher, K., Godleski, S. A., Hart, K. C., Karch, K. M., . . . Ries, E. E. (2009). An intervention for relational and physical aggression in early childhood: A preliminary study. *Early Childhood Research Quarterly, 24,* 15–28.

Pelligrini, A. D., & Long, J. D. (2002). A longitudinal study of bullying, dominance, and victimization, during the transition from primary through secondary school. *British Journal of Developmental Psychology, 20,* 259–280.

Prinstein, M. J., Boergers, J., & Vernberg, E. M. (2001). Overt and relational aggression in adolescents: Social-psychological functioning of aggressors and victims. *Journal of Clinical Child Psychology, 30,* 477–489.

Putallaz, M., & Bierman, K. L. (Eds.). (2004). *Aggression, antisocial behavior, and violence among girls: A developmental perspective.* Vol. 1: *Duke Series in Child Development and Public Policy.* K. A. Dodge & M. Putallaz, Series Eds. New York, NY: Guilford.

Raskauskas, J., & Stoltz, A. D. (2007). Involvement in traditional and electronic bullying among adolescents. *Developmental Psychology, 43,* 564–575.

Rigby, K. (2005). The method of shared concern as an intervention technique to address bullying in schools: An overview and appraisal. *Australian Journal of Guidance and Counseling, 15*, 27–34.

Rivers, I. (2001). The bullying of sexual minorities at school: Its nature and long-term consequences. *Educational and Child Psychology, 18*, 32–46.

Rodkin, P. C., & Hodges, E. V. E. (2003). Bullies and victims in the peer ecology: Four questions for psychologists and school professionals. *School Psychology Review, 32*, 384–400.

Rose, A. J., Swenson, L. P., & Waller, E. M. (2004). Overt and relational aggression and perceived popularity: Development differences in concurrent and prospective relations. *Developmental Psychology, 40*, 378–387.

Salmivalli, C. (2001). Peer-led intervention campaign against school bullying: Who considered it useful, who benefited? *Educational Research, 43*, 263–278.

Scheithauer, H., Hayer, T., Petermann, F., & Jugert, G. (2006). Physical, verbal, and relational forms of bullying among German students: Age trends, gender differences, and correlates. *Aggressive Behavior, 32*, 261–275.

Schonert-Reichl, K. A. (2007, March). *Middle childhood inside and out: The psychological and social world of children 9–12.* Research highlights: A University of British Columbia/United Way of the Lower Mainland Report. Burnaby, B.C.: United Way of the Lower Mainland.

Schwartz, D., Dodge, K. A., Pettit, G. S., Bates, J. E., & the Conduct Problems Prevention Group. (2000). Friendship as a moderating factor in the pathway between early harsh home environment and later victimization in the peer group. *Developmental Psychology, 36*, 646–662.

Schwartz, D., & Gorman, A. H. (2003). Community violence exposure and children's academic functioning. *Journal of Educational Psychology, 95*, 163–173.

Simons-Morton, B. G., Hartos, J. L., & Haynie, D. L. (2004). Prospective analysis of peer and parent influences on minor aggression among early adolescents. *Health Education Behavior, 31*, 22–33.

Sullivan, T. N., Farrell, A. D., & Kliewer, W. (2006). Peer victimization in early adolescence: Association between physical and relational victimization and drug use, aggression, and delinquent behaviors among urban middle school students. *Development and Psychopathology, 18*, 119–137.

Swearer, S. M., Espelage, D. L., Vaillancourt, T., & Hymel, S. (2010). What can be done about school bullying? Linking research to educational practice. *Educational Researcher, 39*, 38–47.

Tapper, K., & Boulton, M. J. (2005). Victim and peer responses to different forms of aggression among primary school children. *Aggressive Behavior, 31*, 238–253.

Totura Wienke, C. M., Green, A., Karver, M. S., & Gesten, E. L. (2009). Multiple informants in the assessment of psychological, behavioral, and academic correlates of bullying and victimization. *Journal of Adolescence, 32*, 193–211.

Totura Wienke, C. M., MacKinnon-Lewis, C., Gesten, E. L., Gadd, R., Divine, K. P., Dunham, S., & Kamboukos, D. (2009). Bullying and victimization among boys and girls in middle school: The influence of perceived family and school contexts. *Journal of Early Adolescence, 29,* 571–609.

Troop-Gordon, W., & Ladd, G. W. (2005). Trajectories of peer victimization and perceptions of the self and schoolmates: Precursors to internalizing and externalizing problems. *Child Development, 76,* 1072–1091.

Unnever, J. D. (2005). Bullies, aggressive victims, and victims: Are they distinct groups? *Aggressive Behavior, 31,* 153–171.

Van Goozen, S. H. M. (2005). Hormones and the developmental origins of aggression. In R. E. Tremblay, W. W. Hartup, & J. Archer (Eds.), *Developmental origins of aggression* (pp. 281–306). New York, NY: Guilford.

Vossekuil, B., Fein, R. A., Reddy, M., Borum, R., & Modzeleski, W. (2002). *The final report and findings of the safe school initiative: Implications for the prevention of school attacks in the United States.* Washington, DC: U.S. Secret Service and U.S. Department of Education.

Walden, L. M., & Beran, T. N. (2010). Attachment quality and bullying behavior in school-aged youth. *Canadian Journal of School Psychology, 25,* 5–18.

Webster-Stratton, C., Mihalic, S., Fagan, A., Arnold, D., Taylor, T. K., & Tingley, C. (2001). *The incredible years: Parent, teacher, and child training series.* Blueprints for Violence Prevention Series, Book Eleven, BP-011. Boulder, CO: Center for the Study and Prevention of Violence.

Wilkinson, N., Ang, R., & Goh, D., (2008). Online video game therapy for mental health concerns: A review. *International Journal of Social Psychiatry, 54,* 370–382.

Williams, K. R., & Guerra, N. G. (2007). Prevalence and predictors of Internet bullying. *Journal of Adolescent Health, 41,* 14–21.

Xie, H., Swift, D. J., Cairns, B. D., & Cairns, R. B. (2002). Aggressive behavior in social interaction: A narrative analysis of interpersonal conflicts during early adolescence. *Social Development, 11,* 205–224.

Appendix: Resources on Workplace Bullying and a Sample Bullying Policy

Michele A. Paludi

SAMPLE ORGANIZATIONS

American Psychological Association Center for Organizational Excellence
www.apaexcellence.org

Bully Busters
www.bullybusters.org

Crisis Prevention Institute
www.crisisprevention.com

Equal Employment Opportunity Commission
www.eeoc.gov

National Bully Prevention Center
www.pacer.org/bullying/resources/

National Education Association
www.nea.org

Society for Human Resource Management
www.shrm.org

Stop Bullying
www.stopbullying.gov

Workplace Bullying Institute
www.workplacebullying.org

SAMPLE BULLYING POLICY FOR AN ORGANIZATION

We foster a civil, open, and interactive community. At (_____), we are committed to maintaining an environment free of bullying and all forms of coercion that diminish the dignity of any member of our organization.

We are committed to providing all employees a safe working environment. Bullying is unacceptable behavior because it breaches principles of respect, dignity, equality, and fairness, and it presents an abuse of power and authority. It also has consequences for everyone involved, including bystanders.

The purpose of this policy is to communicate to all employees and administrators that (_____) will not in any instance tolerate bullying behavior.

This policy shall apply to all employees, regardless of his or her employee status (i.e., managerial vs. hourly, full time vs. part time).

DEFINITION OF BULLYING

Bullying is unwelcome or unreasonable behavior that demeans, intimidates, or humiliates people either as individuals or as a group. Bullying behavior is often persistent and part of a pattern, but it can also occur as a single incident. It is usually carried out by an individual but can also be an aspect of group behavior.

Bullying can be direct (face-to-face) or indirect (via texting or e-mail). Furthermore, bullying can be physical (e.g., pushing, kicking, hitting), emotional (humiliating, tormenting, ostracism), or verbal (name calling, spreading rumors). All forms of bullying are prohibited by (_____).

Cyberbullying is defined as bullying an individual using any electronic form, including, but not limited to, the Internet, interactive and digital technologies, or mobile phones.

MOBBING

Mobbing is a particular type of bullying behavior carried out by a group rather than by an individual. Mobbing is the bullying or social isolation of a person through collective unjustified accusations, humiliation, general harassment, or emotional abuse. Although it is group behavior, specific incidents such as an insult or a practical joke may be carried out by an individual as part of mobbing behavior.

IMPACT OF BULLYING ON INDIVIDUALS AND OUR ORGANIZATION

There are high costs of bullying to individuals. They include depression, feelings of helplessness, decreased productivity, headaches, anxiety, sleep disturbances, and disordered eating. Individuals commonly leave the campus as a consequence of being bullied. Individuals may also face termination, demotion, or denial of promotion and be forced to leave their jobs either voluntarily or involuntarily.

The cost of bullying to our organization includes decreased productivity, deterioration of work, absenteeism, lack of communication and teamwork, and decreased morale.

Individuals who witness incidents of bullying also have their work performance impacted. These bystanders suffer from feelings of guilt that they did not intervene in the bullying incidents. They also become intimidated and perform less efficiently, fearing that they may also be bullied.

(_____) COMMITMENT TO ENSURING A BULLY-FREE ORGANIZATION

We will:

1. Investigate bullying allegations as we do harassment and discrimination complaints.
2. Issue discipline to individuals who violate this policy. In addition, harassment and assault (physical and/or sexual) are violations of our policies and the state criminal code. Individuals who violate this policy/code may face disciplinary action under either or both systems.
3. Ensure that all employees are trained in the organization's antibullying policy and procedures.
4. Ensure that any incident of bullying is dealt with regardless of whether a complaint of bullying has been received.
5. Respond promptly, sensitively, and confidentially to all situations where bullying behavior is observed or alleged to have occurred.

IF YOU THINK YOU HAVE BEEN BULLIED

Call 911 if you or someone else is in immediate danger.
Get yourself to a safe place.
Seek medical assistance when injuries are present or suspected.
Report the matter to _____.

RETALIATION

There will be no retaliation against any member of (_____) for reporting bullying or assisting in the investigation of a complaint. Any retaliation against such individuals is subject to disciplinary action, including verbal and written reprimands, transfers, demotions, and dismissal.

CYBERBULLYING

E-communications services are provided to our organization in support of the administrative functions of the organization. Users of our e-mail services are expected to act in accordance with our Computer Use Policy and with professional and personal courtesy and conduct.

E-communication services include the general use of the organization's wireless network on one's personal devices.

Individual use of e-communications to harass another individual or group of individuals is unacceptable. Harassment may include the sending of unsolicited and unwanted messages after an individual has been told that such messages are not desired. It also includes the use of e-communications to send any threatening, sexually suggestive, sexist, racist, ethnic, homophobic, or otherwise demeaning comments to any individual or group. The use of e-communications to harass is also a violation of state laws. This includes topics covered by the harassment and discrimination policy of (_____).

SAMPLE CIVILITY POLICY

Statement of Purpose

It is the commitment of _____ to ensure our workplace is free from negative, aggressive, and inappropriate behavior, and that the work/learning environment is aimed at providing high-quality services in an atmosphere of respect, collaboration, openness, safety, and equality.

All employees and administrators have the right to be treated with dignity and respect.

Incivility includes, but is not limited to, cursing, name calling, yelling, berating others, using a harsh tone of voice, ostracism, denigration of an individual's work, gossiping, sending demeaning e-mail, making accusations about professional competence, spreading rumors, speaking with a condescending tone, and using intimidating tactics. Incivility thus displays a lack of regard for others.

A civil organization exhibits and promotes the following values:

- Displaying personal integrity and professionalism
- Practicing fairness and understanding
- Being accountable for our actions
- Emphasizing collaborative resolution of conflicts
- Exhibiting respect for diversity and inclusivity

IMPACT OF CIVILITY ON INDIVIDUALS AND OUR ORGANIZATION

Incivility and disrespect can be barriers to effective communication, coaching, and performance. There are high costs of incivility to individuals. They include depression, feelings of helplessness, substance abuse, headaches, anxiety, sleep disturbances, and disordered eating. The cost of incivility to our organization includes decreased productivity, absenteeism, and decreased morale. Incivility can escalate and may lead to other behaviors, including harassment, discrimination, and violence.

INCIVILITY VERSUS LEGITIMATE FEEDBACK

Incivility should not be confused with legitimate feedback and recommendations from administrators for work performance of an individual or group of individuals. Feedback about work performance is intended to improve the employee's performance.

Civility requires that even the most critical feedback be delivered respectfully, privately, and courteously.

RESPONSIBILITIES

All members of _____ are responsible for creating and maintaining a positive and productive work culture. Administrators are accountable for identifying and addressing issues in a timely and fair manner. All employees may request advice and assistance from Human Resources. They will assist in ensuring people communicate openly and listen to one another's point of view.

COMPLAINT PROCEDURE

All complaints of incivility will be taken seriously and followed through to resolution by Human Resources. The investigation will be limited to what is necessary to resolve the complaint. If it appears necessary for the investigator to speak to any individuals other than those involved in the complaint, they will do so only after informing the complainant and the respondent.

The investigator will endeavor to investigate all complaints of incivility expeditiously and professionally in a two-week period. In addition, the investigator will make every attempt to maintain the information provided to them in the complaint and investigation process as confidentially as possible.

There will be no retaliation against an individual for reporting incivility or assisting the investigator in the investigation of a complaint. Any retaliation against an individual is subject to disciplinary action, up to and including termination.

If after investigating any complaint of incivility it is discovered that the complaint is not bona fide or that an individual has provided false information regarding the complaint, the complainant may be subject to disciplinary action.

SAMPLE TRAINING OUTLINE FOR ANTIBULLYING

Welcome
Workplace Bullying Examples
Definition of Bullying in the Workplace
    Overt
    Covert
    Mobbing
Relationship between Schoolyard Bullies and Workplace Bullies
Impact of Workplace Bullying on Individuals
    Psychological
    Physical
    Career
    Social-Interpersonal
    Self-Concept
Impact of Workplace Bullying on the Workplace
Degrees of Bullying
Bullying Profiles
Factors that Increase Risk for Bullying Behavior
Reasonable Care
    Policy
    Investigatory Procedures
    Training Programs
Concluding Comments

About the Editor and Contributors

MICHELE A. PALUDI, PhD, is the series editor for "Women's Psychology" and for "Women and Careers in Management" for Praeger, and the Equal Opportunity and Employee Relations specialist and ADA/504 coordinator for Siena College. She is the author or editor of 52 college textbooks and more than 200 scholarly articles and conference presentations on sexual harassment, campus violence, psychology of women, gender, and discrimination. Her book *Ivory Power: Sexual Harassment on Campus* (1990, SUNY Press) received the 1992 Myers Center Award for Outstanding Book on Human Rights in the United States. She served as chair of the U.S. Department of Education's subpanel on the Prevention of Violence, Sexual Harassment, and Alcohol and Other Drug Problems in Higher Education. She was one of six scholars in the United States to be selected for this subpanel. She also was a consultant to and a member of the former New York State governor Mario Cuomo's Task Force on Sexual Harassment. She serves as an expert witness for court proceedings and administrative hearings on sexual harassment. She has had extensive experience in conducting training programs and investigations of sexual harassment and other Equal Employment Opportunity (EEO) issues for businesses and educational institutions. In addition, she has held faculty positions at Franklin & Marshall College, Kent State University, Hunter College, Union College, Hamilton College, and at Union Graduate College, where she directs the human resource management certificate program. She is on the faculty in the School of Management. Her four-volume edited set, *Managing Diversity in Today's Workplace*, recently received the 2014 RUSA Outstanding Business Reference Source, and the 2014 RUSA/ BRASS Notable Business Reference Source awards.

AFRA S. AHMAD is a doctoral student in the industrial/organizational psychology program at George Mason University (GMU). She graduated in 2008 from GMU with a B.A. in psychology and a minor in Islamic studies. After earning her bachelor's degree, she was selected for a Fulbright fellowship to conduct research in the United Arab Emirates. Currently, she is involved in diversity projects related to age diversity, religious minorities, women and ethnic leaders, and LGBT employees. In addition, she is working on examining the effects of a well-being program to help employees improve their workplace emotions. Ahmad's work has been published in journals such as *Personnel Psychology* and the *Journal of Business and Psychology*.

AMANDA J. ANDERSON is a doctoral candidate in the industrial/ organizational psychology program at George Mason University. Her research interests include workplace diversity, work–family balance, and employee well-being. Her dissertation research examines individual and organizational strategies to reduce hiring discrimination against mothers using an experimental field study. In addition to conducting academic research, she has consulted on projects related to recruitment, training, and selection. Her work has been published in journals such as the *Journal of Business and Psychology* and she has presented her research at conferences including the Society for Industrial and Organizational Psychology, Academy of Management, and the American Association for Public Opinion Research.

JENNIFER BOZEMAN is a PhD candidate at the Asper School of Business, University of Manitoba. Her research interests are in workplace aggression. She aims to understand how victim attributes, such as self-esteem, influence victim coping and other responses to workplace aggression. She is also interested in how victim attributes and the interaction between perpetrator and victim attributes precipitates victimization. She has held a variety of positions, including business development manager, marketing consultant, and director of sales, working in industries ranging from packaged goods to water purification. She earned an MBA from Drexel's LeBow College of Business.

JERRY CARBO is an associate professor of labor relations and business in society at the Grove College of Business at Shippensburg University. He is also a practicing attorney in the State of West Virginia and a founding member of the National Workplace Bullying Coalition. He researches and consults in the areas of workplace bullying and harassment and socially sustainable systems. He has published papers on workplace bullying, socially sustainable business systems, leadership, and workplace harassment. He has a PhD and MILR from Cornell's School of Industrial and Labor Relations, a JD from the Pennsylvania State University, and a BBA in accounting from Texas Christian University.

LILIA M. CORTINA, PhD, University of Illinois, is a professor of psychology and women's studies at the University of Michigan. One line of her research addresses harassment based on sex, sexuality, and gender. She also investigates the contours and consequences of workplace incivility. She publishes in organizational science, social/personality, and feminist journals.

KATHLEEN GARGAN holds two degrees from the College of Saint Rose: a bachelor of arts degree in English and a master of science in education from the College Student Services Administration program. During her graduate work, she was a graduate assistant for the chief diversity officer and the Office of Intercultural Leadership at the College of Saint Rose. She completed her master's program as a graduate intern for the Damietta Cross-Cultural Center at Siena College and returned to the institution to work for Residential Life as a residence director.

SYBIL GELDART is an associate professor of psychology, Wilfrid Laurier University (Ontario). She currently serves as associate editor of *European Review of Applied Psychology*. She has two areas of research; with collaborators from McMaster University, she has explored attributions of accident causes, organizational practices, and employee perceptions of work organization.

CHRISTA GRANT graduated from the University at Buffalo with a bachelor of arts degree, double major in communication and sociology in 2005. Prior to receiving her master's of science in education degree, Grant was the program director at the Boys & Girls Clubs of Schenectady for three years. She began her career as the residence director at Siena College in 2008 and she has been working at the Damietta Cross-Cultural Center since 2011, starting as assistant director, and was appointed to serve in the director role in April 2013. Grant was the recipient of the 2009 Esther Lloyd-Jones Annual Case Study Competition Award.

KATIE E. GRIFFIN received her MA in forensic psychology at City University of New York John Jay College of Criminal Justice. Her research interests include microaggressions and mental health as well as hate crimes and associated legislation.

LAUREN GRIFFITH is an assistant professor in the Department of Clinical Epidemiology and Biostatistics at McMaster University. She holds a PhD in epidemiology from the University of Toronto and a master's degree in biostatistics from the University of Michigan. She is the associate scientific director of the Canadian Longitudinal Study on Aging and her research interests include multimorbidity, physical functioning, injury, and aging.

TED HAINES, MD, MSc, CCFP, DOHS, FRCPC, is an associate professor in the Department of Clinical Epidemiology and Biostatistics at McMaster University. He collaborates widely as a clinician researcher and epidemiologist, focusing on occupational health. He is involved in many occupational epidemiological studies, including stress in the postal sector.

M. SANDY HERSHCOVIS is an associate professor at the Asper School of Business, University of Manitoba. Her research interests focus on the broad topic of workplace mistreatment, including various forms of workplace aggression (e.g., incivility, social undermining, workplace bullying). She is interested in (1) the effects of workplace mistreatment on observer attitudes toward the perpetrator and victim, (2) how the relationship between the perpetrator and victim affects victim responses to workplace mistreatment, and (3) how the interaction between perpetrator and victim attributes and behaviors contributes to workplace victimization. She has published her research in several academic journals, including the *Journal of Applied Psychology, Journal of Occupational Health Psychology*, and *Journal of Organizational Behavior*.

EDEN B. KING joined the faculty of the industrial/organizational psychology program at George Mason University after earning her PhD from Rice University in 2006. She is pursuing a program of research that seeks to guide the equitable and effective management of diverse organizations. Her research integrates organizational and social psychological theories in conceptualizing social stigma and the work-life interface. She is currently an associate editor for the *Journal of Management* and the *Journal of Business and Psychology* and is on the editorial boards of the *Academy of Management Journal* and the *Journal of Applied Psychology*. She was honored to receive the State Council of Higher Education of Virginia's Rising Star Award in 2011.

LUCAS LAVERA is a senior creative arts major at Siena College. He is a student leader at Siena, working for the Damietta Cross-Cultural Center as a Heritage Month coordinator and as a student advocate. In April 2013, he received the Campus Involvement Award as a sophomore. Later that year, he became the Diversity Action Committee First Fellow and developed a presentation about how the college can be more inclusive with transgender students. He intends to obtain his master's degree in higher education administration and work as a college administrator.

ALEX P. LINDSEY is a fourth-year doctoral student in the industrial/organizational psychology program at George Mason University. His research interests include diversity and inclusion as well as the promotion of employee well-being in the workplace. Specifically, he is interested in strategies that organizations, targets of prejudice, and allies can use to reduce workplace discrimination and promote the well-being of marginalized employees, with a special interest in populations with concealable stigmas. In the future, he hopes to obtain an academic position in which he can continue these streams of research while also pursuing his passions for teaching and service.

PAULA K. LUNDBERG-LOVE is a professor of psychology at the University of Texas at Tyler (UTT) and the Ben R. Fisch endowed professor in humanitarian affairs for 2001–2004. Her undergraduate degree was in chemistry, and she worked as a chemist at a pharmaceutical company for five years prior to earning her doctorate in physiological psychology with an emphasis in psychopharmacology. After a three-year postdoctoral fellowship in nutrition and behavior in the Department of Preventive Medicine at Washington University School of Medicine in St. Louis, she assumed her academic position at UTT where she teaches classes in psychopharmacology, behavioral neuroscience, physiological psychology, sexual victimization, and family violence. Subsequent to her academic appointment, Lundberg-Love pursued postgraduate training and is a licensed professional counselor in Texas. She is a member of Tyler Counseling and Assessment Center, where she provides therapeutic services for victims of sexual assault, child sexual abuse, and domestic violence. She has conducted a long-term research study on women who were victims of childhood incestuous abuse, constructed a therapeutic program for their recovery, and documented its effectiveness upon their recovery. She is the author of nearly 100 publications and presentations and is co-editor of *Violence and Sexual Abuse at Home: Current Issues in Spousal Battering and Child Maltreatment*, *Intimate Violence against Women: When Spouses, Partners, or Lovers Attack*, and *Women and Mental Disorders*. As a result of her training in psychopharmacology and child maltreatment, her expertise has been sought as a consultant on various death penalty appellate cases in the state of Texas.

CAROL MACKINNON-LEWIS is a professor in the Department of Child and Family Studies, University of South Florida. She received her

PhD in child development from the University of Georgia. For 25 years, her research focus has been on the identification of family processes as they contribute to children's social-emotional competence and how variations in youths' experiences within their families influence their relationships in other contexts, with a particular interest in their aggressive behavior with peers. Her most recent research, funded by the National Institute on Drug Abuse, tests a technology-based model for the dissemination and implementation of the Strong African-American Families Program, an evidence-based prevention program shown to be efficacious in deterring alcohol use and conduct problems in rural African American youth. She was a scholar in the William T. Grant Foundation's Faculty Scholar Award program. Funded by the National Science Foundation, U.S. Department of Education, National Institute of Mental Health, National Institute of Child Health and Human Development, and the William T. Grant Foundation, MacKinnon-Lewis's work has been published in a number of professional journals including *Developmental Psychology, Child Development, Development and Psychopathology, Journal of Family Psychology,* and *Social Development.*

LISA A. MARCHIONDO, PhD, University of Michigan, is an assistant professor of industrial/organizational psychology at Wayne State University. She researches low-intensity forms of workplace mistreatment, including incivility, and modern discrimination. She also studies leadership experiences and perceptions of women and people of color.

JENNIFER L. MARTIN, PhD, is an assistant professor of education at the University of Mount Union. Prior to working in higher education, she worked in public education for 17 years, 15 of those as the department chair of English at an urban alternative high school for students labeled at risk for school failure in metropolitan Detroit. Additionally, she taught graduate and undergraduate courses in research methods, multicultural education, educational leadership, and women and gender studies. Currently, she teaches graduate courses in curriculum and undergraduate courses in multicultural education, gender studies, and content area literacy. She is committed to incorporating diverse texts in all her courses and inspiring culturally responsive pedagogical practices in current and future educators. She is the editor of the two-volume set *Women as Leaders in Education: Succeeding Despite Inequity, Discrimination and Other Challenges* (Praeger, 2011), which examines the intersections of class, race, gender, and sexuality for current and aspiring leaders from a variety of perspectives. Her current book project is *Racial Battle Fatigue: Insights from the Front Lines of Social Justice Advocacy,* which contains personal stories of the repercussions of doing social justice work in the field and in the university. Activists and scholars share experiences of microaggressions, racial battle fatigue, and retaliation because of who they are, for whom they advocate, and what they study. She has numerous publications on bullying and harassment, educational equity, and issues of social justice. She is currently studying the development of culturally responsive leadership practices.

RONALD MATOS is currently an assistant director with the Public Safety Department at Siena College in Loudonville, New York. Prior to his role at Siena College he served as the acting director of investigations and internal affairs for New York State's Office for People with Developmental Disabilities. During that time, he was charged with the duty of providing supervision and direction to 13 statewide field offices, which were established to investigate abuse and neglect claims on behalf of some of the state's most vulnerable citizens. Before entering state service, he served 21 years with the Albany, New York, Police Department. For the majority of his police career, he was assigned to the criminal investigations unit, where he spent time as a detective and detective supervisor. He retired from the Albany Police Department in March 2012 as the commander of the Office of Professional Standards, where he helped develop the agency's personnel management program.

CESELIE McFARLAND is currently pursuing a master's degree in clinical psychology, with a specialization in neuropsychology, at the University of Texas at Tyler. Prior to enrolling in her graduate studies, she was actively involved in community service projects and provided assistance to underprivileged populations. Currently, she works with at-risk undergraduates as a freshman seminar instructor. The classes consist of psychoeducation, anxiety reduction, stress management, career and academic development, and learning disability evaluations. Between graduate studies and teaching, she works as an assistant to the coordinator of the University Tutoring Center, specifically regulating productivity and academic advancement. Previous experience in the psychiatric field includes the local behavioral health medical facility in stabilizing and treating substance abuse, schizophrenia and psychosis, suicide attempts, personality disorders, and affective disorders. Upon completion of her master's degree, she plans to pursue her doctorate in clinical psychology. Special research and clinical consideration for future endeavors include adolescent and young adult populations with respect to the treatment of eating disorders.

ASHLEY A. MEMBERE is a doctoral student in the industrial/organizational psychology program at George Mason University. She graduated with a BA in psychology from Rice University in 2013. Her primary research interests include workplace diversity and employee well-being. More specifically, her diversity research focuses on how multiple identities can affect experiences of discrimination. Her current research projects involve diversity training and issues faced by female and ethnic minority leaders.

KEVIN L. NADAL, PhD, is an associate professor of psychology at John Jay College of Criminal Justice–City University of New York (CUNY), as well as the executive director of the Center for Lesbian, Gay, Bisexual, Transgender, and Queer Studies at the CUNY Graduate Center. The author of 5 books and over 60 publications, his research focuses on multicultural issues in psychology and education.

WESLEY S. PARKS holds a master's degree in clinical psychology, with a specialization in neuropsychology. For the past decade, he has worked at a private forensic and clinical psychology practice where he has been involved in wide-ranging, and often high-profile, forensic psychology and legal cases. Prior to that, his career involved product- and service-oriented retail management, corporate training, and consulting. Most recently, he has refocused on clinical assessment and therapy. Special treatment concerns in his therapy caseload include affective and anxiety disorders, psychotic and somatic disorders, trauma and abuse issues, career and employment, and neurodevelopmental disorders. His research interests include effects of exposure to traumatic events, comorbidity in major mental illness, groupthink, business and organizational psychology, and the symbiotic relationship between psychology and public policy.

KATHLEEN PIKER-KING is a professor of sociology and criminal justice at the University of Mount Union. Her professional activities include presentations, panels, and workshops at both the regional and national levels. She has served in elected and appointed committees and task forces at the regional and national levels. Presently, she is serving on the American Sociological Association's Advisory Panel for High School Sociology that is responsible for developing national standards for high school sociology courses. Her research interests have most recently focused on interpersonal aggression in educational settings from the primary grade levels through the collegiate levels. During her tenure at the University of Mount Union, she has served as departmental chair and has served on key university committees. Besides serving her institution and her discipline, she has held board positions for various local nonprofit organizations and at private grade schools and high schools. Presently, she serves on the board of directors for Archbishop Hoban High School in Akron, Ohio. Over her professional career, she has won several awards recognizing her contributions to college teaching and recognizing her service to her profession. Her most recent award was given by the Department of Sociology at Kent State University, recognizing her lifetime contributions to teaching.

PHILIP E. POITIER has over 30 years of results-driven experience in school building safety, threat assessment, the prevention of targeted school violence, bullying prevention, crisis intervention, and creation of climates of school safety, and student and parent advocacy as well as law enforcement. His leadership experience includes over nine years as a school resource officer with the New York State Police and an instructor in Street Survival for the New York State Police Academy and currently serves as the director of school safety and security for Burnt Hills/Ballston Lake School District, with 3,000 students. He has worked with thousands of students, faculty members, school leaders, parents, and community groups in multiple urban and rural school districts, governmental agencies, and others on school safety and educational strategies for prevention. This includes large group presentations, action plans for leaders, as well as one-on-one counsel. He regularly serves as an expert adviser on strategies to address crisis intervention as well as the prevention of negative incidents in schools and communities. This includes serving on the New York State Education Department's *Dignity for All Task Force*, in which he is providing guidance on the design of the education commissioners regulations to implement the important new Anti-Bullying Law. He has been featured in numerous news articles and media broadcasts including National Public Radio and is the recipient of multiple awards for his work and results. This includes the Trooper of the Year Award for outstanding service to the Division of State Police—the first time such an award was given by the New York State Police for work with children in schools—and an annual award, the Trooper Phil Leadership Award, now given to students who demonstrate exceptional character. He attended Queens College of the City University of New York, nationally certified by the Federal Community Oriented Policing Services, and was trained by the U.S. Secret Service.

ISAAC E. SABAT is a third-year doctoral student in the industrial/psychology program at George Mason University. His research focuses on all aspects of diversity and discrimination in the workplace, with special focus on invisibly stigmatized minorities. Most of his work deals with understanding the dynamics of stigma identity management within a workplace context and identifying ways to improve the effectiveness of identity management strategies that stigmatized targets can engage in to remediate the discrimination they experience. He is also interested in understanding the psychological and physiological impact that workplace discrimination can have on all stigmatized minorities. He plans to pursue an academic career that will allow him to continue researching these very important topics.

KATHERINE ANN SCOTT has worked in numerous research and academic settings and is currently focusing on expanding her clinical testing and counseling skills. Her primary research interests lie in memory performance and cognitive dysfunction in relation to mild cognitive impairment, Alzheimer's disease and other dementias, and the rates of deterioration associated with the aforementioned disorders. She is also interested in the neurophysiological underpinnings of post-traumatic stress disorder and the consolidation and retrieval of memory related to traumatic experiences. She holds a bachelor's degree in psychology and received her master's degree in clinical psychology with a specialization in neuropsychology in May 2015.

HARRY S. SHANNON, PhD, is a professor in the Department of Clinical Epidemiology and Biostatistics at McMaster University. He has conducted many occupational epidemiology projects, including mortality studies, investigations of organizational factors in relation to work injuries, analyses of workers' compensation data, and studies of work stressors and musculoskeletal disorders.

MARTINA L. SHARP-GRIER is an assistant professor of sociology at an Ohio two-year college. She has a long history of social advocacy and service, having maintained positions in victim advocacy, forensic social work, and criminal justice. Prior to her current position, she served as a lecturer of women's studies at an Ohio four-year institution. She obtained her BS in criminal justice/prelaw and an MA in sociology. She has done postgraduate work in both social work and women's studies and is a licensed social worker for the state of Ohio. As a public speaker, she has addressed audiences on the realities of interpersonal violence. She has provided agency diversity training for nonprofit organizations and has facilitated statewide and national conversations regarding curriculum design and management, student success, and student engagement. Other professional presentations include discussions regarding domestic violence, African American women and identity formulation, habitus and cultural standpoint, and race and lesbianism. Her written work primarily addresses religion and domestic violence. She is a honorably discharged member of the U.S. Army Reserve.

AIMEE STEWART is a graduate student working on an MS in clinical psychology with a specialization in neuropsychology at the University of Texas at Tyler. She obtained a BS in psychology from Louisiana State University. She has worked as a psychometrist in clinical and forensic settings with children and adults for the past five years in Louisiana and Texas. Her current research interests include psychopharmacologic effects on the developing brain and sustained traumatic brain injuries in children. Upon completing her master's degree, she plans to pursue doctoral studies in pediatric neuropsychology.

SUSAN STRAUSS, RN, EdD, is a national and international speaker, trainer, and consultant. Her specialty areas include harassment and workplace bullying, organization development, and management/leadership development. Her clients are from business, education, health care, law, and government organizations from both the public and private sectors. She has authored book chapters and written articles in professional journals and curriculum and training manuals, as well as authored the book *Sexual Harassment and Teens: A Program for Positive Change.* She has been featured on *The Donahue Show*, *CBS Evening News*, and other television and radio programs and also been interviewed for newspaper and journal articles such as the *Times of London*, *Lawyers Weekly*, and *Harvard Education Newsletter.* She has presented at international conferences in Botswana, Egypt, Thailand, Israel, and the United States and conducted sex discrimination research in Poland. She has consulted with professionals from other countries such as England, Australia, Canada, and St. Martin.

CHRISTINE M. WIENKE TOTURA, PhD, is an assistant professor in psychology at Auburn University. Her research to date has focused on the relationship between school and community contextual factors and youth social-emotional and behavioral development. She is particularly interested in understanding the role that settings play in shaping youth experiences, such as bullying, victimization, and related behavioral health issues. She has worked closely with communities, utilizing participatory research practices to evaluate the implementation and effectiveness of public health prevention strategies in promoting youth and community health. She has published and presented extensively in these areas and has received federal, foundation, and local funding to support her research. She earned her bachelor of science degree in psychology from Loyola University Chicago and her master of arts and doctor of philosophy degrees in clinical psychology from the University of South Florida. Additionally, she is a licensed clinical psychologist.

Index